Technologies of Vision

Technologies of Vision

The War Between Data and Images

Steve F. Anderson

The MIT Press
Cambridge, Massachusetts
London, England

This book was set in Stone Sans and Stone Serif by Toppan Best-set Premedia Limited. Printed and bound in the United States of America.

Library of Congress Cataloging-in-Publication Data

Names: Anderson, Steve F., author.
Title: Technologies of vision : the war between data and images / Steve F. Anderson.
Description: Cambridge, MA : The MIT Press, [2017] | Includes bibliographical references and index.
Identifiers: LCCN 2017009919 | ISBN 9780262037013 (hardcover : alk. paper)
Subjects: LCSH: Images, Photographic--Political aspects. | Information visualization. | Video surveillance--Social aspects. | Image processing--Social aspects.
Classification: LCC TR184 .A53 2017 | DDC 770--dc23 LC record available at https://lccn.loc.gov/2017009919

10 9 8 7 6 5 4 3 2 1

I dedicate this book to Holly, Ginger, and Quiller, with love.

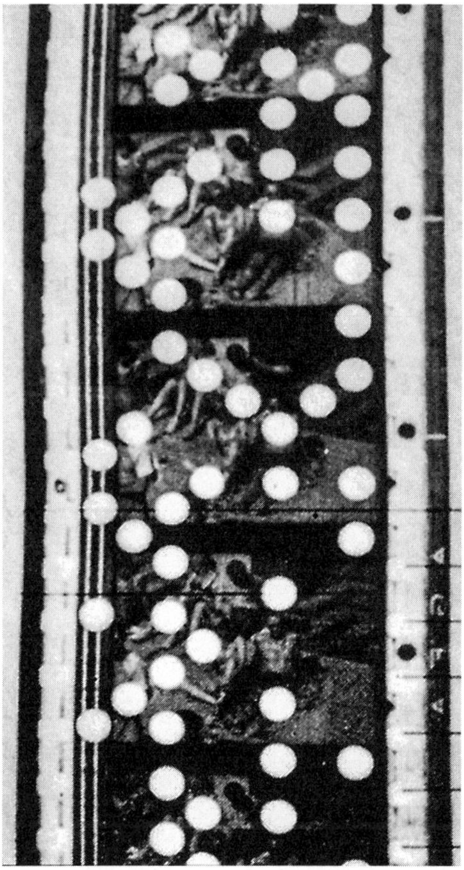

Figure 0.0
Konrad Zuse's Z2 computer used holes punched in 35mm film for data input and program storage. Image courtesy of Horst Zuse private collection.

Contents

Acknowledgments

This book lurched into focus all at once like the resolving of a progressive JPEG loading over a modem. It would have been easier if my writing process had been more like a standard JPEG, filling in one line of resolution at a time from top to bottom, or a vector graphic, tracing a path from beginning to end by the logic of some mathematical algorithm. But where algorithms allow operational complexity and extraction of order from chaos, my own process has benefited from distinctly analog predispositions, meanderings, and tactical inversions of signal and noise.

The timely completion of this project was enabled by the American Council of Learned Societies, from whom I received a Digital Innovation fellowship during the 2015–2016 academic year. However, the book itself began as little more than an afterword—a "print supplement"—to the primary task of assembling a digital media archive and series of video essays examining the emergence of computation in the American technocultural imaginary. This point of origin partially explains the book's emphasis on media, artists, and technology industries centered in North America. The digital component, titled *Technologies of Cinema,* has become an undertaking so pleasurable and ambitious that it remains in a state of perpetual becoming while this engorged print supplement heads off to be rasterized as ink on paper. They serve different purposes as material and intellectual objects and it has been a revelation to operate in three different modes—archive curating, video editing, and word writing—at the same time. I can no longer imagine working any other way.

At a key stage in the writing of chapter 1, I had the opportunity to participate in a months-long Culture Analytics symposium co-organized by Lev Manovich at UCLA's Institute for Pure and Applied Mathematics. These sessions provided blunt and practical glimpses of research on data analytics and visualization that significantly shaped my perceptions of this topic. Chapter 2 was substantially reshaped in response to revelations by Edward Snowden regarding the nature and extent of surveillance technologies deployed by the United States government and I, along with the rest of the nation, owe him a continuing debt of gratitude. The Virtually There conference co-organized by William Uricchio at MIT's OpenDocLab offered a timely snapshot of immersive nonfiction that significantly informed chapter 3. Finally, my longtime proximity to the research labs and projects of the USC School of Cinematic Arts provided the original impetus and practical contexts for considering the abstract contestation of data and images. I remain grateful for the regular access and insights provided by lab directors Mark Bolas, Scott Fisher, Tracy Fullerton, Marientina Gotsis, and Alex McDowell and countless students and researchers in these spaces.

This book would not have been possible without the continued support and interest of my editor Doug Sery and the efficient and professional editorial, design, and production staff at MIT Press. For assistance with acquiring images and reprint permissions I thank Faig Ahmed, Natalie Bookchin, Arnaud Colinart, Sterling Crispin, Nonny de la Peña, Masaki Fujihata, John Gerrard, Ben Grosser, Aaron Koblin, Lev Manovich, Christian Marclay, Alex Melamed, Vincent Morriset, Michael Naimark, Johan Nordberg, Pat O'Neill, Trevor Paglen, Davide Quayola, Casey Reas, Marie Sester, Matthew Shaw, Sally Stein, Clement Valla, JoAnn Wypijewski, and Horst Zuse.

The completion of this book has taken place during a time of personal transition, marked by my move from USC's School of Cinematic Arts to the School of Theater, Film and Television at UCLA, two freeways across town. The change is bittersweet but I am fortunate to have landed among a new community of scholars, makers, and students at UCLA, where I have been warmly welcomed and my work recognized in spite of purported institutional rivalries. My long association with USC—more than two decades—has indelibly shaped my work by virtue of many close personal and professional associations. Particular thanks are owed to the current and former students in the Media Arts + Practice (iMAP) PhD program. This program, which was conceived by Anne Friedberg and Jen Stein, was my privilege to direct for the first few years of its existence and to consider my primary faculty affiliation for the past decade. The students in this program, especially those for whom I served as chair—Veronica Paredes, Susana Ruiz, Laila Sakr, and Amanda Tasse—continue to provide moments of inspiration, light, and hope for the future of academia.

For their readings of various chapters at various stages, I am indebted to Aniko Imre and Andreas Kratky who brought diversely challenging perspectives to bear on the project. I received further input and historical context from Scott Fisher, Mark Bolas, Marie Sester, Michael Naimark, Nonny de la Peña, and Casey Reas. The intellectual and creative context from which this book emerged is inseparable from my decade-long collaboration with Tara McPherson on the *Vectors, Scalar,* and *Critical Commons* projects as well as our continuing work with Erik Loyer, Phil Ethington, Craig Dietrich, and Curtis Fletcher. The only person with whom I can claim forty years of friendship and intellectual camaraderie is Greg Golley and it was with him in mind that many of my favorite passages were composed.

My deepest gratitude is reserved for my partner and colleague Holly Willis, whose innumerable contributions to this project I can no longer distinguish from my own. Far beyond the pages of this book, my life is unthinkable without her intellect, generosity, support, and mindfulness, all of which remind me gently, insistently, and daily what, in the end, really matters.

++++++++++++++++

Introduction

If inhabitants of the twentieth century were tyrannized by images—cinematic, televisual, advertising—we in the early decades of the twenty-first are surely ruled by data. Our whereabouts, health, habits, interests, affinities, social connections, and communications are logged, tagged, located, recognized, interpreted, stored, and circulated in corporate and governmental databases. Photographic images, which were once tasked merely with capturing reflected light on bodies in space, now bear responsibility for a degree of self-knowledge that was unthinkable for the first 150 years of the medium—where they were taken, when and by whom, to say nothing of volumetric data and information about the technologies and contexts in which they are captured, rendered, saved, or shared. It may be something of an overstatement to say that data and images are "at war," but taking the evolution of their relationship seriously means unraveling an entangled history that illuminates the cultural preoccupations, limits, hopes, and anxieties that attend the visual culture of our own age.

A generation ago, Susan Sontag argued that images got in the way of experiencing reality; that photography came to stand in for both the immediacy of experience and the memories that could be called forth later. In today's world, the capture and analysis of data do not yet constitute the same kind of barrier between individuals and their perception of the world, but data has an undisputed impact on the organization of our ways of thinking and what it is possible to know. Sontag's description of photography as co-implicated with systems of power, however, is directly relevant to the discussion of data: "To photograph is to appropriate the thing photographed. It means putting oneself into a certain relation to the world that feels like knowledge—and, therefore, like power."[1] Writing in the early 1970s, Sontag found much to be melancholic about when analyzing the role of photography in politics, memory, and history. Her description of Nixon-era America as "a sad, frightened time" seems no less applicable today.[2] But where Sontag diagnosed the proliferation of photographic images as an attempt—whether conscious or unconscious—to record the disappearance of the premodern world, today's mass extinctions and environmental destruction far outpace the capacity for mere images to remember, even with billions of lenses carried in pockets around the globe.

Despite their elegiac tone, Sontag's words are hardly the stuff of naïve romanticism. She saw with painful clarity the instrumentalization of photography in the interest of suspect ideologies and unreflective power. "Cameras began duplicating the world at that moment when the human landscape started to undergo a vertiginous rate of change: while an untold number of forms of biological and social life are being destroyed in a brief span of time, a device is available to record what is disappearing."[3] Such words ring hauntingly in times that have been described as the early or late stages—does it really matter which?—of the Anthropocene, a reframing in finite terms of humanity's planetary reign. To trace our descent toward global destruction, one needs a different system of documentation, one capable of tracking in real time the gasping downward spiral of a billion points of data. The talismanic function of photography that Sontag describes in service of sentimentality is not available to large-scale data systems. We may feel helpless at the sight of melting glaciers and ice floes, but how does one conjure sentimentality for a data flow? On the contrary: the presence of data to describe epochal patterns of decline mendaciously suggests the inevitability of an institutional response. If such events are well known enough to have their data captured, graphed, and visualized, it is tempting to believe that surely someone must be doing something about it.

Images—and the methods we have developed to study them—have much to teach about today's digital culture, but first we must speak with precision about the evolving relationship of images and data. Although it is early in the game, allow me to put all my cards on the table: this book proceeds from the supposition that no great divide separates pre- and post-digital culture. I put this bluntly as a strategic maneuver, not to disavow the many exceptions to its rule. It is certainly more seductive to argue the opposite, that digital culture offers an opportunity to rethink timeworn cultural and critical paradigms. New critical models and objects of study certainly help illuminate the specificities of digital media, but we should not forget the lessons of the past regarding social consequences and the fact that today's imaging and data systems are just as ideologically inscribed as their predecessors. The best of visual culture theory was never solely about representation. It always engaged systems of power and knowledge alongside the pleasures and politics of perception—all of which remain centrally relevant to the study of digital culture. For the time being, then, we disserve the study of data if we suppose that it requires a whole new set of critical or subdisciplinary paradigms.

I say this advisedly, knowing that some of my most respected colleagues would and do argue otherwise. The emergence of subfields such as software studies, code studies, and platform studies have achieved broad recognition and influence in recent years. But these paradigms offer little that is digestible to historians of visual culture. Equally, the branch of art history that focuses on visual media in the digital era remains ill equipped to address the specifics of hardware and software necessary to produce its objects of study. The benefits of treating this emergent area of investigation as a "new field" are many, including the impetus to create specialized academic apparatuses, such as book series, journal publications, faculty lines, and curricular revisions. These are all predicated on the need to assert the specificity of digital media in order to articulate the new methods and competencies required to properly study them. The danger of this model lies in creating an insular field of discourse that is alienating to those who do not write or understand computer code. A new kind of "digital divide" thereby threatens to exclude many people, especially in the arts and humanities, who might otherwise introduce useful perspectives or alternative voices in the evolution of these fields.

While I remain sympathetic to the many passionate calls for universal code literacy—and I confess that every academic program I have been involved with for the last fifteen years has actively promoted coding as a foundational twenty-first-century literacy—I believe it is ultimately more productive to imagine the critical study of hardware, software, and the media objects they produce as coextensive with critical models developed around analog media and cultural studies. In part, the benefit of such continuity lies in the persistence of hard-won advances in areas such as feminism, critical race theory, and models linking popular culture and technology to issues of class, sexuality, and politics. Starting over with a newly defined subfield allows certain critical perspectives—especially those of the technologically adept—to flourish, but we should also be mindful of voices that may be thereby excluded.

Technoculture in Transition

As I write this, a camera lens is pointed in my direction from the top margin of my laptop screen. My previous computer required a cylinder-shaped camera to be plugged into a USB port, which could then be clamped onto the screen or pointed in any direction. The external camera was admittedly less convenient, but I was never tempted to forget it was there. Now, the tiny lens at the top of my screen has an even tinier green indicator light that goes on, ostensibly, every time the camera is in use. Similar lenses on the tablet and phone devices in the room with me do not. It would be easy to assume that they are simply on all the time, or worse, to forget they are there at all. The lens built into the laptop also points in only one direction, in a fixed relation to the screen; in cinematic parlance, it is capable of a crude tilt, but it doesn't pan or zoom. It doesn't understand the size or shape of the room I'm sitting in, and the software running behind it does not bother to recognize my face, notice where my eyes are looking, or infer my emotional state. The next machine I own may very well do all these things, either on its own or in conjunction with other devices, software, or electromagnetic signals in the room. These abilities will come with certain minor conveniences that may dissuade me from learning how to turn them off somewhere deep in a settings menu. They will begin to seem as natural as the lens that is currently pointed in the direction of my face, and I will begin to assume that they are on all the time. These shifts occur gradually. We may be tranquilized by the seeming inexorability of technological change, or we may work to decode the assumptions and implications of each microstep in its evolution.

My basic supposition is that we are witnessing—and participating actively in—a remarkable transition in visual culture, the root of which lies in the evolving relationship between data and images. I am not referring to the ontological shift from analog to digital photography that sparked a minor crisis among theorists of visual culture some twenty-five years ago, nor even the epochal transition from atoms to bits declared by Nicholas Negroponte in 1995.[4] Images have never stopped lying at any point during the last 150 years. Computers were not needed to invent ways to deceive the eye, but this is not the issue. Let us leave it to our art historians and journalism ethicists to lament the crises of referentiality occasioned by digital imaging. Instead, I would ask, what happens to images when they become computational? An image that is computational is no longer strictly concerned with mimesis, nor even with signification. Computational images may serve as interfaces, carriers, or surface renderings, the real importance of which are their underlying processes or data structures.

This book would not be necessary if it were true—as I am sometimes told—that the difference between images and data no longer exists. We accept such equivocation at our peril if the goal is to think clearly about all that happens when images become as computable as they are representational and data seems incomplete if not visualized. Of concern here may not be the war between data and images so much as the war between computability and mimesis. "Computability" in this context refers to the extent to which computers can act on or process visual information; "mimesis" simply means the extent to which images resemble phenomena in the physical world. Sidestepping contested binaries such as "real" and "virtual," I occasionally observe distinctions between "lens-based" and "computer-generated" imagery, but we should remember that the sharp, intuitive boundary that we currently perceive between them is another transient artifact of our present state of imaging technology. I am not much concerned with remarking on the evolution of digital image making as it moves with alleged inexorability toward an asymptotic "photorealism," but I am interested in mapping the ways in which our vision of the world is differently inflected by the competing historical lineages of data and image.

At stake in this investigation are nothing less than the future cycles of media production and consumption and the terms of analysis for film, TV, games, and media art. A nuanced understanding of the actively evolving relationship between data and images offers a key to thinking critically about the effects of media and technology in the politics of everyday life. In the end, data and images should not be taken as a fixed or truly oppositional binary. The two are complementary—and at times functionally congruent—existing in a dynamic interplay that drives technological development and media making both in and out of the entertainment industries. The implications of this entanglement suggest diverse consequences related to the status of documentary and materiality, the politics of large-scale systems of surveillance and information, and contested issues of space, time, and subjectivity. This book privileges media practices that complicate the ideology driving much technological development and entertainment industry production, but my intent is to avoid outdated models of resistance. In many cases, in the chapters that follow, I seek to map the limit cases or internal contradictions that define areas of practice within a broad spectrum of media arts.

Not long ago, denouncing Hollywood's privileging of emotional identification and illusionistic representation seemed to strike a blow against the bad object of bourgeois culture in favor of radical, underground, or subversive cinema. The data systems we now face are orders of magnitude more encompassing than the emotional plenitude offered by classical Hollywood's three-act structure. They also pose a more direct threat to individual freedom. I believe it is no longer sufficient to favor media that subverts or denies the logics of commercial entertainment. The same systems that capture consumer metrics tell us the number of "views," "plays," "hits," "likes," "shares," and so forth that have been garnered by even the most oppositional works of digital art.

My selection of key media works, technologies, and creators favors reflective practices that contrast the digital allure of realism, seamlessness, immateriality, totality, ubiquity, and convergence with an embrace of the pleasures and complexities—computational, algorithmic, ludic—unique to digital culture. Under consideration is a deliberately eclectic array of examples, albeit one focused on the technologies and practices of media art and entertainment in North America during the last two decades. These geographic and historical boundaries remain permeable, but they are motivated by a practical need to limit the project's scope and should not be mistaken for an implicit argument that excluded works are less worthy of attention. Objects of analysis range from the obscurity of experimental films, digital media, and software art to commercial productions of the entertainment and technology industries, as well as data analytics, social networks, and government databases. To begin, I attempt to articulate a "politics of data" that is informed by—and in dialogue with—the "politics of images" forged by media and visual culture studies.

Politics of Data

Thanks to rapidly proliferating technologies of vision and their counterparts in large-scale data systems, what is at stake in seeing and being seen is much different today than it was only a decade ago. The once voyeuristic gaze of cinema has given way to power relations articulated through computational systems rather than through ocular regimes predicated on reflected light and bodies in space. The academic field that emerged to theorize visual culture in the twentieth century provides a rich critical framework that offers productive continuities, but it is, nonetheless, insufficient for understanding the computational turn of the twenty-first. In the visual realm, we see and are seen by others. This dual status as both viewer and viewed has been rigorously theorized to account for the power of looking, cultural inscriptions of the gaze, and the nuanced differentials of public and private, rich and poor. In the realm of data, we both sense and are sensed, track and are tracked; our data is mined by others, and we voraciously consume the insights gleaned from data aggregators, visualizers, and evaluators.

To speak productively about the "politics of data," we must direct our attention to an informed discussion of four areas: defining, sensing, processing, and knowing. Before data can be considered data, it exists as phenomena in the world—often the results of human activities that are registered by server logs and information sensors. Before data can be captured, it must be desired, identified, and described; correctly sized and formatted repositories must be created that are suited to its capture, storage, and processing. In this way, each stage in the treatment of data implies others in the circuit. In no event, as Lisa Gitelman argues in her book-length polemic *"Raw Data" Is an Oxymoron*, can data be said to exist in a "raw" state—a form that preexists its definition and the creation of a system for doing things with it.[5]

With this requisite definition in place, the politics of data becomes a politics of sensing. This statement bears close resemblance to the politics of looking. What we choose to look at, who is empowered to look, and who gets looked at—all have analogs in the realm of data. Sensors are invented and deployed for specific purposes. They gather certain kinds of information while neglecting others. They belong to a system that is part ideological, part technical, and part social. Above all, they are intentional—that is, imbued with intention. Unlike the discourse of camera lenses, which suggests direct comparison with human eyes, sensors may address specific aspects of the built or lived environment that are not, in themselves, particularly meaningful. They make sense only when collated and integrated with interpretive systems. Thus, we may say that the politics of data is also the politics of processing.

To be processed into legibility, data must first be prepared—outlying samples and anomalies are routinely eliminated or bracketed to exclude them from analysis. This process is often called "cleaning" the data. At scale, data processing focuses on dominant patterns and broad contours. The promise of "big data" is to extract meaning from patterns that are too large to perceive except through intense computation. This data must then be translated into systems of signification that are legible to humans. The importance of this part of the process cannot be overstated, and it is among the driving questions for this book's chapter devoted to data visualization (chapter 1). Here, complex apparatuses of visual semiotics and representation come to the fore; decisions about how data should be rendered visually require conscious choices within the rhetoric of display, computation, and communication.

As a politics of knowing, data becomes most deeply entangled with systems of ideology. Many efforts have been made to schematize the relationship between data and knowledge. Among the most commonly used models is the DIKW pyramid, from the field of information science, which proposes a hierarchy rising from a large base of discrete and decontextualized "data" on the bottom, to contextualized "information" on the next tier, followed by "knowledge" that has been interpreted or operationalized, culminating in "wisdom," presumably denoting especially useful knowledge that occupies a comparatively tiny space at the apex of the pyramid.

In his afterword to *"Raw Data" Is an Oxymoron,* Geoffrey Bowker references a graph generated by Google's Ngram Viewer, which is used to track the frequency with which particular words or combinations of words appear in millions of books published over a period of years, decades, or centuries. Bowker used the Ngram Viewer to illustrate the decades-long statistical decline of the terms "knowledge" and "wisdom" alongside the coincident ascendance of the terms "data" and "information."[6] Bowker's wry humor invites readers to conclude that data was vanquishing wisdom, as certain sectors of the humanities have long feared. But this is neither the time nor the place to address the differences between causation and correlation.

Google's Ngram Viewer is no different from any other computational system in requiring a second order of analysis. An animating precept behind Gitelman's book is that we must always "look *under*" the data in question to ascertain how, why, and by whom it was defined, acquired, processed, and interpreted. This book extends that logic to argue that we must also "look under" the systems and assumptions by which data and images are positioned in relation to each other.

Johanna Drucker has argued that usage of the term "data" is itself misleading, in part because of its etymological origins, which assume the preexistence of phenomena independent of definition or observation. Drucker instead advocates use of the term "capta," which emphasizes that data must be actively taken and does not exist in a given or "natural" state.[7] For other writers, the proliferation of data—regardless of whether it is given or taken—is sufficient to confer meaning and value. In 2008, *Wired* editor Chris Anderson proclaimed that big data would bring about the end of theory as a means of explaining the functioning of the world and its societies. Anderson argued that models on the scale that a young company called Google was imagining them, would displace virtually all theories of human behavior.

> This is a world where massive amounts of data and applied mathematics replace every other tool that might be brought to bear. Out with every theory of human behavior, from linguistics to sociology. Forget taxonomy, ontology, and psychology. Who knows why people do what they do? The point is they do it, and we can track and measure it with unprecedented fidelity. With enough data, the numbers speak for themselves.[8]

Anderson's uncritical epistemology of data has been rightly eviscerated by social scientists,[9] but the sentiment remains all too common in the hyperbolic discourse of big data in industry. Pinboard founder Maciej Cegłowski, in his keynote address at an industry conference devoted to big data and sponsored by Strata + Hadoop, offered a rare critique of data science, titled "Haunted by Data," from the perspective of a technologist and an entrepreneur:

> The promise is that enough data will give you insight. Retain data indefinitely, maybe waterboard it a little, and it will spill all its secrets. There's a little bit of a con going on here. On the data side, they tell you to collect all the data you can, because they have magic algorithms to help you make sense of it. On the algorithms side, where I live, they tell us not to worry too much about our models, because they have

> magical data. We can train on it without caring how the process works. The data collectors put their faith in the algorithms, and the programmers put their faith in the data. At no point in this process is there any understanding, or wisdom. There's not even domain knowledge. Data science is the universal answer, no matter the question.[10]

Cegłowski's contrarian response to the prevailing celebration of data illustrates the gap between promise and reality in the field of data analytics. From my perspective, paying attention to the scale on which data is acquired and processed is of secondary importance. This allows me to sidestep the bandwagon syndrome as many current theories about data are revised to become theories of big data. I do not mean to be flippant about the importance of understanding how data is differently processed on a massive scale; it is simply not a central concern of this book. In fact, I would compare the phenomenon and functioning of big data to the parallel emergence of noncomputational high-density image formats seen in ultrahigh resolution, high dynamic-range photography, and ultrahigh frame-rate cinema. On one hand, these formats change everything about the capturing and postprocessing of lens-based images; on the other hand, these formats and the discourse that often surrounds them uncritically reinforce much about the status quo in visual culture. If a lot is good, a *huge* amount must be better. All this leads me to suspect, as I explore in chapter 2, that our era may be aptly described as caught up in a "frenzy of the digital."

In *Minima Moralia*, Theodor Adorno famously revised Georg W. F. Hegel's declaration "the true is the whole" to "the whole is the false."[11] If we have learned nothing else from large-scale data analytics, surely we now know that "the whole" is a theoretical impossibility, even if the encyclopedic affordances of digital systems suggest it as an alluring ideal. Although Adorno did not write directly about computation, he worked on *Minima Moralia* in Germany and in the United States, homes of the two most vibrant computing industries of the 1940s. In both countries, computing machines had already been deployed on entire populations, whether in the form of census calculators in the United States or the tabulating machines deployed in Nazi Germany's pursuit of genocide. It is tempting to say that data is uniquely susceptible to the logic of totality. Data processing often relies on samples that are meant to represent a whole. Humans designed computers partly to maximize efficiency and economy. But the logic of totality—the "encyclopedic" affordance of digital technology identified by

Janet Murray—represents only one possible application.[12] I would argue instead that although data is readily mobilized in the interests of totality, it is just as likely to be deployed for ends that are nontotalizing. Totalization represents one possible outgrowth of the logic of computation, but it is far from the only one.[13]

Even the largest data sets must be understood as inevitably situated, motivated, and partial. Routine processes of sampling, translating and interpreting—to say nothing of "cleaning"—data, even on a massive scale, are not synonymous with the philosophical whole imagined by either Hegel or Adorno. Indeed, Hegel's notion of "the universal" necessarily took account of the particular, thereby forming part of the basis for the logic of dialectics. In the context of data analysis, a similar tension plays out between the situated specificity of individual data "points" and the much larger "sets" into which they are integrated. But the promise of interpreting data at scale is precisely a generalizable form of knowledge—a degree of certainty by which one could map a corporate strategy or shape a candidate's platform to maximize profits or electability. Within such a system, particularity does not effectively assert itself dialectically against the universal; it is taken into account statistically even if its effect is infinitesimal.

In Gitelman's book, "data" is assiduously—and somewhat obtrusively—treated as a plural noun. Her introduction notes, "Data's odd suspension between the singular and the plural reminds us of what aggregation means. If a central philosophical paradox of the Enlightenment was the relation between the particular and the universal, then the imagination of data marks a way of thinking in which those principles of logic are either deferred or held at bay."[14] For my purposes, data is neither singular nor plural; I am tempted to speak of a "data effect," which would obviate such distinctions and allow us to focus on its implication in broader systems of power, knowledge, and representation. Following Allan Sekula's interrogation of photography's role in the politics of documentary, we might ask, "What type of exchange is implied" by the capturing of data?[15] Is it an exchange between equals? Does encouraging amateur visualization (e.g., of one's social network) imply a mendacious pluralism in the possible uses of tracking data? Do local, recreational visualizations make more totalizing data systems appear misleadingly domestic and benign?

An emphasis on function also reminds us that data and its interpretations require a class of specialists as well as a complex technological apparatus. Ironically, data analysis systems simultaneously appear to be endlessly open and adaptive as well as (drawing the ire of critical theorists) self-contained systems of knowledge and belief. The more we learn about data, the more directly we confront the uncomfortable truth that, in the eyes of marketers and government agents, we *are* the data we generate: metadata, records, traces, trajectories, profiles. As we will see in the following discussion of the nineteenth century's competition between photography and biometrics in the science of criminology, the abstractions necessitated by computation contrast sharply with the particularities of the photographic record for identification. Perhaps this desire to recapture one's capacity for self-representation is precisely what lies behind the current trend of self-documentation online; the arm's length composition of digital self-portraits constitute a reassertion of the visible self as a gesture of defiance at having one's identity reduced to abstract metadata.

I would also compare this awareness of how data functions in market analytics with the TV-era realization that we (viewers) are the real objects sold by broadcasters and bought by advertisers, that our identities as viewers have relative value based on the income and shopping habits of our demographic. An even more insidious and indigestible realization attends our transformation into a digital-era aggregation of habits, keystrokes, clicks, scrolls, searches, views, likes, location data, browsing history, and so on. The comparatively gross definition of demographics is replaced by aggregated specificities in an age of data mining. As TV viewers were defined as split subjects by their capacity to function as consumers and as citizens, digital consumers are also split, knowable in their particularities if one assembles the available metadata, but more commonly reduced to an infinitesimal point within an aggregated flow. The data effect is thus always hybrid—we perceive it through channels and semiotic protocols that are inflected with meaning, even as they purport to represent the detachment of scientific instrumentation or applied mathematics.

Finally, we should remember that data is defined, collected, and interpreted within a social hierarchy that privileges large, technologically endowed corporate interests. In systems that offer both paid and free access, ironically, those who refuse to pay are more likely to be tracked, while those who presumably have greater resources—a bigger prize for companies harvesting consumer data—can afford to opt out of tracking systems. For all its bigness, big data is not all-inclusive. Kate Crawford notes that "with every big data set, we need to ask which people are excluded. Which places are less visible? What happens if you live in the shadow of big datasets?"[16] Crawford goes on to argue against the continuing fetishization of big data in favor of developing an ethic she calls "data with depth";[17] others have argued convincingly on behalf of "thick data," following the model of deeply contextualized cultural analysis promoted by anthropologist Clifford Geertz.[18] The topic of this subsection—the politics of data—in turn should not be reducible to an easy formula. We need not ask *whether* data has politics, only how deep we want to dig to reveal its secrets.

When, in 1971, Michel Foucault contrasted the *longue-durée* trajectories of macrohistory with the focus on disruption and dislocation within fields that might be regarded as "applied history" (that is, histories of literature, science, philosophy, etc.), he was describing the very intervention in modes of human thought that attended development of the mainframe computer. Although computation as such is not dealt with directly in *The Archaeology of Knowledge*, issues of scale, precision, totality, recall, disruption, categorization, and codification lie at the center of Foucault's historical models.[19] What questions are more insistently provoked by the invention of a machine for large-scale storage and analysis of data than those of historiography and epistemology? In each instance of the data image we find evidence of the ideological, historical, and technical conditions in which it was produced. Hence, understanding the politics of data is only possible within a context that accounts for both technological development and cultural meaning.

Certain themes persist across the decades of computing's rise. Computers are electronic, mechanical, automatic; they work with numbers, calculations, digits; their utility may be universal or specific. The status of "data," which was once a synonym for quantitative information, has been downgraded over time to denote instead an unprocessed intermediate state in the production of information. The regime of data challenged, then quickly surpassed, the visual positivism that had driven scientific imaging technologies and practices of the late nineteenth and early twentieth centuries. Although the critique of positivism was well established in the human sciences, the critique of photography's unique buttressing of visual positivism was still on a distant horizon when data became ensconced in the scientific establishment as the epitome of accuracy, verifiability, and objectivity. Data did not so much inherit the mantle of photographic empiricism as it forestalled the eventual demise of photographic mimesis.

Allan Sekula was at some pains in his writings about photography to insist on the medium's implication in a history that included instrumental applications—scientific, military, cadastral, criminological—alongside its favored—formalist, pictorialist, illusionist—siblings. For Sekula, the goal was to rethink the history of photography as enmeshed in a tangled web of ideology and state power as much as in the eye of the beholder. Data has never had this problem. Data has always been shamelessly instrumental and is readily characterized as such. Even such dubious instrumentalities as online tracking data—the logging and aggregating of our search terms, clickstreams, likes, interests, and associations, as well as keywords appearing in private communications—are presented as shopping aids and time savers for users of e-mail and search engines. Data, we are assured repeatedly in the context of social media and networked communication, is a friend whose friendship grows more rewarding the more we share.[20]

Online tracking is only one example of how the logics of neoliberalism have broadly infused everyday technologies. "Information technology," according to David Harvey, "is the privileged technology of neoliberalism" because of its role in creating and optimizing a framework where the logic of markets can prevail.[21] Under neoliberalism, politics and contestation are subsumed by efficiency and rationality; political interest groups and ideologically aligned collectives are replaced with the notion of "stakeholders" and collaborative participation in processes of problem solving. The horizontal networks—both technological and human—celebrated by evangelists of digital culture are easily digested as part of neoliberalism's shift from hierarchical modes of governance to rational problem solving. Neoliberalism's focus on market exchange as the model for all human action "requires technologies of information creation and capacities to accumulate, store, transfer, analyze, and use massive databases to guide decisions in the global marketplace."[22] Is the shift from optics to computation, then, simply an escape from the frying pan into the fire?

Echoing Harvey, political scientist Wendy Brown differentiates neoliberalism from other diagnostic models for critiquing the deleterious effects of capitalism by emphasizing its radical extension of the logics of "the market" into virtually all aspects of everyday life:

> Importantly, this is not simply a matter of extending commodification and monetization everywhere—that's the old Marxist depiction of capital's transformation of everyday life. Neoliberalism construes even non-wealth generating spheres—such as learning, dating, or exercising—in market terms, submits them to market metrics, and governs them with market techniques and practices. Above all, it casts people as human capital who must constantly tend to their own present and future value.[23]

Although Brown does not focus on technology in her critique of neoliberalism, it would be difficult to miss how large-scale informatics systems are implicated in the logic of neoliberal society and economics that she describes. If the industrial age brought an increase in the power of machines and the demotion of humans to the role of operators and consumers, the digital age has further lowered the status of consumers from humans needing to be seduced into buying particular goods to data points within trackable patterns of consumption. In data systems, we are no longer the individuals we once believed ourselves to be, but this realization brings neither the anxiety of modernism nor the nihilism of postmodernism. A properly trained neoliberal subject instead wants a piece of the action, to shape data flows and profiles consciously to profit from the insights and access they provide.

The term "neoliberalism" is all the more insidious in preemptively dashing the traces of hope that were once inscribed in the term "late capitalism." Describing capitalism as "late" suggested that its end was, if not near, then at least conceivable. "Neoliberalism" carries with it a hint of despair, a concession that the once redemptive quality of liberalism has become just as co-optable as the conservatism once invoked by its pejorative predecessor, "neocon." The "neo" in neoliberalism suggests that we are not at a stage of lateness nearing relief, but at a point of renewal in a cycle that shows fewer signs than ever of letting up.

Perhaps the deepest and most destructive paradox of the role of data in consumer culture is the extent to which it mobilizes the power of multiplicity across a population, while individuals whose actions are logged are deprived of any type of collective agency. Whether through passive or active engagement with data collection and analysis, we occupy a subject position that is individuated: every choice, search, and purchase "matters" as part of a larger market-tracking system. At the same time, however, our ability to act is restricted to severely constrained individual choices: what brand to buy, not what political or environmental priorities should be supported by our representatives. In this sense, we are never meaningfully disaggregated from our demographic, nor are we capable of directly steering how our actions are interpreted. We are monads in a vast leviathan of traced actions, yet we experience no lasting sense of individual agency or collective interest. Giorgio Agamben diagnosed this insistence on "desubjectifying" the individual as a key to constructing "the most docile and cowardly social body that has ever existed in human history."[24] We are, if anything, tempted toward fatalistic resignation, cynicism, or apathy by the statistical insignificance of any single gesture. Ironically, it is joint collective action undertaken at a scale that could only be realized through digital networks that offers the only viable alternative.

What would it take to transform large-scale data systems into effective tools for social change? First, technologies of data would need to be somehow disaggregated from the larger apparatuses of neoliberal economics and ideology from which they emerged. No small task! In addition to its seductive cultural rhetoric, neoliberalism aligns with a daunting range of existing political power structures embedded in mainstream party politics, economic infrastructures, legislative reforms, and judicial decisions. For those of us who hold out hope for the socially liberatory potentials of digital networks, many of the tenets of neoliberalism have been rallying cries against the imaginary threat of monolithic cultural regimes that were hierarchical, centralized, and prescriptive—the hegemony of late capitalism and state bureaucracy. The affordances of networked computing aligned neatly with alternative movements that favor collaboration over competition; horizontal networking over vertical hierarchy; best practices over regulation; stakeholders over interest groups; consensus over doctrine—but these terms all turn out to be drawn directly from the playbook of neoliberal governance!

The result, according to Brown, is the displacement of power as the focal point of political critique. In its place, neoliberalism promotes cooperation without collectivization, facilitating connection and communication among disparate groups, yes, but without the sense of shared interests that might drive and sustain a political movement.[25] All of this, Brown aligns with what Foucault calls modern government's technique of "omnes et singulatim" (all and each), by which a population may be simultaneously gathered but isolated; amassed and distinguished; massified and individualized.[26] A key factor is neoliberalism's emphasis on rational self-interest, in which individuals are encouraged to act, within certain bounds, as individuated participants in a more or less rational market economy. As market actors, we are variously aware that each action, decision, or movement, however passively it may be undertaken, feeds data into an overall information system that tracks these activities and generates meaning. Unless we are targeted for specific investigation—say, by agents of law enforcement, immigration, or intelligence—no single action may be said to have much significance on its own, but increasingly, neoliberal subjects come to understand their *selves* to be aggregated statistically. Individual particularities remain latent in data systems, lying dormant until called forth in the service of an externally imposed narrative.

There is no small irony in systems that seek most actively to undermine the hegemony of data operating through multiplicity and overproliferation, often mixing "good" data with "bad" to obfuscate the reality of one's inter/actions in digital space. The Tor browser offers a case in point, along with the technology underlying the Wikileaks platform. Both systems operate by exploiting the limited capacity of computational data mining to distinguish relevant from irrelevant data. This tactic is presumably of transient utility, given the rapid pace of developments in artificial intelligence and data processing. Rather than merely concealing or encrypting data intended to remain private, multiplicity depends on limitations in the capacity of computers to intelligently sift through an avalanche of data. Such operations may well prove trivial to circumvent in the future, but for now, the tactic of resistance through proliferation marks a revealing limit case for the function of data in systems of knowledge and control. When speaking of the "politics of data," I don't know whether it is ironic or simply appropriate to paraphrase Jean-Luc Godard when concluding that the issue, ultimately, may not be to make political data but to make data *politically*.

Visible Culture

In *Programmed Visions,* Wendy Hui Kyong Chun highlights one of the challenges associated with parsing the relationship between visual and digital culture in a chapter subtitled "Invisibly Visible; Visibly Invisible":

> Computers have fostered both a decline in and frenzy of visual knowledge. Opaque yet transparent, incomprehensible yet logical, they reveal that the less we know the

more we show (or are shown). Two phenomena encapsulate this nicely: the proliferation of digital images (new media as "visual culture") and "total information" systems (new media as "transparent").[27]

Our ability to talk about the conjunction of visual-digital culture is founded on an internal contradiction, or at least the divergent extremes of visibility and invisibility. Chun's paradox suggests that what is at stake exists not primarily in the realm of the visible, but in the nonmimetic domain of computation, and she reminds us that the artifacts and practices of today's digital technologies are all too readily embraced by the instrumentality that underpins neoliberal economics and culture. In Sean Cubitt's introduction to *The Practice of Light*, he notes, "Historically, much of visual culture has concerned itself with making the invisible visible. ... The universe of numbers generated by an informational society draws on this history of visualizing to make itself visible, and in turn the particular organizational modes typical of informatics begin to impinge on modes of visualization."[28] Cubitt's analysis of the political embeddedness of technologies of vision within culture is exemplary, illuminating a wide swath of political and theoretical implications. For both Chun and Cubitt, the invisibility of digital processes is functionally analogous to the operation of ideology—the more widely it is disavowed, repressed, or denied, the more it is clearly determinative of cultural beliefs and actions. Correspondingly, in Chun's model, one's ability to decode the operations of the most abstract and invisible digital processes is dependent on the sophistication of one's understanding of how these systems operate.

A similar privileging of technical knowledge occurs in Benjamin H. Bratton's *The Stack*. In Bratton's terms, the deeper we are able to drill critically into the "accidental megastructure" of "The Stack," the more complete our understanding of its functioning will be. Bratton's Stack comprises digital culture by means of a vertically integrated system that includes all the particularities of hardware and software along with their interfaces and governing protocols, but also those infrastructures that subtend them (mineral sourcing, electrical grids) and those that operate them (humans, robots). Bratton's model is both philosophical and practical, offering a far-reaching exploration that is worthy of taking as its object of study "the digital." Bratton's work is also intended as a practical intervention in design, refusing to settle for articulating a new theoretical model. In *The Stack*, Bratton operationalizes his theoretical principles, laying out a roadmap for designers and architects as well as systems engineers and cultural theorists.[29]

The aspirations of this book are more modest. I do not seek a philosophical nor deeply technological understanding of the origins or essence of digital culture. My aim is rather to address the functioning of visual-digital culture in some particularity, observing overarching historical trends, yes, but with a focus on specific instances and aberrations. My goal is not to redraw the map of visual culture, but I would like to demonstrate the benefit of revisiting received historical models that continue to shape our thinking about the technological present.

The method of this book is partly inspired by media archaeology, particularly as it derives from the historiographical models—fractious, non-teleological, eccentric—advanced by Foucault and others. The scope of the project is a discontinuous, but still in-depth, exploration of the "technocultural imaginary" and its manifestations at particular moments. The investigation is thus not *about* technology; rather, I analyze how specific technologies serve as historically situated prisms for exposing, expressing, or engaging our most pressing cultural concerns. Digital media are often symptomatic of the processes by which technologies have become banal, invisible, and accepted, even in their most troubling manifestations. My goal is to expose the systems of power by which we govern our own behavior; the technological, corporate, and governmental elites in whom we place (or from whom we withhold) our trust, the premises and constraints we accept, and the myriad microcapitulations by which power maximizes its efficiency in an increasingly technologized world.

The proliferation of theoretical writings about "new media" during the 1990s seemed to parallel the pace of late twentieth-century technology industries. As the world hurtled toward the end of the millennium, this period was dubbed—as if in some urgent computer shorthand—Y2K. It was widely perceived and described as an era marked by radical disjunctions, paradigm shifts, and potential catastrophes, all of which afforded enticing opportunities for reinventing the terms of its theoretical understanding. Fetishists of the "new"—often unapologetically inspired by the futuristic literary genre of cyberpunk fiction—were subsequently criticized by a countervailing critical genre skeptical about the proclaimed "newness" of new media, pointing to numerous instances in which categories of "old" and "new" were rhetorically and historiographically bankrupt.[30] Some of these challenges deployed a form of historical parallax, drawing attention to the euphoric discourses that attended previous generations of technology, implicitly reminding readers just how silly those exceptionalist proclamations sound in retrospect. The model of historical parallax, practiced with rare virtuosity by Anne Friedberg and Lisa Gitelman, in which technologies from radically different moments in time are placed in critical juxtaposition, provided inspiration for the primary method of this book. Outlined in some detail below, my adaptation of the parallax concept hinges not on historical anachrony but on drawing attention to the convergent/divergent relations that are expressed between the realms of data and images.

My goal in writing this book is not to convince readers of the inevitability of any particular future but to produce a critical subjectivity that is both historically aware and technologically informed. Hopefully, the lessons of 1990s cyberculture have been articulated and internalized to the point where we no longer need to march through the usual litany of denunciations: technological determinism; utopia/dystopia; euphoric proclamations/moral panic; and so on. However, I will selectively mine the history of this body of critical literature for evidence of the interconnectedness of cultural criticism and cultural production. Media archaeology offers a useful model for investigating the media technologies and critical literature of the late twentieth century. Over the course of the two decades straddling the millennial turn, roughly 1990–2010, citizens of technologically privileged societies were retrained to experience the world in terms of procedural logic governed by interoperable systems. The subfield new media studies emerged to address these shifts and developed a sometimes awkward vocabulary for speaking about digital*ness* across various domains of culture. Turning this body of not-so-distant theoretical writing into objects of archaeological study allows us to examine not so much the correctness of any given work of scholarship, but its presuppositions, limits, and thresholds. In other words, we may learn as much by examining this work in terms of what it does *not* say as from what it *does* say.

The archaeological approach attempts to find patterns of discourse through an examination of material conditions and the systems governing them. This model is further predicated on excavating complex systems, not in their totality or as components of a cohesive historical narrative, but as fragments from which to extrapolate and propose insights into human behavior and systems of thought. I hope it is not immodest to set the sights of this project on such a large span of media and technologies. Faced with an overwhelming data set, stretched across decades of complex evolution, we have no choice but to be selective with our objects of study. By establishing a critical conceit that is specifically oriented to address the resonances and conflicts of data and images across a range of media platforms, this project will privilege cases that are in some way liminal, hybrid, or uncontainable by one category or the other.

Finally, this investigation is bounded by the methods and concerns of visual culture studies on one side, technology studies on another, and ("new") media studies on a third. With visual culture I share concerns about how we make meaning out of the visible world and the critique of signification, representation, tropes, and metaphor, but I choose to confront—and even embrace—the disruptions occasioned by digital imaging. With technology studies I share a respect for material context in mapping the history of technological development. My aim here is not to recapitulate the history of apparatuses or inventions—and certainly not *great men*—but to pay attention to the reciprocal, sociocultural, economic, and political motivations that drive them. From media and new media studies, I build on longstanding concerns with the politics of seeing and being seen—perhaps I should say of sensing and being sensed?—the interrogation of systems of power and ideology, and an underlying critique of capitalism and its consequences.

Parallax Views

Data tells stories.[31] It is also used to capture and convey information about the world. Like images, this information and its modes of conveyance are contested and nontrivial to decode. I base this book's critical method on the data/images dyad not to propose a structural binary, but as two components of a "parallax logic" that can be brought to bear on numerous moments throughout the history of technology. At the risk of overburdening the metaphor, I would explain this strategy as follows: as with the optical properties of parallax, information about a viewed object may be gleaned through perceived differences in the distance between two viewpoints. In certain cases, data and images operate in close proximity, informing, cross-pollinating, and inspiring each other; at other times, their relationship seems to be philosophically quite distant, motivating antithetical pursuits, methods, and results. Parallax also allows the eyes—and thence the brain—to perceive and deduce spatial information from occlusions caused by one object getting in the way of another. In other words, we can derive information from things that are unseen, obstructed, or perhaps misrecognized, as well as from those that are perceived with clarity and wholeness.

Images and data suggest differing knowledge regimes, the relative ascendance of which, at any given moment, correlates with ways in which we culturally process issues of political and social significance. What does it say about the epistemic regime of a historical moment if all efforts—cultural and technological—insist on concealing the differences between competing ways of knowing about the world? A critical dynamic that problematizes values such as realism, convergence, totality, automation, and ubiquity suggests a very different role for the developers and users of digital technology. Within industrial practice, an implicit commitment to the synthetic mode has long dominated the conventional wisdom about data and images. The accepted narrative maps a trajectory of linear progression toward ever more convincing approximations of the real world. Graphics engines used for 3D games become ever more photorealistic, for example, while film and television productions increasingly merge lens-based and computer-generated images at the stages of production, postproduction, and previsualization. While certain aspects of technological development indeed reflect this narrative, the reality of the situation is both more complicated and more interesting.

The idea that moving images can (and should) provide audiences with an asymptotic approximation of "reality" was fully articulated in writings by film theorists of the early twentieth century. André Bazin associated emerging cinematographic techniques, such as long takes and deep focus (which were themselves enabled by the increased light-gathering capacity of film emulsions), with a perceptual experience that resembled the real world.[32] Bazin's argument that this constituted cinema's greatest potential is barely distinguishable from the realist discourse that attends the recent resurgence of virtual reality and contemporary visual effects such as motion capture. Outside the promotional context of industry marketing, it would be naïve to return to such a model, ignoring decades of film scholarship devoted to unraveling the assumptions underlying both Bazin's telos and the deterministic view of technology that underlies it. This project instead acknowledges the persistence of a desire for "the real"—in this respect I agree with Brian Winston that we remain "addicted" to at least the idea of realism—but I would insist that the most provocative dialogue between data and images occurs when "realistic" representation is not the primary goal.[33] My hope is that this taxonomy will help illuminate the operative strategies across a broad spectrum of media making, allowing us to defamiliarize some seemingly self-evident motivations in the media and technology industries, and ultimately to identify strategies for misusing or misappropriating these technologies for socially and creatively beneficial ends.

The notion of parallax also enables us to throw the relations between data and images into relief—to observe points of convergence when they occur without privileging them in a general sense. Parallax—as with its functioning in the ocular world—allows for the perception of both sameness and difference; it presupposes a split viewing position and the ability to process differences in perspective and perception. The concept of parallax further allows us to consider the active dynamics of the relationship between data and images at specific moments. This model emerges in part from the observation that particular media forms may exhibit either a convergence or a divergence of images and data. To think systematically about these dynamics, I propose the following taxonomy of modes to describe the functional relationships between data and images.

Supplemental

The supplemental mode may reasonably be considered the most straightforward and intuitive of the modes outlined here. In this mode, images and data relate to each other in an additive way. The supplemental mode allows deficiencies in the descriptive capacity of images to be supplemented by those of data and vice versa. This model can be traced back to the nineteenth-century Bertillon card, a variation of which is still in use for driver's licenses, passports, and criminal records. In this mode, neither regime (data or images) challenges the other epistemologically; instead they work together in a parallel process that demands no systemic reconciliation. One advantage of the supplemental mode is the potential to simply add new information as it becomes available. In the case of the Bertillon card, this may be seen in the addition of fingerprints to identification cards. Fingerprints, which were not part of Bertillon's original system in the 1880s, were simply added to the bottom of existing cards once fingerprinting became a viable technology in the early 1900s. Thus, the photographic mug shot, biometrical measurements, and fingerprints all function in parallel, with no crossover or effect on the adjacent systems of identification; each may be used to cross-reference or verify the other, but the systems themselves remain discrete.

Multiperspectival

The multiperspectival mode has historical roots in Eadweard Muybridge's multicamera array, used for the study of human and animal locomotion. The multiperspectival mode is fundamentally lens-based, and the conjunction of multiple images from multiple perspectives does nothing to disrupt the mimetic function of each individual lens and the image it renders. Images in the multiperspectival mode are not abstracted or translated into computable data; they continue to generate meaning through their indexical relationship to a profilmic body. In the multiperspectival mode, images captured from multiple points in space are used to compose a data set of visual information that remains rooted in the photographic. Meaning is then created through the juxtaposition or compositing of the images, which are unshackled from their original time base and location in space.

Translational

The most common exemplars of the translational mode may be found in motion capture and facial recognition systems. These technologies use visual information captured photographically to generate an array of data points, which are then mapped onto a Cartesian plane or volume. This mode has its historical roots in the time-motion studies of Etienne-Jules Marey, which he dubbed "chronophotography." In Marey's system, photographic images were abstracted and converted into a combination of points and lines in space, ultimately effacing the photographic representation and original bodies entirely. Another historical example may be found in the grid-based tracing process enabled by the portable camera obscura. The translational mode values the photographically or optically perceived image, but only as a source of convertible data, not an end in itself. The translational mode also works in the opposite direction, beginning with data sets—including sonographic, radiographic, and backscatter data—that express meaning to humans only when translated to the visible register.

Aspirational

Software has been long capable of generating "realistic-looking" images without any photographic referent at all. In this case, designers create volumes, shapes, and surfaces through a combination of manual and procedural modeling. Textures may be created directly by software or by adapting prerendered patterns or samples from photographic originals. The environments of most contemporary 3D games are created this way, resulting in fully navigable and responsive environments that have no indexical relation to the physical world. In many cases, however, these artificially created worlds approximate photorealistic—or, more accurately, *cinematically* realistic—imagery. In this case, the basic relationship between data-based imagery and lens-based imagery is that of iconic resemblance, not literal translation. Just as the multiperspectival mode articulates a relationship between image and image, the aspirational mode articulates a relationship between data and data. The goal of this work is a product that is entirely digitally generated but increasingly indistinguishable from lens-based images.

Synthetic

The synthetic mode is perhaps the most familiar because of its current dominance in the entertainment industries. The synthetic mode includes a cluster of technologies—virtual and augmented reality, holographic projection, previsualization, virtual cinematography—all of which deploy variations on the synthesis of data and images. The synthetic mode has evolved over many years to dissolve the hierarchy between image and data, or data and metadata. Workflow in the visual effects industry, for example, no longer involves "adding" metadata to filmed images; rather, images and data are captured via integrated systems that ascribe no necessary hierarchy to the two types of data. Increasingly, lens-based images and volumetric or positional data are captured in tandem and remain mutually interdependent throughout the postproduction and display process.

Negotiated

I have termed the final mode of digital imaging "negotiated," to signify models of digital imaging that deploy selected aspects of the strategies described above to ends that are not adequately described by any single mode. The negotiated mode is so-named in homage to Stuart Hall's negotiated stance described in his reception theory of encoding/decoding. Here, it denotes a way to describe instances that seem to be negotiating the unstable relationship between data and image. At their most revealing, these negotiations include elements of self-reflexivity that invite reconsideration of the data/images binary in both general and specific terms. Instances of the negotiated mode often highlight internal contradictions of the data/images binary and make this a part of the work itself. Among the exemplars of this mode is Casey Reas, whose work has consistently blurred the boundaries between referential and computational image making, which I discuss in chapter 1.

To expand on the parallax modes outlined above, each subsequent chapter of the book is devoted to a conceptual realm—space, visualization, surveillance—wherein various instances of these modes are deployed. While this introduction sketches a broad historical and conceptual framework for parsing relations between data and images, the chapters that follow operationalize this framework to analyze specific cases. I believe the parallax modes outlined here offer a useful vocabulary for critiquing the conjoined practices of visual-digital culture, but I would not want to suggest that this paradigm is either comprehensive or exclusive. Barely a generation ago, the technologies of vision through which the relationship between data and images was negotiated would not have sustained this type of investigation. Though today's media, technology, and entertainment industries are dominated by a logic of synthesis that has come to seem increasingly natural and inevitable, this approach follows a long period of ascendance of the translational mode during which images were consciously reimagined as visual information and digitized into formats that could be acted on by computers. My aim throughout this book is to decenter naturalized paradigms of translation and synthesis to recognize the value of other modes that invite different kinds of experimentation and aberration.

Finally, parallax is part of a conceptual toolkit that enables us to make sense of the evolution of imaging technologies and to bring a demystified critical perspective to bear on both the practices of data/image making and the systems by which they gain cultural significance. In a practical sense, articulating these parallax modes frees us from dealing with the perpetual cascade of new or anticipated technologies. As history has taught repeatedly, no technology—and certainly no single corporation—should be mistaken for a permanent fixture of the technocultural landscape. I therefore strive, when possible, to examine the functioning of these modes in a general context, rather than anchor my observations to even the most promising new—or currently dominant—technology, trend, or corporate entity.

A Symbolic History of Data/Images

A symbolic point of origin for this book lies in the virtually concurrent conception in the early 1830s of mathematician Charles Babbage's protocomputational difference engine and the precinematic phenakistoscope. The phenakistoscope shares a genealogy with several other optical/philosophical toys of the nineteenth century, but Babbage's difference engine is unthinkable without the technical apparatus and mechanical sensibility of the industrial revolution. Both, as Anne Friedberg has noted, share the ability to modify units of meaning from one state to another and to create meaningful associations as a result, but the two could hardly be more different in terms of their material origins and philosophical precepts.[34] In these two inventions—the phenakistoscope and the difference engine—images and data are aligned with entirely divergent epistemological regimes.

Along with numerous other optical toys related to cinema's prehistory, the phenakistoscope constructed a visual experience that approximated the perception of movement experienced by the eye. Each device that prefigured cinematic motion deployed a slightly different strategy for alternately presenting images and the gaps between them, but all were predicated on sequences of varied images to create a composite illusion of movement. Like its sibling technology the zoetrope, movement of the disks in the phenakistoscope was initiated by a highly variable gesture of the human hand, and the speed of the resulting animation typically went from too fast to too slow, with a sweet spot in the middle when things momentarily seemed about right. The experience, in other words, was fundamentally imprecise, analog, and variable, the very antitheses of the mechanical repeatability on which the conception of a calculating machine was necessarily based.

While Babbage devised the concept for the difference engine and its successor, the analytical engine, he owned a silk portrait of Joseph Marie Jacquard, inventor of the Jacquard loom. Created in 1801, Jacquard's loom produced extraordinarily intricately woven graphical images. One history of computing goes so far as to describe the loom itself as a protocomputational apparatus. "In a sense, Jacquard's loom was a kind of early digital

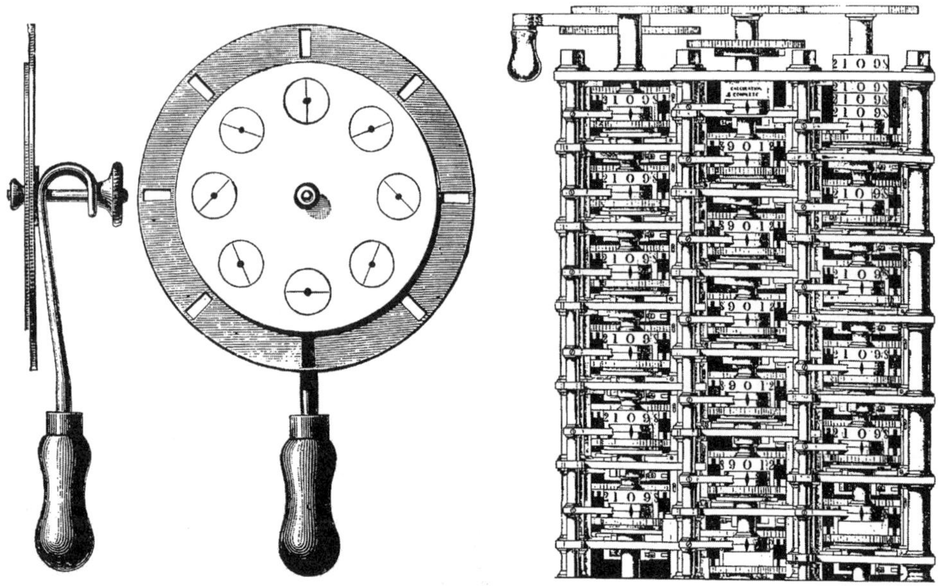

Figure 0.1
Simultaneous, but oppositional, regimes of knowledge aligned with the logics of data and images to manifest in the phenakistoscope and difference engine (ca. 1839).

graphics computer."[35] The portrait owned by Babbage, in fact, was created from more than twenty-four thousand punch cards, and the complexity of the graphical information they represented provided partial inspiration for the two computing machines designed—but never actually built—by Babbage. Quite literally, then, the concept for encoded data, and even the specific form of the punch card that would be deployed by the analytical engine, originated in the domain of images. This convenient origin myth aside, subsequent systems of representation and knowledge that emerged in the nineteenth century were more commonly characterized by an oppositional relationship between data and images.

One such opposition can be found in the nearly concurrent development in the late 1830s of photography and telegraphy, arguably the two most important communication technologies of the nineteenth century. Samuel Morse's system for telegraphic communication would not be considered computational by today's standards, but it was nonetheless a binary data system on which the instrument of the telegraph was capable of

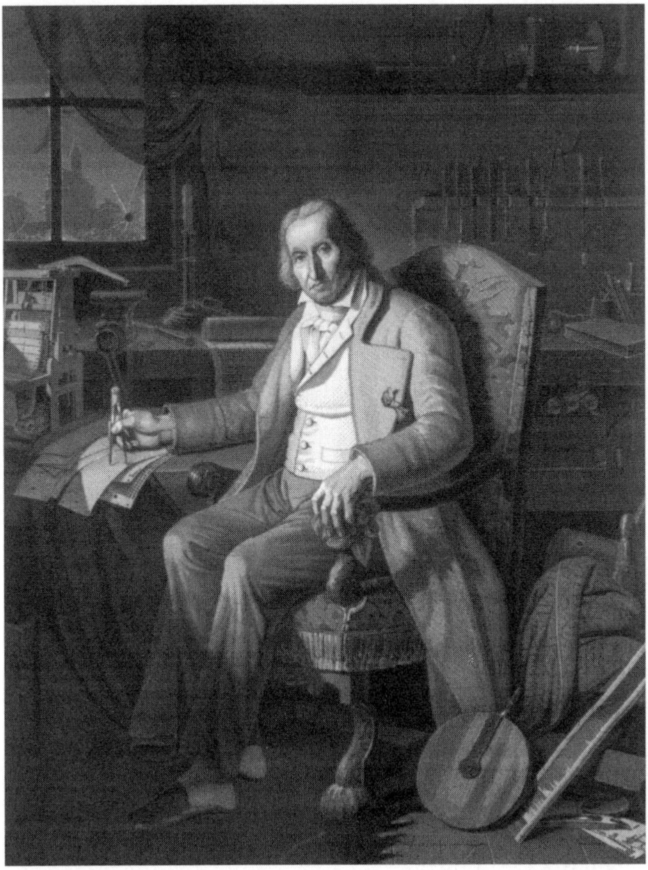

Figure 0.2
A woven silk portrait of Joseph Marie Jacquard illustrates the use of punch cards for data storage (ca. 1839).

acting. Furthermore, the symbolic expressions used in telegraph communication could be regarded as a precomputational system of algorithmically generated codes. Katherine Hayles makes this argument in her book *How We Think: Digital Media and Contemporary Technogenesis* (2012), noting that approximately 90 percent of all nineteenth-century telegraphic communication was first abstracted by operators using code books.[36] This process of encoding/decoding might be correctly understood as an instance of human computation that closely portends the systems for electrical computation that would emerge in the decades to come.

From the beginning, photography was overtly linked with the objectivity of science, and the men who perfected it were technicians born of the Industrial Revolution. Photography's acceleration of the transition within modern painting from representation to abstraction is well known, as is the transformative impact of mechanical reproducibility on the experience of artworks. The virtually concurrent development of photography and telegraphy benefited from the general milieu of nineteenth-century technological innovation, but the two otherwise shared virtually no technological affordances. More important, the two were separated by an epistemic divide that privileged, on one hand, an indexical, photochemical trace of visible phenomena in the world, and on the other, an entirely abstracted, electromechanical translation of symbolic information into pulses and gaps. The oppositional mental models represented by telegraphy and photography are further affirmed by the fact that it took more than forty years for the two technologies to meaningfully converge. Although a patent for sending graphical symbols—a device known as the pantelegraph—was issued within just a few years of the invention of telegraphy, the conversion of photographic images into a binary form that could be effectively transmitted by telegraph was not commonly practiced until early in the twentieth century, when it was found to be useful for law enforcement.[37]

Additional historical bifurcations of data and images are the concurrent experiments in time-motion study undertaken in the United States by Eadweard Muybridge and in France by Etienne-Jules Marey. These examples are well known and I will not recapitulate their contributions to the prehistory of cinema here. For the purposes of this discussion, these two projects are noteworthy because of their radically different uses of the shared technology of photography in service of competing commitments to mimesis and computability. Whereas Muybridge deployed multiple cameras to produce isolated frames that were displayed sequentially, Marey developed a system of motion analysis that captured multiple exposures within the frame of a single image. While Muybridge's multiple camera arrays fragmented the smooth movements of bodies through space into discrete instants, Marey's multiple exposures on a single plate were abstracted from their photographic specificity and reduced to the most relevant data points.

For Muybridge, human and animal bodies were very much at the center of his work, and the naked, unruly bodies he photographed were replete with idiosyncrasy and particularity. On several occasions, Muybridge

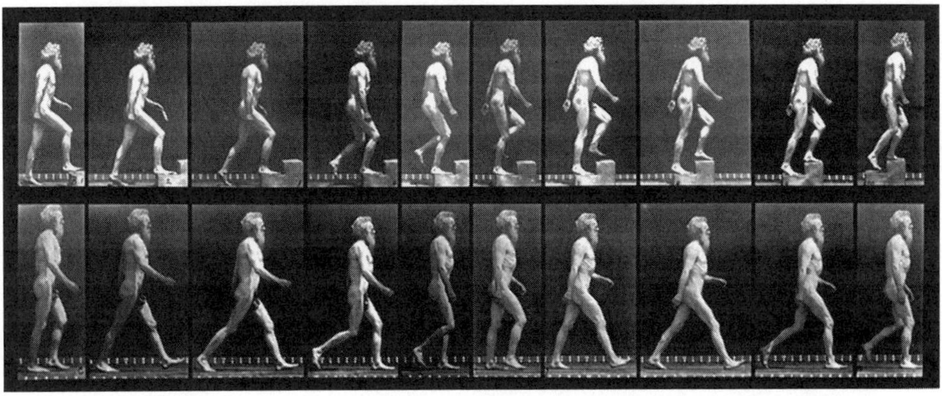

Figure 0.3
Motion studies by Eadweard Muybridge (pictured here) reveled in photographic specificity and bodily idiosyncrasy.

appears in image sequences that might be considered a form of narcissistic self-portraiture. The scale of Muybridge's project, which comprised hundreds of thousands of image sequences, was marked by obsession, as Thom Andersen observes in his film *Eadweard Muybridge Zoopraxographer* (1975), a desire for totality that bordered on pseudoscientific mania. Over decades, Muybridge experimented with various formats for his image sequences, but they were most often presented in grid or sequential form. Although his subjects were frequently positioned in front of a grid, he did not systematically extrapolate from the visual records contained in each individual frame. That is, he did not attempt to apply statistical averaging or create translations of the photographic images into quantified data.

Marey, by contrast, actively suppressed the specificity of the bodies he photographed by having his subjects wear black suits and hoods that concealed facial features and bodily anomalies. His subjects were further outfitted with white dots and lines marking joints and limbs. Marey's system of chronophotography captured multiple superimpositions on a single image plate, which emphasized the contrast of white lines and dots against hooded black bodies and dark backgrounds. Thus, Marey's result maximizes the computability—or at least the measurability—of bodily movements as they are translated into quantifiable points and lines. Marey's "data points" were destined not for computation, as such, but for statistical analysis, which was, in turn, designed to maximize the efficiency and regularity of

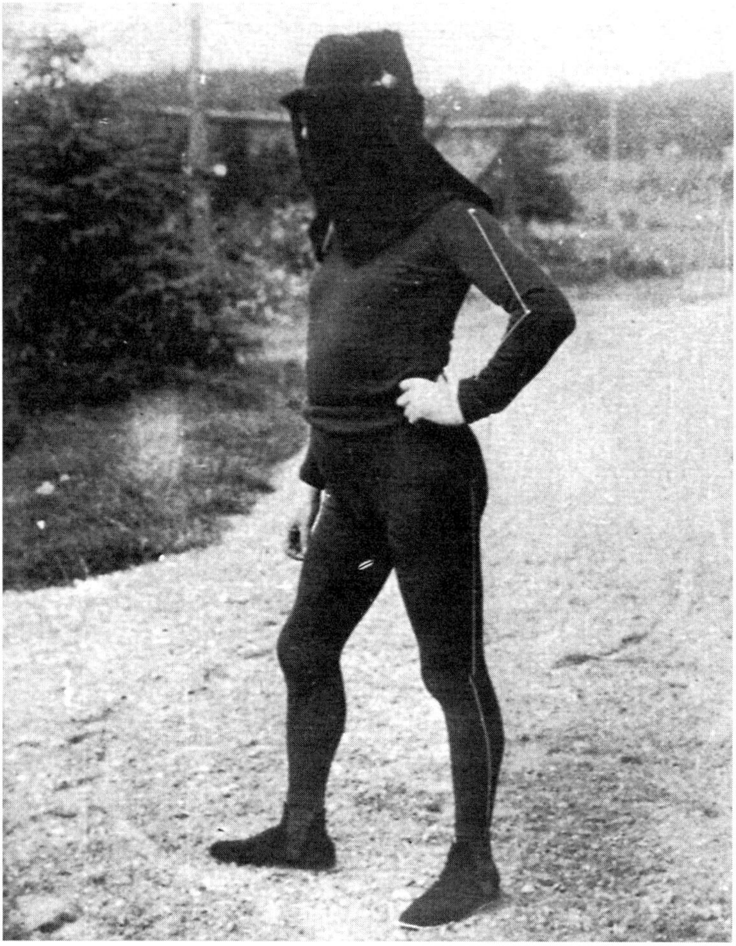

Figure 0.4
Etienne-Jules Marey's single-plate chronophotography abstracted bodily movements and particularities into quantifiable points and lines.

bodily movement. Marey's work was funded by the French military, partly in hopes of bringing regimentation to soldiers' movements in the field, presumably to impress upon participants in colonial uprisings the overwhelming mechanistic and industrial power of the French military. The bodies captured by Marey were like uniformed soldiers whose individuality had been erased, their images abstracted beyond recognition. In some cases, Marey even traced over his photographic originals, reducing them to pure points and lines on paper. In these tracings, bodies are relegated, along with photography itself, to the role of generating data.[38]

A final historical instance of divergent uses of data and images is the work of French criminologist Alphonse Bertillon and the English eugenicist Francis Galton. Both Bertillon and Galton were active users of photography in the late nineteenth century, and both viewed it as a scientifically valid means for social betterment. Although much has been written on these historical figures, I focus briefly on a structural parallel between Bertillon and Muybridge, on one hand, and Galton and Marey, on the other. Both Bertillon and Muybridge used strategies of fragmentation and multiplicity to generate knowledge about the human body; whereas Marey and Galton both made use of image composites within a single photographic frame to minimize the significance of differences between individual bodies. These divergent strategies may be understood as exemplifying the competing logics of data and images in operation at the end of the nineteenth century.

Like Marey, Galton was interested less in the particularities of his photographic subjects than in a process of statistical averaging, designed to suppress irregularities while highlighting shared visual attributes across multiple faces. In his primary investigation, Galton used the photographic equivalent of mathematical averages—that is, single-plate photocomposites—to identify the facial characteristics that could be associated with an essential "type." Referring to these composites as "pictorial statistics," Galton devised a method of multiple superimpositions using a specially designed photographic apparatus and a careful protocol for capturing the photographs. These images purported to distill the recognizable essence of a particular category of humans—not just criminals, but also the poor, unintelligent, immoral, ethnic, or infirm—by printing or projecting a series of precisely registered faces one on top of another. The more images that contributed to the composite, Galton theorized, the more accurate and revealing the visible essence would become, but Galton's composites were generally produced from fewer than a dozen originals. So intoxicating was this conjunction of the still-developing science of statistics with the art of photography that Galton enthusiastically lectured and published on the subject for many years, sometimes staging elaborate illustrated presentations using multiple magic lanterns to create live superimpositions.

In the end, Galton's system of photocomposites remained a novelty that never gained much traction among criminologists. As a practical matter, police investigators and technicians were more interested in systems they could operationalize to catch and identify criminals than in Galton's underlying goal of breeding undesirable humans out of existence. This stereotypical instance of nineteenth-century scientific racism was deeply informed by concurrent cultural discourses of phrenology, physiognomy, and Galton's own term, eugenics. Although the idea of "pictorial statistics" resonated with the growing science of statistics, its resulting visual composites were more useful for the abstract purposes of proclaiming the inferiority of

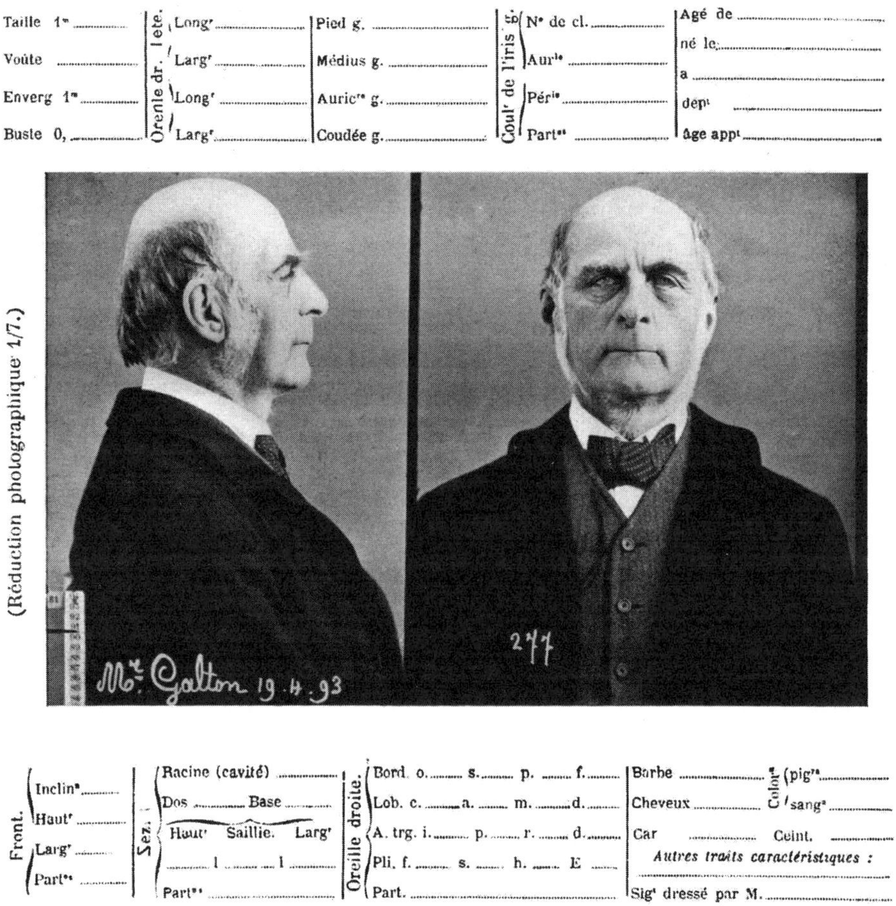

Figure 0.5
A Bertillon card featuring English eugenicist Francis Galton includes a photographic likeness but not biometric data.

certain "types" than for actually preventing crime. The appeal of Galton's photocomposites rested in their promise to make the complex mathematics behind statistical analysis readily understandable through visible means.

Alphonse Bertillon, in contrast, privileged the realm of data over that of images in attempting to prevent criminal recidivism. His system of bodily measurement, known as anthropometrics, was supplemented by a codified system of photographic representation, the mug shot. Bertillon's two-image (frontal and profile) protocol for police bookings is still standard practice in the American legal system today. Perhaps more significant was Bertillon's system for linking these photographic representations to the bodily measurements that he regarded as a more accurate and mathematically verifiable form of identification. Bodily measurements also provided the primary means of storage and retrieval for each card, with photographs used only as secondary visual confirmation of an accused criminal's identity. Once Bertillon's system was implemented, the Parisian police quickly amassed a collection of more than one hundred thousand cards, leaving them with the logistical nightmare of reliably storing and retrieving the data on the cards. Bertillon's filing system clearly anticipated the need—especially among law enforcement officials—for large-scale, high-speed, networked databases.

Evidence that large-scale data generation long predates the existence of computational systems is easy enough to find. Bertillon's filing system functioned as an analog human-powered database predicated on a standardized system for classification, ordering, and cross-referencing. This system accurately prefigured—or perhaps demanded—the invention of a computerized system for automated retrieval. Or maybe we only see the blueprint for modern computing in Bertillon's system because we observe it through the overdetermining haze of twentieth-century history, which is unimaginable without the rise of computation. As evidenced by the concurrent rise of photography and biometrics, the use of statistical and numerical systems for documenting and understanding the world did not depart from the parallel pretensions of scientific photography until well into the twentieth century. For Bertillon and many who followed him, images and data functioned in parallel, without duplicating, converging with, or obviating the other.

We could carry on selectively mining the nineteenth century for evidence of technologies that diverge in their approach to data and images. Even the Hollerith machine, which was used to perform the first

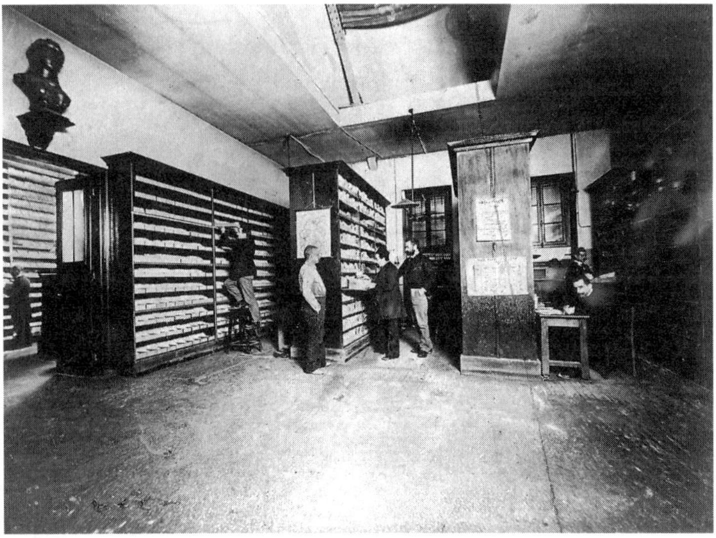

Figure 0.6
Filing cabinets, which were central to French criminologist Alphonse Bertillon's anthropometric system of criminal identification, anticipated the need for networked databases.

mechanical tabulation of the U.S. census in 1890, might be placed next to the invention of cinema that same decade as evidence of a technological bifurcation that would drive competing industries centered in the northern and southern regions of California. But enough. It's time now to shift discussion, in the chapters that follow, to more contemporary matters.

Examining the relationship between data and images at this point in time is revealing precisely because the outcome of their contestation is not yet determined. The conditions of technological possibility and cultural meaning remain productively unresolved. To be clear: I regard this uncertainty as a feature, not a bug. I have no particular interest in being "right" about what the future holds and even less in having this examination prove not to be dated in its interests or critical framing.[39] I would likewise embrace the idiosyncrasy and transience of my own interests, which are themselves ephemeral artifacts of the historical moment in which they were conceived. When it comes to digital technologies, the concept of ephemerality has multiple, contradictory meanings.

Unlike the billions of lines of software code written for soon-to-be obsolete applications and operating systems, the material detritus and environmental destruction of the industrial age will not allow themselves to be forgotten anytime soon. For all this book's talk about data and images, it is important to remember that the computers on which they depend require physical manufacturing, the mining of raw materials, the extrusion of various plastics, and the disposal of waste products of varying degrees of toxicity related to all of these processes. Computer operation, likewise, requires electricity—enlarging humanity's collective carbon footprint proportionate to the number and speed of the processing cycles required. All of this comes at a measurable cost—both monetary and environmental. I am also thinking specifically of the ideological systems to which we tacitly and often innocently submit: what we perceive as our own limits of technical capability, and who is thought to correctly have dominion over data and the tools with which it is organized and disseminated. The more we imagine ourselves to be marginal to such systems, the more disempowered we are in broader systems of social and economic power. I argue unambiguously in this book that the "othering" of technological elites is among our era's most severe collateral damage. The displacement of real anxieties with imaginary ones distracts from critical thinking about the role technology should play in everyday life and, more important, the role that a thoughtful, technologically empowered public can play in shaping the design, development, and regulation of our technological future.

As is probably already apparent, I am neither a futurist nor a historian. Yet, writing about technology requires one to take seriously both the lessons of the past and the implications for the future. I aim for this book to be a document of its time, not a series of prescient pronouncements nor monuments to the forgotten. I do my best to resist the gravitational pull of futurism, where ever-quickening cycles of obsolescence and renewal make it difficult for sustained cultural critique to perform its primary function: thinking clearly about power-suffused infrastructures and suggesting ways to respond. There is much to learn from previous generations of technology, especially those that turned out to be more or less transient than their inventors expected. Historians will surely one day look back at the promises made on twenty-first-century Kickstarter pages with the same bemusement we bring to claims made in the technology pavilions at world's fairs of the early twentieth century.

In *Techniques of the Observer,* Jonathan Crary looks back on the emergence of numerous technologies of vision in the nineteenth century in order to articulate a history that complicates the teleology of precinematic narratives. In Crary's critique, the appearance of cinema at century's end provided a narrative "conclusion" that foreclosed understandings of the alternative directions the investigation of imaging technologies otherwise might have taken. What links the disparate array of optical toys and technologies to which Crary attends—thaumatrope, phenakistoscope, zoetrope—is that they are "not yet cinema."[40]

We do not yet have the benefit of hindsight in considering contemporary technologies of vision, but it is all too easy to recognize the patterns of historical forces that shape the questions we are able to ask. In this investigation, the great mass media of the previous century continue to cast a long shadow, but the epistemic shift suggested by the transition from radio, TV, and film to computational media offers hope for renewed insight. We seek not a definitive, singular, or nonteleological narrative, but rather the capacity to ask the right questions and to recognize when their answers support systems of power whose interests do not align with our own. In other words, our goal is to think critically and look unblinkingly at the interdetermining forces of media, technology, and power. It is to unpacking these relationships that this book is, finally, devoted.

1 Data Visualization

Painting by Numbers

Internet users of a certain age will recall a moment in the latter half of the 1990s when a duo of artists working under the name Komar and Melamid rose to fame online. After emigrating from the Soviet Union to New York in the late 1970s, Alexander Melamid and Vitaly Komar achieved a degree of success in the art world as founders of a movement they called Sots-Art, a blend of conceptual art and playful critiques of Stalin-era Soviet realism. The work was witty and biting, merging irony and politics to the point where it was sometimes difficult to tell which was which. In 1994, Komar and Melamid launched a project with the support of the Nation Institute, for which they hired a professional opinion polling firm to ascertain what features of fine art painting were most and least popular among Americans.

In a telephone survey, more than one thousand respondents were asked approximately one hundred questions designed to elicit preferences in artistic content and style. Respondents were asked about their favorite colors and seasons of the year, as well as their preference between "wild or domestic" animals, "indoor or outdoor" scenes, "religious or non-religious" themes, representations of "reality or imagination," figures that are "historical or contemporary," "men, women, or children," "nude, partially clothed, or fully clothed," and so on. They were also asked to rate formal properties of the paintings, including such factors as "modern or traditional," "sharp angles or soft curves," "expressive brush-strokes or smooth canvas," and whether they preferred paintings that were the approximate size of a dishwasher, refrigerator, TV, magazine, or paperback book. Komar and Melamid then used the aggregated response data to create two paintings, one that possessed as many of the preferred features as possible, and

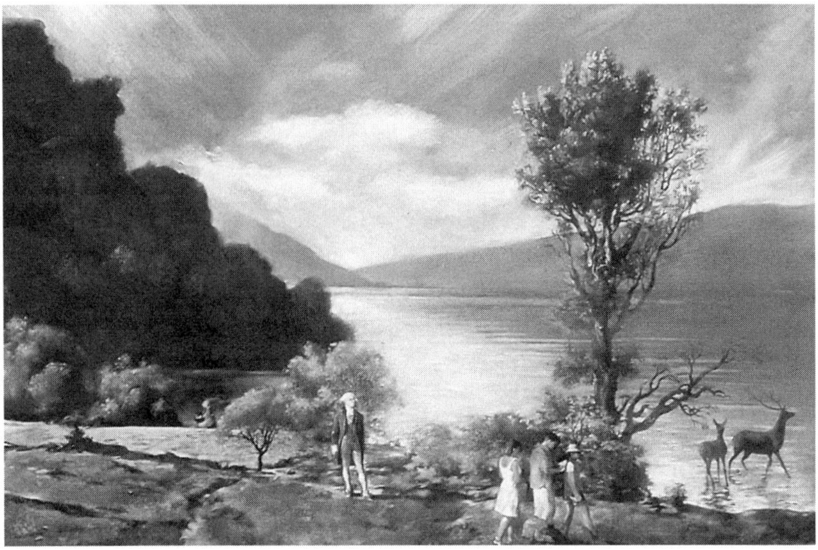

Figure 1.1
Artists Alexander Melamid and Vitaly Komar translated data gleaned from public opinion polls to create an idealized vision of America's *Most Wanted* artwork. Image courtesy of the artists.

another that exhibited as few as possible. They were titled *Most Wanted* and *Least Wanted*, and both paintings were exhibited at the Alternative Museum in New York in a show titled *People's Choice*.

The March 14, 1994, issue of the *Nation* magazine included an interview with Melamid by editors Peter Meyer, Victor S. Navasky, Katrina vanden Heuvel, and JoAnn Wypijewski.[1] Wypijewski would later go on to edit a book titled *Painting by Numbers: Komar and Melamid's Scientific Guide to Art*,[2] which featured an interview with the artists, a witty DIY paint-by-numbers outline of the *Most Wanted* painting created for the cover of the *Nation*, and an essay by art critic Arthur C. Danto, who sketched an appreciative history of Komar and Melamid's body of work since their immigration to New York. In both the *Nation* issue and Wypijewski's book, the seriousness—if not of intent, then of implications—of Komar and Melamid's work was examined in detail, with an image of the artists emerging as provocateurs digging mercilessly into the soft spot between art and politics in America. Both the critics and the artists themselves took the opportunity to address issues related to instruments of democracy, taste culture, and the relationship between art and commerce. While many dismissed the project as a cynical hoax, Sean Cubitt's 1999 essay in *Millennium Film Journal*, "Cartographic Instruments, Narcissistic Illusions, Regimes of Realism in CGI," sets aside the reading of Komar and Melamid as disingenuous pranksters to focus on interrogating serious dimensions of the work.

> [A] second possibility proposes itself: that the artwork is undertaken quite seriously, and that its object, therefore, is neither public taste nor contemporary painting, but the structure which public taste acquires when viewed through the lens of statistical sampling. This has the virtue of allowing us to accept at face value the artists' statements of the seriousness of their undertaking, and removes the necessity to imagine an elite in-group of ironist snobs.[3]

It is difficult to imagine a similar discussion of Komar and Melamid's project taking place today for several reasons. First, the proliferation of "ironist snobs" winking at each other's cleverness over the internet no longer requires a leap of the imagination. Second, and more important, anxieties about potential undue influence of opinion polls and statistical sampling on shaping everything from product marketing to election outcomes has been justifiably eclipsed by parallel concerns about the power of data analytics. Opinion polls, although still widely conducted and cited, don't begin to compete with the scope or speed of large-scale data systems, which now dominate cultural concerns over the dehumanizing tendency of statistics. Cubitt's essay is primarily directed toward the analysis of the structure of public taste, but he also provides an insight into Komar and Melamid's work that is relevant to our investigation:

> What Komar and Melamid add to this process is the form of their final presentation of data: not tables or diagrams but paintings. In this sense, both the illusionistic and the geometrical paintings are representational. And both are abstract: they represent a statistical result, which in turn represents the stated preferences of a sample, which in turn represents the taste of a population; and those phases of representation indicate a process of abstraction from individual response to statistical aggregate.[4]

In other words, the *Most/Least Wanted* project is significant not because of the data derived from statistical sampling or opinion polling, but because it translates that data into tangible, visual form via the medium of painting. Although the translation passes through several stages of abstraction, Komar and Melamid's work delivers a glimpse of the laborious process, circa the mid-1990s, by which data could become image.

Admittedly, Komar and Melamid's paintings are more of an artistic interpretation than a literal translation of the data gathered by the opinion polls. Though survey respondents expressed a clear preference for natural landscapes that include, for example, a body of water, historical figures (fully clothed), wild animals, and the color blue, Komar and Melamid made a series of specific decisions to include a mountain, blue sky, a lake, male and female deer, and a uniformed George Washington in the frame. Where did this archetypal vision of an ideal artwork originate? Komar and Melamid's survey results were possibly shaped by the broad commercial success of American painter and entrepreneur Thomas Kinkade, whose signature bucolic landscapes had gone into mass production shortly before the survey was undertaken. It is even possible that Komar and Melamid's attempt to "scientifically" capture the taste of American art buyers was motivated by an art world contempt for the unabashed commercialism—and corresponding financial success—of Kinkade. Perhaps to Komar and Melamid, Kinkade's idyllic landscapes, which frequently included rustic dwellings or lighthouses as evidence of the harmonious conquest of nature by man, suggested a distinctly American version of the disingenuous utopianism underlying their old nemesis, socialist realism.

In any case, the notoriety of Komar and Melamid's project, which included a review by Andrew Ross in *Artforum* in January 1995,[5] would certainly have caught the attention of Kinkade, who, in turn, would not have been above incorporating elements of the survey results into his repertoire. Although Kinkade's signature style had been well established by the end of the 1980s, drawing inspiration from nineteenth-century landscapes by Albert Bierstadt and Thomas Cole, the mass-produced images at the heart of Kinkade's success continued to feature many of the exact elements seen in Komar and Melamid's *Most Wanted*. Further linkage between Kinkade and Komar and Melamid's *Most Wanted* might be found in the artist "Favorability Ratings" captured by the opinion poll. The highest favorability rating was received by Norman Rockwell (81%), followed by Rembrandt (79%), Picasso (64%), and Monet (57%), with the lowest ratings going to Jackson Pollock (15%), LeRoy Neiman (25%), Georgia O'Keeffe (30%), Salvador Dali (32%), and Andy Warhol (33%). Kinkade cited Rockwell among his most important influences and famously experimented with a line of paintings inspired by French impressionism, completed under the pseudonym Robert Girrard. Although Kinkade enjoyed more than two decades of steady market growth—albeit marred by charges of fraud, labor issues, bankruptcy, and the artist's own untimely death from alcohol poisoning in 2012—his formally polished work was rarely greeted with the seriousness that attended Komar and Melamid's overt chicanery.[6]

So, did Kinkade's highly visible mall-based galleries (or "malleries") influence public taste in landscapes to the point where it affected the "scientific" data captured by Komar and Melamid? Or might the data resulting from the *Most/Least Wanted* survey have filtered its way into Kinkade's own work? These are chicken-and-egg questions that I am not particularly concerned with resolving. What makes the juxtaposition useful is the parallel evolution of explicitly data-driven artistic production, effectively parodied by Komar and Melamid, and Kinkade's mode of artistic production, which was both responsive to and partially constitutive of market forces. Kinkade, in this sense, was no different from other practitioners of commercial entertainment (film, TV, digital games) who aspire to artistic legitimacy along with financial profit. By this logic, opening weekend box office figures, unit sales, or viewership patterns could reasonably be considered the "data" that drives production in today's entertainment industries.

Based on the success of the Alternative Museum's *People's Choice* exhibit, Komar and Melamid received a commission from the Dia Arts Foundation in 1995, with funding from Chase Manhattan Bank, to hold a series of town meetings in Upstate New York to gather qualitative input and solicit requests for specific painting contents. The commission also supported expansion of the quantitative survey to additional geographic regions, including China, Denmark, Finland, France, Germany, Holland, Iceland, Italy, Kenya, Portugal, Russia, Turkey, and Ukraine. Dia specified that exhibition of the resulting works should take place exclusively on the internet—only the second time the foundation had sponsored an online-specific commission. By expanding the number of countries included in the survey, Dia opened the door for cultural comparison, which indeed dominated much of the project's second round of public discussion and, for Cubitt, provided the key to deriving serious insights from the project.

Except for a few outliers (Italy, Holland, Germany), Komar and Melamid's nation-specific *Most Wanted* landscapes appear strikingly similar, depicting a mountain on the left, with a field of grass in the foreground and a body of water behind. Various wildlife—mostly deer, with the occasional moose (Finland) or hippopotamus (Kenya)—frolic or graze at the edge of the water. Most paintings also feature human figures of some sort: for Turkey, children recline and play; for France, a naked woman watches over naked children; for Belgium, ballet dancers twirl in white tutus. While Americans preferred their painting to be the size of a dishwasher, most of the other countries preferred the size of a TV. Scanning the column of paintings generated on behalf of various countries, one cannot help but narrativize the summary vision they offer: "Of course Icelanders would prefer a verdant landscape." Holland, the only country to favor abstraction, may be read as disavowing the cliché of its own art-historical tradition: "Enough with the landscapes and dramatic skies already!" In contrast with today's data analytics, the deliberate eccentricity of Komar and Melamid's polling instrument, customized for each country, seeds these national narratives.

Just three years after *Most/Least Wanted*, another project would take up the issue of opinion polling as an engine for generating art. Created by Michael Mateas, Steffi Domike, and Paul Vanouse, Terminal Time (1999) was billed as "a history 'engine': a machine which combines historical events, ideological rhetoric, familiar forms of TV documentary, consumer polls and artificial intelligence algorithms to create hybrid cinematic experiences for mass audiences that are different every single time."[7] I have written previously about the historiographical significance of Terminal Time,[8] but here what interests me is the continuation of Komar and Melamid's focus on opinion polling as a vehicle for parodic—yet still serious—critique. In each presentation of Terminal Time, audiences respond via an applause meter to a series of multiple choice questions about the values they hold prior to viewing a historical documentary. Terminal Time was a remarkable apparatus for its day because of its capacity to dynamically assemble a video sequence in real time, using text-to-speech synthesis for narration and drawing on a database of historical audio and visual materials. Unlike Komar and Melamid, Terminal Time's creators wanted to be sure that audiences were in on the joke by running the apparatus at least twice at every performance and encouraging audiences to select varying responses to the opinion poll. The resulting differences in the historical narrative, in turn, showcased the system's ability to rescript its narrative and select and combine media elements to suit audience preferences. Ultimately, Terminal Time was a performance apparatus that focused audience attention on the editing algorithm, as opposed to a method for visualizing serious polling data.

Each of these examples—Komar and Melamid's *Most/Least Wanted*; Thomas Kinkade's malleries; and Mateas, Domike, and Vanouse's Terminal Time—shares a moment in the history of technology that narrowly preceded the emergence of data analytics as the successor to market surveys and opinion polls. More important, the technological literacy of Americans who experienced these projects had not yet been cultivated to understand marketers' ability to trace, aggregate, and analyze data as a means of discerning consumer patterns and preferences. This is partly due to the deliberate obfuscation of systems for capturing consumer data. The media production and distribution company Netflix, for example, harvests data concerning its users' preferences under the guise of improving the company's "recommendation engine." After watching a film, viewers are asked to rate their experience, with the promise of enabling the company to improve its suggestions for future viewing. One marketing solicitation offered, "Let us show you some hidden gems that you may have missed or forgotten about. Remember, the more you rate, the smarter we become at giving you suggestions."[9] Similar strategies are deployed by many other services and social networks, and indeed, the preferences they gather may well benefit consumers through customized recommendations. In fact, the perceived quality of Netflix's recommendation engine is so important to the company's public relations apparatus that it once sponsored a challenge offering $1 million to anyone who could improve the accuracy of its engine by 10 percent.[10] The contest ran for three years, between 2006 and 2009, when a winner was finally declared, but as Wendy Chun points out, the winning algorithm was never incorporated by Netflix.[11] Rather than improving its engine, the campaign primarily served a PR function, publicizing Netflix's commitment to optimizing its subscribers' viewing experience. It also marked a revealing case study for the blurring of boundaries between algorithms and culture.[12]

Netflix has admitted the importance of earning and maintaining the trust of its subscribers in making active use of the recommendation system.

> We want members to be aware of how we are adapting to their tastes. This not only promotes trust in the system, but encourages members to give feedback that will result in better recommendations. A different way of promoting trust with the personalization component is to provide explanations as to why we decide to

recommend a given movie or show. We are not recommending it because it suits our business needs, but because it matches the information we have from you: your explicit taste preferences and ratings, your viewing history, or even your friends' recommendations.[13]

All of this underscores the importance of the human element in otherwise algorithm-driven analysis. In Netflix's case, this extends to the use of professional human taggers to parse the contents of its vast catalog of media, a practice that the company publicly acknowledged in 2012.[14] Although the processing of recommendations is performed by computer, Netflix's data structures, categories, and ratings all originate with humans. This supports Ian Bogost's argument that the algorithms that allegedly dominate our everyday lives are too easily occulted when considered apart from their concrete human and cultural contexts.[15] Ironically, except for a few extreme cases such as Google's Deep Learning project, it is the human labor that is most frequently occulted in discussions of data analytics. I will return to this easily neglected fact when discussing computer vision later in this chapter.

Thus far, I have focused on recommendations resulting from Netflix's user ratings, a process that is of decreasing importance to the company in comparison with its real-time data analytics.[16] Ratings-based recommendations are structurally equivalent to brief opt-in consumer satisfaction surveys and are entirely dependent on capturing good-faith responses from viewers who choose to respond. It is not difficult to imagine the algorithms programmed to identify and respond to patterns associated with particular genres, actors, directors, and so on. Reflective viewers might even deliberately modify their ratings in an attempt to preclude unwanted responses from the recommendation engine. "I may have liked the *Bourne* movies, but *please*, no more Matt Damon!" What Netflix viewers may be less aware of is the company's ability to precisely monitor the real-time viewing patterns of its streaming media subscribers. This enables Netflix to know, for example, which episode in a given season resulted in viewers being sufficiently "hooked" to watch the remainder of that season,[17] or specific narrative events or characters that may have induced a significant percentage of viewers to abandon a particular episode, film, or series. Netflix also captures data related to its users' time spent on the company's website, searching the collection or managing their account, including factors such as "scrolls, mouse-overs, clicks, or the time spent on a given page."[18]

Although the company is notoriously secretive about its viewership numbers[19] and refuses to release data supporting the purported popularity of its offerings, the exposed parts of its recommendation system, which Netflix refers to as "one of its most valued assets,"[20] allows glimpses of the categories it uses to organize its collection. In 2014–15, *Atlantic* writers Ian Bogost and Alexis Madrigal created a data-scraping system that reverse-engineered a list of more than seventy-six thousand potential categories—or microgenres—that could be generated based on the vocabulary used in Netflix descriptors. Bogost and Madrigal then did what any procedurally minded media critics would do and created an online tool for generating sample categories that mimic Hollywood clichés, actual Netflix genres and a third setting dubbed "Gonzo" that creates "ultra-niche" categories highlighting the potential for absurdly granular categories and combinations. These included "Romantic Post-Apocalyptic Small Town Fantasy Movies Based on Real Life Set in Africa About September 11 Starring Jackie Chan," "Talking-Animal War Documentaries Set in Asia Starring Wynton Marsalis," and so on. Although amusing, the Gonzo setting on Bogost and Madrigal's microgenre generator did not aim to produce any real insights into how Netflix uses its data. Nonetheless, the generator might have contributed something to the procedural literacy of *Atlantic* readers, who were invited to denaturalize the demographic categories that drive marketing strategies in different parts of the entertainment industry.[21]

As audiences become more aware of the functioning and limitations of recommendation systems, they also become more critical. Following a proposed dramatic expansion of its presence in international markets in early 2016, Netflix began exposing more parts of its recommendation algorithm. In a February 2016 blog post, Netflix discussed the challenges it faces in refining its algorithms to account for massive variability among viewers and data input from a proposed 130 new international markets. Netflix's blog readers responded with acerbic critiques of the functioning of the recommendation engine, often citing the incongruous or inaccurate selections they already receive from the company.[22] Rather than simply managing their own ratings and recommendations, viewers are showing the ability to critique the functioning of the system as a whole and, by implication, the logic of algorithmic culture broadly.

If the connection is not already apparent, my point is that the original series produced by Netflix may be seen as an interpretive visualization of its viewer data. Like America's *Most/Least Wanted* paintings, this visualization should be understood not as a literal translation, but as an artistic manifestation of the demonstrated preferences of the company's viewership. Yet, there is a potentially disturbing, majoritarian logic to the deployment of viewer data to reverse engineer original content. Successful genres that reach the company's most desired subscriber demographics may favor white middle-class audiences over "niche" profile categories such as "African-American" or "gay and lesbian." Netflix's data analytics are presumably capable of anticipating the audiences for specific identity groups, but judging by the company's selection of original programming thus far, these groups have seemingly not yet crossed the profitability threshold. The secrecy that shrouds Netflix's most valuable asset ensures that this is only speculation, but the continuity between data-informed production and old-school Hollywood suggests the operation of the same kind of circular logic that has long served to maintain the status quo in the entertainment industries.[23]

For a brief period in spring 2016, roadside billboards advertised the Netflix original series *Fuller House*, a decades-later sequel to the white-bread family comedy *Full House*, which aired on ABC from 1988 to 1995. The billboard was free of text except for the title of the series and the Netflix text treatment in its signature red font; nothing else needed to be communicated by means as clumsy as words. The image depicts a large family of creamy-skinned sitcom characters riding in an oversized classic red Cadillac convertible with the Golden Gate Bridge in the background. The surrounding hills are lush and green; skies are blue. The position and expressions of characters in the car suggest a combination of interpersonal dramas and running jokes poised to pick up where the original series left off. Each element of the billboard could be read as an object lesson from Roland Barthes's *Mythologies* (1972), each semiological gesture designed to deliver a piece of a puzzle aimed at inviting viewers to watch, to log in, and ultimately to subscribe to a monthly streaming plan. In the wake of our protracted discussion of Komar and Melamid, it is tempting to read each element of the billboard as a response to a public opinion poll or, in the case of Netflix, a carefully harvested synthesis of user data portending success for the series.

What type of family do you prefer? White? Black? Asian? Hispanic? Other?
Should the family be: Attractive and well off? Scruffy and resourceful? Offbeat and zany? Dark and brooding?
Do you prefer narratives that are funny, dramatic, scary, adventurous, or mysterious?
Do you prefer cities, suburbs, or rural areas?
If cities, East Coast or West Coast?
If West Coast, Los Angeles, San Francisco, or Seattle?
If San Francisco, what is your favorite landmark?
Do you prefer landscapes that are hot and dry, wet and lush, or cold and snowy?
What kind of car do you prefer? Compact, sedan, SUV, convertible?
Do you prefer contemporary cars or classic cars?
And so on.

Of course, Netflix need not ever administer such a crude instrument. These questions—and many others—are answered with far greater nuance by analysis of streaming patterns among viewers of finely parsed demographics. The insights offered by these analytics may then be incorporated into decisions about original programming. In this sense, then, original programming by a company such as Netflix begins to resemble an ouroboros, with data-informed media being used to produce new streams of data to refine future productions, which, in turn, generate new data for analysis. Just as television was once outed for its role in "delivering people," today's media production must be held accountable for its role in delivering data.

When artists Richard Serra and Carlota Fay Schoolman created their classic work of video art *Television Delivers People* in 1973, in which a scrolling text offers a critical analysis of television, it was still possible to speak to TV viewers in the second person as a mostly homogenous group defined by its relationship to mass media. The text includes a series of statements:

There is no such thing as mass media in the United States except for television.
Mass media means that a medium can deliver masses of people.
Commercial television delivers 20 million people a minute.
In commercial broadcasting the viewer pays for the privilege of having himself sold.
It is the consumer who is consumed.
You are the product of t.v.
You are delivered to the advertiser who is the customer.
He consumes you.
The viewer is not responsible for programming------
You are the end product.
You are the end product delivered en masse to the advertiser.
You are the product of t.v.

It is necessary, in light of the conjoined practices of data analytics and data-informed media production, to amend Serra and Schoolman's declarations. Viewers in the 2010s may not be directly responsible for programming, but aggregated data is acknowledged as part of the decision process for Netflix in choosing its in-house productions. Actor and producer Kevin Spacey, in his keynote lecture at the *Guardian's* 2013 Edinburgh International Television Festival, explained the difference between the standard, pilot-oriented model of American television and how the dramatic series *House of Cards* (Netflix 2013–) was received. "Netflix was the only network that said, 'We believe in you. *We've run our data and it tells us that our audience would watch this series.* We don't need you to do a pilot'" (emphasis added).[24] Please don't misunderstand. I do not believe that images—much less entire TV series—are somehow imprisoned in data, waiting to be released. Nor is it my intention to diminish the creativity or sincerity of the producers of *House of Cards* or other Netflix original productions. My point is simple: the television consumer is consumed no longer by advertisers but by data.

The type of analytics available to Netflix represents a difference that is of both scale and kind. Hollywood has long deployed strategies for capturing viewer feedback, ranging from focus groups to Nielsen ratings, to shape its production decisions. In *George Gallup in Hollywood* (2006), historian Susan Ohmer describes the entertainment industry's uneasy adoption of social scientific methods for analyzing and predicting audience taste in the 1940s and 1950s. Founded in 1935, the Gallup organization had quickly earned a reputation as the preeminent opinion polling firm in the realm of American politics and advertising. In 1940, Gallup founded the Audience Research Institute to bring its analytical methods to the film industry. This move was not welcomed by many in the entertainment industry, where studio moguls famously relied on artistic instinct or "hunches," based on years of industry experience, to predict financial success. So long as studio profits remained high, most major studios resisted parsing variations in box office returns. But as film industry profits began to decline later in the 1940s, the "scientific" methods offered by Gallup gained traction. Gallup's methods, like those of Komar and Melamid several decades later, were entirely noncomputational, relying on telephone-based and door-to-door interviewing to derive a combination of quantitative and qualitative data. The use of computers to guide production strategy in the film and television industries evolved steadily and with increasing influence in the decades that followed. Yet, the distance between contemporary computational analytics and the tabulated polling data pioneered by Gallup is as great as that between a viewer's opt-in survey ratings and the data generated by real-time streaming patterns.

The passively generated data resulting from viewers' real-time streaming provides a degree of insight surpassed only by real-time biofeedback, a technology that is starting to make its way into the market, swimming cautiously against the tide of well-justified public suspicion. The closest analog to this type of data might be found in the controlled use of real-time feedback systems that invite test audiences to evaluate material, such as advertisements and TV pilots, by turning a knob to indicate relative levels of attention or amusement. By comparison, the massively scaled data analytics available to streaming media companies such as Netflix, Hulu, and Amazon evaluate both broad patterns and granular specifics, reflecting actual viewer behaviors in their native habitats.

Netflix's commercial success at operationalizing viewer analytics is consistent with the company's alignment with the data-driven sensibility of Silicon Valley in contrast to the box office and ratings orientation of the film and TV industries. Media content, as much as it continues to resemble familiar cinematic and televisual genres, is also a tool for generating an increasing volume and sophistication of viewer data. In the end, what matters is not the existence of a circular relationship between viewing data and media production, but the *absence* of the kind of public discussion around questions of taste, art, and democracy that was occasioned by Komar and Melamid's *Most/Least Wanted*. Consumers who have been sufficiently familiarized with the logic of corporate data mining and procedurality may focus on optimizing their own experience or mocking the obtuseness of recommendation engines rather than engaging in public dialogue or cultural intervention on the subject. On bad days, I view this as approaching precisely the neoliberal cynicism that Cubitt warned against or, indeed, the supplanting of theory by "big data" as celebrated by *Wired*'s Chris Anderson. On better days, the development of even self-serving modes of algorithmic literacy suggests the potential for beginning a much-needed conversation about the role and limits of data mining in everyday life.

Another Parable of Visualization

More conventional histories of data visualization begin with work by nineteenth-century figures such as Charles Joseph Minard, John Snow, and Florence Nightingale, all of whom were valorized by contemporary information visualization guru Edward Tufte. Along with his many disciples, Tufte has passionately advocated for visualization strategies driven by principles of efficiency and clarity, preferably executed by professional designers.[25] Tufte draws a sharp contrast between the hygienic precision of his own economical design style and the excess and imprecision that results from putting digital tools for graphic design in the hands of amateurs.

Tufte's well-publicized diatribes against poorly designed presentations created with Microsoft's PowerPoint software came to a head in 2003 in a public "debate" between Tufte and musician David Byrne, former lead singer of the Talking Heads, who had produced a multimedia artwork using PowerPoint. Their pro-con argument about the platform resulted in concurrent articles in the September 2003 issue of *Wired*, published under the subtlety-challenged titles "Learning to Love PowerPoint" and "PowerPoint Is Evil."

Motivated in part by the public sensation surrounding this debate, Byrne went on to publish a book with a title that parodied Tufte's series of self-published design manifestos. Byrne's book, which was sold with an accompanying DVD containing twenty minutes of animated images and sounds created or assembled in PowerPoint, bore the title *Envisioning Emotional Epistemological Information* (2003). Sometimes shortened to *EEEI*, Byrne's title is at once a parody of Tufte's *Envisioning Information* (1990) and an anagram of the electrical engineering organization IEEE (Institute of Electrical and Electronics Engineers), which counts among its subfields the development of tools for data analysis and visualization.

Like Tufte, Byrne's book sales undoubtedly benefited from the widely publicized difference of opinion over PowerPoint. Both writers, however, share a familiar binary, favoring professional creatives (musicians, designers) over ordinary users of a software program designed for a limited range of business applications. The positive attributes that Byrne finds in PowerPoint's automated animation and presentation features actually do little to address Tufte's attack on algorithmic information visualization. Byrne writes, "I began to see PowerPoint as a metaprogram, one that organizes and presents stuff created in other applications. ... What's more, the application can be made to run by itself—no one even needs to be at the podium. How fantastic!"[26] In fact, Byrne's admission that PowerPoint is most effectively used not as an authoring tool but as an aggregator for externally generated content undermines the ostensible premise that he was defending PowerPoint against the charges leveled by Tufte.

Byrne's DVD consists of five short videos, with animations created using text, graphics, and occasionally the background-generator features native to PowerPoint, along with retro transition effects such as pixelated dissolves, gradients, and wipes. The audio track is lush with instrumentation, alternately melancholic, lyrical, and discordant, providing nonverbal accompaniment to the cascade of visuals that is in every way antithetical to the business aesthetics of PowerPoint's intended consumer base. But like many of the graphical elements that Byrne simply animates with the software, the music has been entirely composed outside the presentation software, which serves only to synchronize sound and image for playback.

Byrne's animations mostly use PowerPoint to critique the presumptions and aesthetics of business software and marketing, with one notable exception. The final composition of the five videos, titled "Physiognomies," deals with the then nascent technology of facial recognition, which Byrne positions on a continuum with physiognomy, a nineteenth-century pseudoscience. Physiognomy was devoted to deriving a scientific basis for racist and eugenicist ideology, proposing linkages of bodily features, especially cranial size and shape, with degrees of intelligence or moral character. In the book's introduction to this piece, Byrne notes the reappearance in the digital realm of long-ago discredited methods associated with physiognomy. "Digital Physiognomy uses a sophisticated neural network to identify correlations between facial features and psychological characteristics using photo-identification techniques recognized by law-enforcement officials."[27] Although Byrne's critique is only obliquely implied in the video, his linkage between biometric technologies of the nineteenth and twenty-first centuries is apt. (I return to linkages between the translational strategies of nineteenth-century biometrics and more recent technologies of facial recognition in chapter 2.)

Focusing on more conventional uses of PowerPoint, Tufte compares the software to a drug with unacknowledged side effects that "induced stupidity, turned everyone into bores, wasted time, and degraded the quality and credibility of communication."[28] Although he offered no evidence to support his implication that it was widely or uncritically used, Tufte's diatribe inveighed most bitterly against the tyranny of automated design, PowerPoint's admittedly dubious feature that automatically generates information visualizations from spreadsheet data.

> Applying the PowerPoint templates to this nice, straightforward table yields an analytical disaster. The data explodes into six separate chaotic slides, consuming 2.9 times the area of the table. Everything is wrong with these smarmy, incoherent graphs: the encoded legends, the meaningless color, the logo-type branding. They are uncomparative, indifferent to content and evidence, and so data-starved as to be almost pointless. Chartjunk is a clear sign of statistical stupidity.[29]

In his article, Tufte presents unsightly examples of graphs generated using this tool, but his charges ring hollow in the absence of evidence that PowerPoint users were broadly duped into mistaking them for good design. At the heart of Tufte's denunciations is a conventional reassertion of the amateur-professional hierarchy, occasioned by the spread of desktop publishing and presentation software that promised to erode this distinction in favor of nonprofessionals.

The real problem, in the historical context of the early 2000s, was the general lack of awareness about the functioning of algorithms within digital culture. Even enthusiastic, early adopters of digital authoring software may not have recognized multiplicity as one of the key affordances of algorithmic transformation. However, Tufte's categorical privileging of visual economy should be regarded, like all reductive epistemological models, with a degree of skepticism. Tufte's influential but single-minded desire for direct, minimalist translation of data into visual form represents only one possible response to the spread of algorithmic culture. In fact, what I have dubbed the "translational mode" of converting between images and data is sufficient to describe only a narrow—and far from the most interesting—slice of the overall field of data visualization. Of particular interest, following the discussion of Komar and Melamid above, are those instances where algorithm-based processes of translation are negotiated by humans and/or alloyed with alternative parallax relations.

Data Epistemologies

The stage-managed controversy between Tufte and Byrne marks a transition in the discussion of data visualization from the purposes of art and entertainment to the realm of epistemology. First, we should remember that images were once similarly vilified as simplifiers of complexity, agents of consumerism, and manipulators of democracy. Writing in 1962, historian Daniel Boorstin referred to his century's "graphic revolution" as a symptom of the debasement of mass media. For Boorstin, commercial media, especially television, marked a point of no return for visual culture's addiction to banality.[30] Though Boorstin's critique has long been superseded by more generous and nuanced analyses of popular culture, the sentiment that images pose a threat to traditional text literacy has proved surprisingly tenacious.[31] In an age of data visualization, however, images have come to serve the opposite function. Compared with the abstract realm of data, images are now seen as consummate and efficient conveyors of meaning.

Computational research has a long and controversial history in the humanities, where literary scholar Franco Moretti's advocacy of "distant reading" marks only the most recent example. Moretti's position is deliberately provocative, advocating departure from the humanities' most tried-and-true strategies of close reading. "We know how to read texts," Moretti famously prodded his peers across the academy. "[N]ow let's learn how not to read them."[32] A nondefensive reading of Moretti reveals many more nuanced points that have found their way into mainstream literary studies. In the computational analysis of literature, text encoding can be viewed practically, not as an end in itself but as a means to sort through unimaginably vast quantities of text—more than could be read by many humans in many lifetimes—to refine an area of investigation or test a research hypothesis before undertaking closer analysis.

The introduction of large-scale data analytics within literary studies does not imply a necessary either/or; the two may readily sit side by side, and indeed the logical relationship between them is one of reciprocity. Building on Moretti, Matthew Jockers adopts the term "macroanalysis" to suggest a parallel with the acknowledged benefits of coexistence between the complementary fields of microeconomics and macroeconomics. Macroanalysis, in this context, is a complement to microanalysis, with close and distant reading simply yielding different insights and avenues of investigation.[33] For Lisa Gitelman, among the benefits of introducing a "distant" perspective on humanities research is a reminder that "when we put our own critical perspectives into historical perspective, we quickly find that there is no stance detached from history, which is to say that there is no persistently objective view."[34] In other words, Moretti's methods afford not just a widened critical corpus but a reconception of literary analysis itself as a set of identifiably embedded and delimited historical practices.

Gitelman further argues that we should treat data "as a matter of disciplines—rather than of computers."[35] Here, Gitelman distinguishes between computational humanities work that deploys computers for analysis of large-scale cultural corpora and the need for computationally literate analysis of the ways in which data has functioned in cultural contexts as diverse as astronomy and slavery. In framing her *Raw Data* anthology, Gitelman consistently foregrounds cultural and disciplinary contexts as crucial to the meaningful use of data. This supports my contention that digital culture studies should remain in dialogue with visual and cultural studies; but that dialogue continues to unfold unevenly, depending on disciplinary contexts. As Gitelman further notes, "Few literary critics want to think of the poems or novels they read as 'data,' and for good reason."[36] She continues, "The skepticism within literary studies about Franco Moretti's 'distant reading' approach, which in part reduces literary objects to graphs, maps, and other data visualizations, testifies to the resistance the notion of literature as data might provoke."[37] At its best, the disruption sparked by Moretti should provoke reflection on unspoken or infrequently challenged disciplinary conventions. The defensive posture that frequently results seeks to reassure those in academia that human interpretation is "still necessary." Carried to its logical conclusion, however, the real message is not "we are still relevant" but the opposite—with the way things are going, one day we surely won't be.

Visualization is just one among many strategies that has fueled digitally enhanced scholarship. In fact, efforts at large-scale quantitative research in fields such as linguistics long predates "humanities computing" as it was conceived in the 1950s. American linguist George Kingsley Zipf conducted research on language frequency as early as the 1930s.[38] Although Zipf's work did not involve computation, it did require a corpus of linguistic data to be divided into tabulated components that could be tracked across geographic regions. Decades later, the use of computer algorithms to analyze artistic styles closely followed the model established by text analytics, prompting similar results, headlines, and anxieties within the fields of art history and visual culture.[39]

It is possible to trace multiple historical trajectories for what is now termed the digital humanities, not all of which involve computational analysis, encoded text, or large-scale data sets. Tara McPherson has asserted a historical origin for digital humanities that privileges expressive, affective, and embodied forms of communicating humanities research, looking back on work by Charles and Ray Eames in the late 1950s. McPherson also cites the art-science collaborations of the Experiments in Art and Technology (EAT) collective beginning in the late 1960s as evidence of a vibrant historical collaboration between artists and engineers.[40] Large-scale, complex multimedia installations and performances offer an alternative historical lineage for the digital humanities. This history is quite different from the canonical history of humanities computing that is most often traced back to Roberto Busa's *Index Thomisticus* (1946–1974), an electronic concordance to the written works of St. Thomas Aquinas, which was undertaken with the support of IBM.[41] Within the digital humanities, the legacy of Busa's work can be found in the computational analysis of large-scale digital archives, but this is as likely to result in conventional, text-based publication as in electronically enhanced or richly mediated scholarship.

Within the expansive field of digital humanities, scholars find continuing evidence of a bifurcation that may be grossly described in terms of differing approaches to the study and use of data and images. Dramatic differences in the scholarship resulting from text encoding or data analytics compared with that of, say, videographic scholarship prompted Holly Willis to propose an alternative category she dubs the "cinematic humanities." For Willis, what sets the cinematic humanities apart is its simultaneous investment in "humanistic inquiry enhanced through the practices and modes of cinema, even as cinema continues to expand into what has been dubbed 'the post-cinematic.'" Envisioning a "post-cinematic" future, Willis sees the potential "to imagine critical practices that are immersive, embodied, gestural and virtual, and to engage in acts that integrate thinking, writing, coding and designing."[42] Critical work modeled on the cinematic arts may be uniquely attuned to issues such as space, affect, movement, dimensionality, and the subjectivity of viewers and interactors, all factors that are more readily conveyed by established paradigms of images as opposed to data.

Let's Build a Smarter Planet

For more than six decades, the art and design patronage of International Business Machines (IBM) Corporation has resulted in a striking combination of corporate image building and visionary experiments with computational and protocomputational media. From artist residencies by John Whitney and Charles and Ray Eames in the 1950s to IBM's sponsorship of grandmaster chess (Deep Blue) and *Jeopardy!* (Watson) challenges, IBM has worked for many decades to bring computational literacy to the public. IBM has also been among the most active corporate players in engaging the cultural effects of computerization in the workplace (Walter Lang's *Desk Set*, 1957), in museums (the Eames's *Mathematica* exhibit, 1961), and in daily life (Ogilvy & Mather's Let's Build a Smarter Planet advertising campaign, 2010). The historical trajectory of IBM's ongoing public relations efforts maps a revealing shift in parallax, from the hermetic separation of data and images in the Eames's work to a series of infuriating equivocations in the visually stunning design fictions for Let's Build a Smarter Planet. Although each of the art and design works resulting from IBM's patronage is deserving of analysis on its own, in the context of a discussion of data visualization, I focus on the series of four short videos that launched the company's Let's Build a Smarter Planet advertising campaign.

Let's Build a Smarter Planet included a variety of print and online materials that combined to create a rich visual vocabulary for the idealized synthesis of data and images. Along with it, IBM announced that "smart" technologies could solve a vast array of the world's problems, from health care to transportation and energy use. IBM's advertising agency, Ogilvy & Mather, won numerous awards for the campaign, and IBM has continued to expand its connection to smart technologies and responsible global citizenship as an integral part of the company's brand.

Three of the four short videos that contributed to the campaign—"Data Baby," "Data Energy," and "Data Transportation"—were produced by the Los Angeles–based design firm Motion Theory, while the first video, "Data Anthem," was produced by James Frost of Zoo Films, in partnership with The Mill. The videos themselves, described as a form of "data-driven design,"[43] do not present a visualization of any actual data. This distinction is intended not to privilege "real" over "fake" visualization, only to recognize the difference between visualizations based on literal translations of data, compared with computer-generated motion graphics that are strictly expressive. As examples of the latter, these videos are free of any mathematical connection to measurable phenomena in the world. The politics of these videos therefore lie not in the realm of data acquisition or processing but in visual rhetoric. If authenticity had been the goal, it would certainly have been possible to include "real" visualizations of data pertaining to electricity usage, urban transportation, or a baby's vital signs. Instead, these ads invite us to reconceptualize the visible world as data space, frequently deploying the visual vocabulary of 3D modeling software, including point clouds that seamlessly morph from one shape into another.

The first of the series, "Data Anthem," begins with a colorful radial burst resembling an exploding star, which spins to form a glowing cluster of downtown high-rises. Meanwhile, a disembodied camera performs a rapid fly-through into the heart of a city and tracks around a vehicle composed of glowing bits; the virtual camera completes a semicircular arc before pivoting to an overhead position from which we witness the car transforming into a human figure on a hospital gurney. The camera then pushes through the hospital scene to follow high-voltage electrical wires, zooming down to the scale of an excited electron, then back out—an apparent homage to the Eames's *Powers of Ten* (1977)—to reveal a planet glowing and pulsing with spikes indicating worldwide electricity usage or possibly data production. Finally, the earth explodes into a glowing, pulsing Let's Build a Smarter Planet logo, which in turn shatters and reconstitutes as an oozing, neon version of Paul Rand's venerable IBM logo. This dense thirty-second spot contains not a single cut, which might suggest a threat to the continuity and seamlessness of IBM's synthetic vision of the world.

The accompanying voiceover offers IBM's vision of the central role of data in reshaping every aspect of technology, health care, and urban planning.

Our planet is alive with data.
It's generated by cars on a freeway,
patients in a hospital,
electricity in the grid.
The more we understand data, the more answers we find.
Patterns are easing traffic in over 400 cities,
detecting disease faster,
reducing energy costs by ten percent.

On a smarter planet, we can analyze all the data we now see,
to make the world work better.
Let's build a smarter planet.

Although the narrator's key assertion, "On a smarter planet, we can analyze all the data we see to make the world work better," is predicated on identifying patterns within data that has been translated into the visual register, the video's depictions of "data" shows no trace of the prosaic mechanisms by which real data is captured or processed. Ignoring the need for material apparatuses such as sensors, electrodes, and transducers, the video instead presents colorful, translucent waves that emerge organically from the landscape, from bodies, and from objects in space. The result is a misleading naturalization of data's existence in the visible register, coupled with an ironic suppression of precisely the type of computing hardware that IBM is best known for manufacturing.

In aggregate, the videos that launched the Let's Build a Smarter Planet campaign were an influential model for the vocabulary of data visualization that was rapidly infusing visual culture in the early 2010s. The grammar of visualization seen in these videos reveals the desires we now invest in data as a key component of contemporary knowledge production. Framed by IBM's declaration that 2010 marked the opening of a "decade of smart," variations on the vocabulary of data visualization seen in these spots has filtered into many other contexts, from feature films and television, to newspaper graphics and advertising. Most important, simulated visualizations like this have shaped cultural expectations for what data visualization can or should look like, setting expectations that are often misleadingly high.

The ability to see and interact with waves of data has subsequently become a common cinematic and televisual trope via fictional characters who develop enhanced mental abilities that allow them to directly access information from the electromagnetic spectrum. We may regard these as Hollywood design fictions for an idealized, hardware-free interface by which humans interact with digital information. Like the IBM ads, rainbow-colored sine waves naturalize the encoding and decoding of data as if it were not governed by digital protocols or accessed through physical technologies that require human labor, industrial capital, and a calculable amount of environmental damage simply to appear on screen. In erasing the underlying technology of both software and hardware, these visions of an evolved bodily interface flatten distinctions among the diversity of electromagnetic signals, which are already widely misunderstood, even without imagining that they can be directly accessed by the human senses of sight or touch.

Two recent examples include Scarlett Johansson's eponymous character in the Luc Besson film *Lucy* (2014), whose cognitive abilities have been chemically expanded. Another is the autistic character Gary Bell (Ryan Cartwright) on the Syfy TV series *Alphas* (2011–12). Both Lucy and Bell are able to reach out and touch the streams of data emitted from unseen towers and transmitters, using gestures familiar from screen- or motion-based controls, such as swiping, pinching, and tapping. Not only do the IBM ads and these Hollywood design fictions erase the infrastructures that make them possible, they represent a convenient fiction for Hollywood in the midst of its ongoing rivalry with Silicon Valley. If only human cognitive and perceptual abilities could be amplified to the point of obviating the need for computers and game consoles, then Hollywood's victory over the consumer technology industries would finally be complete. Industrial rivalries aside, it is worth taking seriously the question of whether data visualization creates pseudoknowledge about the world or offers the key to understanding the deluge of cultural data in which we currently reside.

Translational Visualization

The volume and complexity of data generated by machines in the twenty-first century exceed human comprehension. This is nothing new within the discourse of computation or, indeed, that of analog information storage and retrieval. Encyclopedias and physical archives hold more information than the human brain can reliably manage; Bertillon's filing system handled more suspected criminals than any squad of detectives could track. Most contemporary data processing has no visual component, literally no point of entry for the unaided human sensorium to meaningfully engage it. Self-driving vehicles, for example, need not generate real-time models of their environment from the sensor data used for navigation. The most important interactions in such a system take place between machines and other machines, or software and other software. Only when the goal of a data system is to aid human understanding does the translation of data into visual form become necessary. Fields ranging from journalism to the sciences have made a conscious effort to codify the terms under which data is rendered legible to nonmachines and nonspecialist humans. Like any other field of visual expression, data visualization should therefore be understood in terms of cultural rhetoric and not merely as the result of technical processes.[44]

The availability of data, the tools for visualizing it, and the cultural sensibility required to understand it have all dramatically increased in the past decade. In 2012, the *Harvard Business Review* named data visualizer the "sexiest" profession of the year.[45] Data visualization has also proliferated in mainstream journalism. The *New York Times*, to enhance visualization efforts begun in 2008, enlisted the talents of data visualizer Jer Thorpe, who served as data artist in residence at the *Times* R&D Lab from 2010 to 2012, helping to develop the graphical vocabulary of the paper's visualizations in static and dynamic contexts. For journalistic and scholarly purposes, visualization emphasizes reliable translation from the abstract to the evocative or evidentiary, posing logistical and creative challenges. As the *Times* was developing its own expressive style for print and electronic visualization, the paper also opened its data API, allowing anyone with the technical skills and access to create their own visualizations. This led to evocative external projects such as Tim Schwartz's NYT Data Grapher, Command Center, and Geohistoriography, among many others. The *Times* thus became a central conduit in the two-way flow between data and visualization, simultaneously making the paper's contents available for use by others and elevating visualization as a key strategy in the beleaguered evolution of news journalism.

In addition to its utilitarian applications, data visualization has found its way into various artistic forms, ranging from studio art to music video. Among the most prolific and accomplished data artists is Aaron Koblin, who has been a key collaborator on numerous groundbreaking projects, including Chris Milk's "The Wilderness Downtown" (2010) music video for Arcade Fire, and the crowd-sourced music video "The Johnny Cash Project" (2010). Koblin's creative experimentation dates back to his time as a graduate student in the Design Media Arts program at the University of California, Los Angeles (UCLA), where he studied with Casey Reas, cocreator of the programming language Processing. Koblin's MFA thesis *Flight Patterns* (2005) used Processing to translate publicly available flight data from the Federal Aviation Administration (FAA) into colorful traces showing the paths of airplanes over North America during a single twenty-four-hour

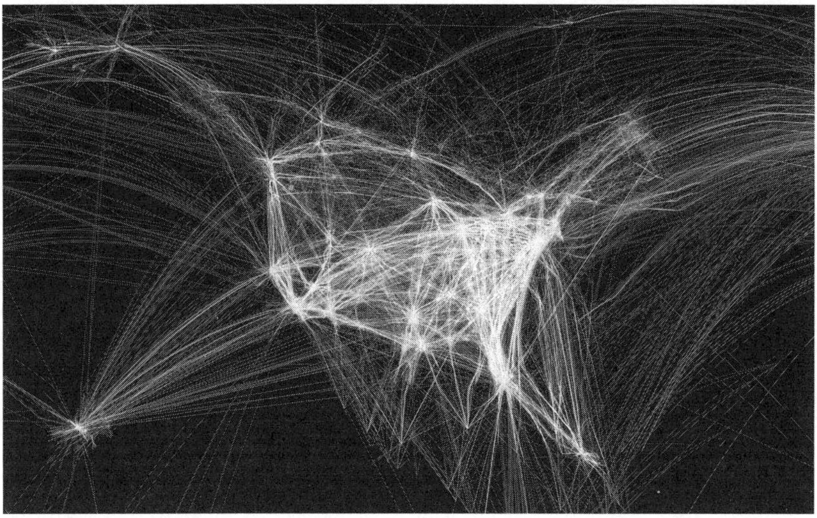

Figure 1.2
Visualized flight-tracking data creates an aestheticized portrait of North American air travel in Aaron Koblin's *Flight Patterns* (2005). Image courtesy of Aaron Koblin.

period. Although Processing performs an automated—or algorithmic—translation of abstract FAA data into aesthetic forms, there is nothing natural or automatic about the way the visuals are produced. Koblin made a series of formal decisions, which were encoded into a Processing sketch that converted FAA data into lines, colors, and durations.

If keyed to their original data—the colors on Koblin's map signify different kinds of airplanes, for example—the resulting image could be thought of in terms of the straightforward translation of information into an arbitrarily codified visual system. The aesthetic pleasure of *Flight Patterns*, however, does not lie in its conversion of abstract air traffic data into "understandable" forms. In its time-based version,[46] *Flight Patterns* tells the story of a day-in-the-life of North American aviation. A video running less than a minute traces flight paths during slightly more than twenty-four hours. Only two items of information are provided, the time of day and the number of planes, ranging from about four thousand to nearly twenty thousand being tracked at any given moment. With repeated viewing, several patterns emerge, confirming viewer expectations about the ebb and flow of national and international passenger flights. Likewise, geographic contours of the continent and its cities emerge from the darkness, with hub cities erupting like fireworks across the Midwest as the day begins. International flights arc across the sky like comets with slowly dissipating tails, then disappear abruptly at their destinations. Close inspection reveals that the rendered flight paths are remarkably noisy, quivering and zigzagging along their route, suggesting the limits of the system's ability to translate physical space to digital trace.

Another prototypical visualization project is Jer Thorpe's GoodMorning! (2009). Created during his tenure in the *New York Times* R&D Lab, Thorpe mined the Twitter API for instances of the phrase "good morning" in various languages around the globe. The messages were then aggregated and visualized by language, time of transmission, and the number of users saying "good morning" in any given place. The resulting dynamic 3D model shows waves of colored pistons erupting around the globe, roughly following the sun, and shifting hues to reflect linguistic differences. Although it is possible to derive some meaning about global time zones, and the densities of Twitter users or multiple languages in various geographic regions, GoodMorning! is less about information transmission than a kind of naïve assertion of global sameness. Despite all our differences, the project suggests, the shared ritual of a banal morning greeting unites worldwide Twitter users in rainbow-hued, graphical harmony.

Even before the beginning of IBM's "decade of smart" had officially begun, an array of DIY tools for converting abstract data sets into evocative forms had been widely integrated into knowledge production and dissemination. Among the most prominent and influential was Martin Wattenberg and Fernanda Viégas's Many Eyes (2007), a tool created as part of their work in the IBM Visual Communication Lab from 2005 to 2010. With the stated goal to "'democratize' visualization, and experiment with new collaborative techniques,"[47] Many Eyes was among the first genuinely robust, publicly available online systems for data visualization. Until the project was shuttered by IBM in 2015, Many Eyes allowed users to upload data sets to create multiple formats of visualization. "Data visualization," Wattenberg noted in 2008, "has historically been accessible only to the elite in academia, business, and government. But in recent years web-based visualizations … have reached audiences of millions. Unfortunately, while lay users can view many sophisticated visualizations, they have few ways to create them."[48] Offering fewer graphical presets than the open visual architecture of Processing favored by many artists, Many Eyes nonetheless brought sophisticated tools for visualization to a broad, nonspecialist user base.

Although their mandate from IBM was to facilitate practical, utilitarian strategies of visual communication, Viégas and Wattenberg indulged parallel, creative aspirations for their work. Writing outside their role as IBM researchers, the two were prone to wax artistic when describing the insights that data makes possible, framing their goals in markedly intimate, somatic terms: "Our work explores the joy of revelation: the special electricity of seeing a city from the air, of hearing a secret, of watching a lover undress." Describing themselves as "proponents of expressive visualization," Wattenberg and Viégas continue:

> [W]e believe visualization to be an expressive medium that invites emotion. We aim our tools at "data sets" that range from hip hop songs to Walt Whitman's poetry, from arguments on Wikipedia to expressions of carnal desire. We strive to expand the practical craft of visualization beyond function to create objects of social engagement, pleasure and revelation.[49]

I quote this at length out of respect to Viégas and Wattenberg, whose genuinely pioneering work offers much to be admired. On a personal level, the pair seems determined to follow in the footsteps of Charles and Ray Eames in confounding the domains of art and science, joyfulness and technology. But what specifically are we to make of the romanticist underpinnings of their statement as it careens from sentimental to sexual, technical to sublime? The statement was composed during Wattenberg and Viégas's early days at IBM—also once home to the Eames—and has followed them to their position since 2010 as codirectors of the Big Picture Group data visualization lab at Google. Perhaps part of the statement's tenacity lies in its shock value, the unexpected conflation of decidedly human carnal pleasures as a foil for the cold impersonality of computation. Is this a virtuosic turning inside-out of technocratic discourse or a giddy foray into naïve poeticizing?

In Viégas and Wattenberg's own binary, the scientific and computational realms are placed in stark opposition to the human, poetic, sexual, and artistic. Likening the tools of computation to those of science—microscopes, telescopes—Wattenberg and Viégas revisit the nineteenth-century fascination with phenomena that elude perception by the unaided eye. Scientists and nonscientists alike have long recognized the aesthetic pleasures of their objects of study—the formal beauty of astronomical or microscopic phenomena, for example—as an ancillary feature of their primary pursuit of knowledge, or perhaps as a vehicle for promoting their work to nonspecialists.

There is no doubt of the aesthetic pleasures offered by much of Wattenberg and Viégas's work, some of which alludes gracefully to abstract art, as in Wind Map (2012), while other works brush against the erotic, such as Fleshmap Touch (2008). For Wind Map, Viégas and Wattenberg scraped data indicating wind speed and direction across the United States once an hour from the National Weather Service's National Digital Forecast Database. Using Javascript and HTML, they generated animated lines and swirls that play as a loop until the next data update occurs. The scale of the project necessarily reduces a massively complex and variable weather system to a limited number of homogenous visualizations, ensuring that the project can present only the grossest patterns of actual wind data, pleasingly rendered like the swirled brush strokes of a cloud formation by Van Gogh. As with Koblin's *Flight Patterns*, broad patterns become discernible in relation to known geographic features, such as mountains and bodies of water, or weather events, such as hurricanes, but overall the point of the project is formal pleasure rather than meteorological or epistemological clarity.

Described as "an inquiry into human desire,"[50] Viégas and Wattenberg's Fleshmap Touch attempts to visualize erogenous zones of the human body. To create the project, Wattenberg and Viégas selected images of idealized, white, naked male and female bodies from 3D.SK,[51] then created an online survey via Amazon's Mechanical Turk (a low-cost online system that matches low-wage laborers with projects requiring short-term attention) and invited paid respondents to answer two questions: "How good would it feel to touch this area?" and "How good would it feel to be touched in this area?" Frontal and rear images of the male and female bodies were encoded with 707 potential points of contact, and an interface invited survey respondents to express their preferences for touching and being touched. Wattenberg and Viégas then performed statistical analysis on the responses—including demographic data for respondents, such as gender, sexual orientation, and age—and mapped this data back onto the relevant male and female figures, generating a heat map of desire for sexual touching. In aggregate, the results of the survey largely conform to cultural norms for bodily eroticism.

In an essay titled "Beauty and Danger: The Aestheticization of Information in Contemporary Art," Melissa Ragona articulates a withering critique of Fleshmap that is typical of objections to the knowledge-producing capacity of aggregated data.[52] Visualizations that favor the "signal" of consensus over the "noise" of variation, Ragona argues, may confirm broad trends at the expense of minority opinions. Visualizations that are dominated by the logic of averages and majority opinions are particularly detrimental to projects like Fleshmap that seek to mine individual desire, which is surely more interesting in its capacity for variability and idiosyncrasy than its tendency toward consensus. Ragona mercilessly denounces Fleshmap's failure to do anything but confirm obvious generalizations, noting, "Surprise, surprise: men's favorite zone to be touched is the penis."[53] The results of Fleshmap Touch, for Ragona, remain "enigmatic at best, and obfuscating at worst."[54] Data visualization's ability to express complex phenomena is precisely what confers its power as well as its potential for oversimplification. It is not enough simply to embrace the inevitability that anything that *can* be visualized *will* be visualized. What is needed is an orchestrated retraining of expectations related to the visualization of cultural data, resulting in technically sophisticated and methodologically aware systems of meaning making.

Analyzing Cultural Analytics

Cultural analytics has thrived over the past decade as the central initiative within Lev Manovich's Software Studies Initiative research lab. The cause taken up by Manovich and his team is a laudable one, to bring computational analytics to a wide variety of cultural artifacts as data sets: old and new, high and low, commercial and experimental. The lab's signature inversion of traditional scientific hierarchies privileging quantitative over qualitative data allows humanities researchers to engage directly in computational analysis—and has also opened the door to funding from entities such as the National Science Foundation—bringing issues of visual culture into the realm of digitally enhanced cultural theory.

Broadly, cultural analytics aspires to make a seat at the table of big data available to artists and humanists. Manovich defines cultural analytics as "the analysis of massive cultural data sets and flows using computational and visualization techniques."[55] Projects undertaken in the name of cultural analytics have worked to bring this logic to bear on a diversity of cultural phenomena using an innovative set of software tools and methods.

At the time of the lab's inception, Manovich was a faculty member in the Department of Visual Arts at the University of California, San Diego, and many of the group's projects continue to be exhibited in fine arts contexts, especially gallery spaces and hybrid art-science spaces, such as the Highly Interactive Parallelized Display Space (HIPerSpace) display system at the California Institute for Telecommunications and Information Technology (Calit2). The Software Studies Initiative has subsequently expanded operations to the Graduate Center of the City University of New York (CUNY), where Manovich made the transition from a department of visual arts to one of computer science. The work continues to have relevance across domains of art, design, technology, social science, and cultural criticism. In 2016, Manovich co-organized a months-long institute at UCLA's Institute for Pure and Applied Mathematics, where professional contexts ranged from artificial intelligence to advertising. In addition to establishing best practices for analytics and visualization, one of the benefits of the lab's eclectic range of activities is to catalyze collaborations across unexpected fields of expertise and practice.

In 2013, Manovich distilled many of the research questions of cultural analytics pertaining to the issue of "software epistemology" in his book *Software Takes Command* (2013). He argued for the permanent extendibility of the computer as a "metamedium" that gives rise to an evolutionary system supporting the emergence of multiple new "media species."[56] These are intelligible for Manovich through the lens of software studies, which analyzes in detail the technological affordances of software in specific stages and contexts of deployment. Software studies fills a gap in the literature of media and technology studies, where the affordances, precepts, and limitations of basic tools of cultural production too easily lose their specificity. Software studies takes pains to situate software—both in development and in use—within a historical context that accounts for commercial, technical, and cultural influences.

Cultural analytics likewise promises new ways of viewing and analyzing cultural data. Hence, it is appropriate that frames drawn from Dziga Vertov's documentaries *Man with a Movie Camera* (1929) and *The Eleventh Year* (1928) provided early data sets for analysis. Vertov's human-machine Kino-Eye sought precisely the kind of hybrid vision and ubiquitous capture that would come to drive a whole spectrum of the consumer electronics industry nearly a century later—an intelligent, mobile, mechanical agent for re-visioning the world. When Vertov grafts his brother's camera onto the human body and brings it to life, he endows the apparatus of cinema with both agency and autonomy—a prescient glimpse of contemporary machine vision and mobile media. It is easy to forget, however, that Vertov's intervention in the emerging languages and technologies of cinema was deeply enmeshed in a politics of seeing that was inseparable from the utopian pretensions of the pre-Stalin-era Soviet Union. The significance of this moment in cinematic (and indeed revolutionary Soviet) history is irreducible to the kind of formal properties (close-ups of faces, tonal ranges, shot transitions, etc.) that computers are currently able to recognize. Such analysis might well result in insights related to the formal properties of the film in terms of cinematography, visual effects, or editing, but is less suited to engage issues of politics and history.

In his essay "Visualizing Vertov," Manovich is clear on the complementary methodologies at work in cultural analytics:

> In some cases, we use digital image processing software to measure visual properties of every film frame such as average gray scale value, contrast, number of shapes, number of edges, the relative proportions of different colors, texture properties, and so on. ... In other cases, we don't measure or count anything. Instead, we arrange the sampled frames from a film in ... single high-resolution visualizations in particular layouts. This use of *visualization without measurements, counting, or adding annotations* is the crucial aspect of my lab's approach for working with media data sets, and I hope that it can add to other approaches already used in quantitative film studies and digital humanities. (emphasis in original)[57]

The Vertov study represented an attempt to put the tools of cultural analytics to the test with a full-scale interpretation of Vertov's work based on image analysis, providing an especially revealing comparison with films made by Sergei Eisenstein during roughly the same period. The resulting insights confirmed, but also challenged, certain aspects of the conventional wisdom about Soviet montage practices and Vertov's own assertions about Kino-Eye. These computational analyses, as Manovich notes, are powerful and fast, saving time for researchers and providing glimpses of potentially fruitful areas for future research. They are also, he reminds us, not intended to supplant the conventions of human-based analysis. They are simply another tool available to media and cultural scholars, a way to augment one's existing expertise.

Manovich aptly compares computational analysis of Vertov's film with the Eames's *Powers of Ten*. Where the Eames created a series of analytical

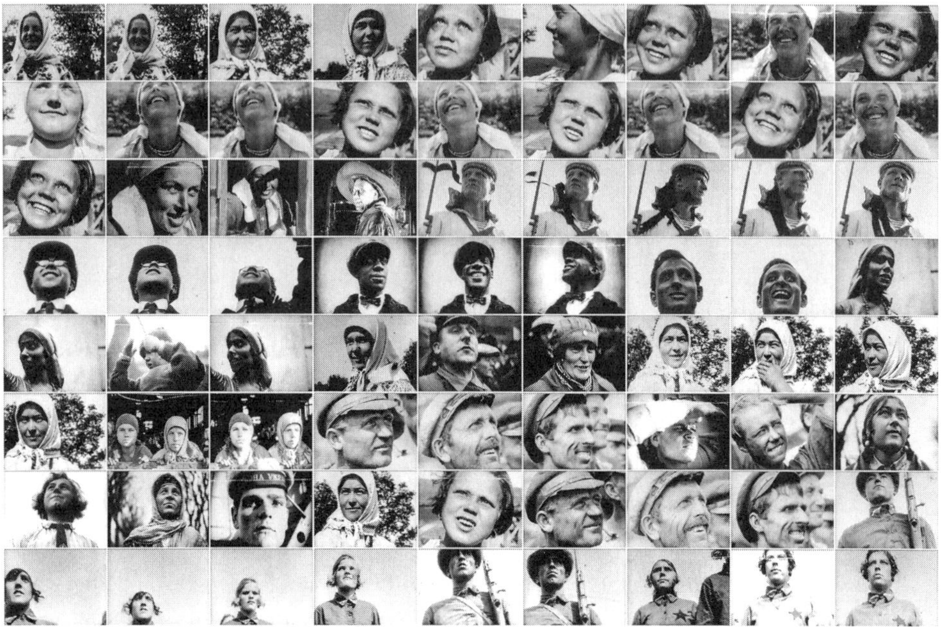

Figure 1.3
Machine vision software for cultural analytics extracts closeup faces from Dziga Vertov's *The Eleventh Year* (1928). From Lev Manovich, "Visualizing Vertov," *Russian Journal of Communication* 5, no. 1 (2013): 44–55. Image courtesy of Lev Manovich.

zooms through space, from the farthest reaches of the galaxy down to the level of individual atoms, the Vertov project performs a kind of temporal zoom, ranging from the whole of cinema history to the level of individual shots and frames. This massively variable perspective enables a single researcher to bring a shared analytical framework to bear on the entire corpus of early Soviet film, then to zoom in on Vertov's body of work, followed by the entirety of *Man with a Movie Camera* or *The Eleventh Year*, which are further dissected into individual sequences, shots, and ultimately, individual frames. Manovich describes the overall project of cultural analytics as a combination of "browsing" and "exploring," a process by which one discovers questions to ask within an otherwise impenetrable data set.[58]

A persistent problem with computer-vision-based analysis lies in the limitations of its analytical paradigms. If we accept the form-based constraints of machine vision, we may gain some insights into patterns within the text being studied. Manovich maps these onto a meaningful analysis of the films, contrasting or supporting conventional wisdom about montage editing. Presumably, part of the justification for selecting Vertov's work derives from the formal interests of the early Soviet filmmakers themselves. But formalism was not the only—or even the most important—concern for Vertov and his successors. Whereas machine vision is entirely capable of recognizing cuts or close-ups of faces, providing insight into editing or shooting strategies, other types of cultural signification—such as class status or embodiment of revolutionary ideals—which were also central to Vertov's visual rhetoric, remain elusive.

Computer models offer seductive mechanisms for analysis, and carefully selected data sets may yield useful insights. In a historical context, it is important to remember that computational analysis arose at the very moment when minority discourse began to assert a viable mainstream presence within the academy. As feminist histories, postcolonial histories, and a range of alternative, often racial or ethnic, microhistories were achieving credibility, computers enabled the smoothing over of such differences in favor of more readily quantifiable parameters. We need not challenge the veracity of insights yielded by this process, but it is legitimate to question which issues on the vast landscape of cultural analysis are most vital to address at any given time. Even more important, we should ask what our analytical models and technological affordances lead us to do next. For such research to have significance, it is—or should be—a precursor to tangible social action.

Manovich's cultural analytics lab has adopted an open source ethos, allowing free access to a range of custom software tools and analytical paradigms. These include Image Montage, a plug-in for the software ImageJ, which was originally developed by the National Institutes of Health (NIH) for medical imaging and analysis.[59] Adapted by researchers in the cultural analytics lab, Image Montage facilitates the analysis and visualization of formal elements of cinema, such as shot lengths, cuts, close-ups, and transitions, as well as the tonal qualities of individual film frames. As the project has progressed, the range of objects and parameters under consideration in the name of cultural analytics has expanded far beyond cinema, proving especially useful for examining the overwhelming profusion of user-generated content circulated via digital networks.

Among these, the Selfiecity (2014) project has taken an integrated approach that makes use of both human labor and computational image analysis. Selfiecity drew on images posted to the online photo-sharing service Instagram, each geotagged from one of five cities around the world. The images were then processed through Amazon's Mechanical Turk to identify images that were consensually regarded as "selfies." Those images were also rated in terms of perceived age and gender, based on a male/female binary. Researchers then subjected the images to mood analysis based on facial expression and degree of head tilt, enabling them to look for answers to questions such as, "Which city's residents smile the most and who has more reserved looks? Which apparent ages and genders take the most selfies? Do angry people tilt their heads more strongly? What is a characteristic mood for people in Moscow? Do Sao Paulo women actually tilt their heads more? Do New Yorkers or Berliners look older?"[60] The Selfiecity website features an animated frontispiece that cycles through a sequence of dozens of selfies positioned in precise registration based on the eyes of the photographer-subject. The images dissolve from one to the next to the next—too quickly to recognize the specific visual characteristics of any individual. The result is a kind of dynamic Galtonian composite that favors general facial and compositional patterns distilled from the broader data set. The relative uniformity of the self-portraits analyzed in Selfiecity facilitates their dual function as carriers of visual and computable information, though we might still challenge the association of quantifiable factors like head tilt with subjective interpretations, such as expressiveness or anger.

Cultural critic Elizabeth Losh insightfully describes the data set subtending Selfiecity as evidence of a shift from seeing to sensing, noting, "[W]e can observe how the human-computer interaction modeled in Selfiecity depicts users wielding their smart phones as collections of semi-autonomous sensors rather than as neutral instruments that extend their own vision or tools that gives them mastery in subject-object relationships."[61] In Losh's framing, humans serve as extensions of the computers' sensory-input system, simultaneously complicating presumptions about authorship and transferring the resulting photographs to the realm of computable data. Losh also positions selfies in relation to the art-historical discourse of portraiture and feminist discourses of self-representation. Such insights precisely exemplify the sort of contextual and historical critiques that elude strictly machine-vision-based analytics.

Historically, it is important to note the parallel proliferation of selfies and technological systems devoted to facial recognition and data mining.

As discussed at greater length in the next chapter, faces are among the most exhaustively studied phenomena in machine vision. Technologies for facial recognition are the subject of ongoing research for multiple purposes, including government surveillance and identity tracking, as well as seemingly benign uses, such as improving the tagging and locatability of individuals in image archives and on social networks. The selfie obliges a unique conjunction of data and metadata—automatically linking one's name and face with foundational metadata, such as computer IP addresses and geolocation coordinates. Whatever else selfies may be, they are all neatly packaged gifts to facial recognition algorithms and data-tracking systems.

Like Selfiecity, the Phototrails project, led by Nadav Hochman and Manovich, sought to extrapolate broad insights about cities by analyzing specific features of photographs uploaded by their inhabitants. Launched in 2013, Instagram Cities attempts to visualize shared aspects of selected cities worldwide, based on fifty thousand uploads for each city sampled from more than 2.3 million Instagram images. Computational analysis was used to produce a series of visualizations of each city, with contours shaped by factors such as how late people stay up, what kinds of filters they apply to their photographs, and how light, dark, or colorful it is in various parts of the city at different times of the day or night. The result is a series of striking composite images variously described as "visual signatures," "visual rhythms," and "cultural patterns."[62]

The tools used for Instagram Cities also allow mapping time and date as well as the upload activities associated with individuals and locations. Among other things, this allows distinct patterns to emerge in response to cultural events and natural disasters, as well as observations about usage patterns over time—whether a city's "signature" results from many users uploading individual photos from a single location or a few individuals uploading many photos from multiple locations, and so on. In the end, the insights offered by this type of analysis work best when they either overtly contradict expectations or strengthen an anticipated hypothesis. The project website situates Phototrails midway between close analysis and distant reading. "As opposed to privileging 'close reading' (analysis of singular texts) or 'distant reading' (analysis of large scale patterns), we use interactive visualizations to perform a multi-scale reading—moving between the global-scale cultural and social patterns and the close-ups revealing patterns of individual users."[63] Each resulting "signature" is suggestive of the realms of both data and image, resembling nothing so much as a point cloud, which would ordinarily be used to describe 3D spaces. In this case, each "point" is signified by an iconic representation of a single image. The composites also offer a radically distilled visualization of the formal qualities of each image, mapped radially in terms of hue and luminance around a central axis.

In combination, Instagram Cities images offer synoptic hypotheses about the behaviors of each city's residents—at least those who upload images to Instagram. At a glance, one may conclude that Instagram users in Tokyo and San Francisco share images with similar patterns of hue and brightness; while the uploads in Bangkok are more deeply saturated compared with those in New York. The problem is that—in mobilizing our desire for, and belief in, the translational and synthetic potentials of data and image—these images lay claim to a more totalizing meaning than their method actually supports. And here I want to tread carefully. The project documentation profusely anticipates and accounts for such objections. Hochman and Manovich acknowledge that, "as a reflection of social reality or, more precisely, as a giant photograph of social reality, Instagram only captures the curated lives of some members of society and not others."[64] The project website also acknowledges additional limitations of the source data, especially regarding Instagram's own demographic and geolocation tagging.[65] These qualifications are not present in the visual rhetoric of the images, however, and uninformed viewers might reasonably perceive the composites as claiming insight into essential characteristics of the cities themselves. Manovich more convincingly disarms charges of homogeneity and stereotyping when he notes, "[B]y rendering the same set of images in multiple ways, we remind viewers that no single visualization offers a transparent interpretation."[66] Indeed, strategies of multiplicity, coupled with the lab's commitment to open data sets and tools, demonstrate a commitment to inquiry that does not foreclose on alternative readings, hypotheses, or analytical vectors.

In any case, challenging the integrity, limits, and origins of source data misses the point of cultural analytics, which consciously straddles the line between art and social science. Methodologically, I would question a different aspect of these projects. The research agenda for each cultural analytics project derives from a pregiven combination of available source data and technological affordances. In a design context, this is known as "technology push." Ordinarily it originates with a client who funds designers or researchers to develop compelling applications for a new or existing technology in the hopes of expanding its marketability or redirecting future development efforts. This relationship introduces certain obvious constraints that predetermine the nature of the experiments or the applications that follow. This, in turn, represents an inversion of the ideal workflow for design research, in which researchers begin not with the need to make use of a specific technology, but with a question motivated by issues of social consequence. Researchers then look for—or create—an optimal combination of tools and data to address the issue.

Like many archive-driven projects, the research questions available to projects like Instagram Cities and Selfiecity emerge from the available objects of study and tools for analysis. Instead of looking at the world and asking what problems need to be solved, researchers begin by looking at a given data set and the mechanisms they have available to analyze it. Together, these structure the questions that may be productively addressed through data analytics. The metadata captured by Instagram, like any commercially motivated media source, will inevitably support certain kinds of inquiries—*in which cities do women tilt their heads more when photographing themselves?*—at the expense of others. What is gained in terms of scale and access in such projects may be lost in the constraints of questions that are possible to ask. The great potential offered by cultural analytics and related efforts is not to provide the answers to complex cultural questions but rather to use strategies of data analytics and visualization to identify the most productive avenues of inquiry; in other words, making sure we are *asking* the right questions, rather than necessarily relying on existing data systems to *answer* them.

While cultural analytics remains the most prolific and widely recognized project operating at the intersection of research in the arts, humanities, and data analytics, strategies of data analysis and visualization have also infused numerous other realms of cultural practice. Chicago artist Jason Salavon, for example, is part of a generation of artists expanding the horizons of data visualization into an area that might be termed "computational aesthetics." At first glance, the work is seductive. Salavon's series *Homes for Sale* (1999/2001/2002) and *100 Special Moments* (2004) offer a wry critique of the sameness of American (apparently mostly white) middle-class culture. Working from large collections of publicly available online images, Salavon generates multiple superimpositions in which no single image is clearly visible, but which, in aggregate, suggest the repetitive contours of cultural rituals. These composite images draw out broad formal resonances across large data sets of iconic images, such as "curb shots" from real estate advertisements and wedding photos (with bride on the left).

While the images retain their aesthetic appeal, the *critique* implied by Salavon's work quickly wears thin. Salavon's technique, which he terms "averaging," aims to address individual uniqueness and large social patterns simultaneously, but it's hard not to feel that the resulting images cynically mock conventions of photographic remembrance at the expense of those who participate in them. The irony implicit in Salavon's title *100 Special Moments* takes an easy shot at the misplaced sense of uniqueness and self-importance evinced by photographic tropes: weddings, Santa Claus shots, graduations, little league photos. Salavon's point is an obvious one, and he makes it repeatedly. The literal insights yielded by these composites fall somewhere between trivial and obvious: skies are sunnier in Southern California than in the Pacific Northwest; lawns are larger and greener in Dallas than in Chicago, and so on.

The point of Salavon's work is not knowledge production, and the artist does not pretend otherwise. For a more generous and nuanced anthropological reading of the "home mode" in photography, one should look not to Salavon but to Richard Chalfen's *Snapshot Versions of Life* (2008). In articulating the parameters of the home mode, Chalfen focuses on the "deep structures" that underlie the production and circulation of codified "home mode" images within an insular economy of prescripted (and, indeed, prescriptive) family narratives. But these interests are nowhere to be found in Salavon's composites, which do not even attend to potentially revealing historical dimensions, such as race and class, instead choosing to focus on normative data sets without interrogating the presuppositions and "sameness" inscribed in his process.

Salavon describes his interests in "pattern in general and individuality and uniqueness; in the antithesis of that—group dynamics; the large social group—thinking in terms of large entities and thinking in terms of individuals as entities." In this context, Salavon states, "'Averaging' is one way to speak to those things simultaneously."[67] The question then emerges whether the dialectical relation between individuals and large social groups is adequately mobilized through the process of "averaging." Salavon's work, in fact, demonstrates the insufficiency of this aesthetic strategy to reveal actual cultural insight.

A more complex interrelationship between data and images can be found in Salavon's projects *The Loop* (2007) and *City* (2008), both of which are composed from digitally generated images of Chicago. Unlike Salavon's other series, these composites were created not from photographs taken and shared by real people but from digitally generated images simulating the view from the city's trains as they circumnavigate downtown Chicago. Although they are computer generated, Salavon's composites privilege common sites for tourist photographs, presenting digital simulations that are idealized and lacking any of the defects or detritus of lived urban spaces. These abstract but distinctly urban—perhaps even distinctly Chicagoan—images evoke the general category of city*ness*, while insisting on the *constructed*ness of both the physical city and its simulation in digital space.

Technologized Vision

This chapter pairs data visualization with machine vision because they are reciprocal, technical phenomena, each serving, in its own way, as an intermediary between the visual and computational registers.[68] Structurally, however, this model offers no insight into the politics of vision played out across the array of technologies discussed here. It would be entirely possible to focus on affordance and process at the expense of social consequence. Technology too easily distracts from the questions of power, privilege, and ideology that rightly dominated visual culture during the previous century; to ignore them now mendaciously suggests that today's technologies of vision are somehow absolved of responsibility for the very phenomena most imperative for them to reveal. Practicality prevents us from carrying forward all the theoretical models that might be productively adapted from twentieth-century visual culture. For now I will mention just two—Jean-Louis Comolli's apparatus theory of cinema and Donna Haraway's technofeminist critique of scientific imaging—both of which resonate productively with what we now call "machine vision."

Although Comolli's influential 1971 essay "Machines of the Visible" focuses on cinema, its framing of the interdetermination of human and technological apparatuses of seeing offers useful insights into machine vision. Building on Martin Heidegger's answer to the "Question Concerning

Technology," Comolli positions the importance of cinema's apparatus not in the realm of the technological but in that of the social. Technological components, he argued, came and went; they thrived not on inventions or breakthroughs but on their ability to be integrated into social practices and needs. A "new" invention such as the cinema had its roots in a half-century or more of image culture that prepared viewers for the cinema's commercial implementation.

So it is with digital technology, the basic components of which existed long before they became a part of most people's everyday lives. The transition from technological possibility to social integration requires decades of infiltration and acculturation. A "digital logic" had first to be infused in the consciousness of the culture that would eventually embrace it, even if, like its end users, it did not fully digest the terms of service for what it was agreeing to. For Comolli, the iconic visibility of the film camera stood as a metonym for "the whole of the technics"[69] underlying the medium. But what would such an icon look like for digital culture? A supercomputer with banks of flashing lights from a Hollywood prop house? A server farm with cooling towers and backup generators? A microprocessor? Perhaps the mobile devices that many of us are connected to stand in for the sum of all digital technologies. When dozens of individuals on YouTube upload videos of smashing, burning, microwaving, or blending their old cell phones, it's hard not to suspect that the conjoined industrial cabal of hardware and telecommunications is being assaulted in effigy. The absence of any single metonym for "the digital" may be part of the reason digital apparatus theory remains splintered and ineffectual as a vector for social critique.

Writing in the context of the early 1970s and influenced by theories of postcolonialism, Comolli drew a straight line between looking and capturing, with the result that "the visible" is implicated in social apparatuses of colonization and control. Knowledge, according to this model, correlates not only with power but with possession. Comolli assumed that a fundamental characteristic of the visible is that it may be appropriated and owned by one in possession of the photographic apparatus. But the rights of individuals operate differently in the realms of image acquisition and data tracking. Private citizens are generally entitled to a degree of control over how their photographic image may be captured and used. But when those same individuals traverse data space, their movements, choices, and other trace data (time, location, duration, connection, etc.) are captured by default, often after a compulsory licensing agreement relinquishing all right to know, limit, or control how that data might be aggregated, interpreted, or sold.

When thinking about the relationship between seemingly organic, biological vision and the technologized processes by which visual information is transformed into computable data, we should not ignore Donna Haraway's two-decade-old warning about the perils of disembodied vision and the troubling imbrication of scientific technologies of vision that are inextricably tied, in her critique, to "militarism, colonialism, capitalism and male supremacy."[70] These were forcefully articulated in her 1997 article "The Persistence of Vision."

> The "eyes" made available in modern technological sciences shatter any idea of passive vision; these prosthetic devices show us that all eyes, including our own organic ones, are active perceptual systems, building in translations and specific *ways* of seeing, that is, ways of life. There is no unmediated photograph or passive camera obscura in scientific accounts of bodies and machines; there are only highly specific visual possibilities, each with a wonderfully detailed, active, partial way of organizing the worlds. All of these pictures of the world should not be allegories of infinite mobility and interchangeability, but of elaborate specificity and difference and the loving care people might take to learn how to see faithfully from another's point of view, even when the other is our own machine.[71]

Haraway privileges subjugated viewpoints but she does not do so naïvely. Visions "from below" are preferable because they allow for disruptions of the fundaments of power inscribed from above. But this perspective is not easily come by—it requires a highly skilled and self-critical stance that is as complicated as the "highest" stratum of technoscientific visualizations.[72] Haraway goes on to describe a litany of seemingly unlimited "visualizing technologies" capable of enhancing and extending primate vision. The twentieth century's enhancements to the eye created the possibility of "seeing"—by means of visualized sensor data—the vast reaches of the solar system and the inner workings of biological organisms. Today's fusion of data and images promises to reveal a different order of invisible phenomena, namely the conceptual rendering of information flows and patterns. Such data has no logical or immanent visual form; viewing information as colorful or animated graphics has begun to seem natural only by convention. Rather than be seduced into epistephilic complacency, and out of respect for these models of politicized vision, let us always ask, at what cost and in whose interests are these visions of the world constructed? As Haraway asks pointedly, "With whose blood were my eyes crafted?"[73] The answer may be as relevant to what we see with our biological eyes as it is to the visual apparatus of our computers.

Machine Vision/Human Vision

YouTube is not about video; Facebook is not about social networking; and Snapchat is not about sharing images. These companies capture and store collections of media on a massive scale as a basis for refining algorithms for machine vision, marketing analytics, and artificial intelligence. The surface operations of these online platforms provide services of sufficient utility to draw participation from as large and diverse a population as possible. The social network Facebook, for example, is also by far the largest image archive in the world, storing and possessing unlimited usage rights to hundreds of billions of images, with hundreds of millions more being added every day. YouTube reported in 2014 that it was receiving three hundred hours of video uploads every minute, with a total running time in excess of sixty thousand *years*. As collections of images requiring the attention of human beings, such archives are useless. Although humans continue to play a crucial role in training computers to recognize the visual content of images and video, these massive collections only become valuable to their keepers in proportion to the speed and precision with which they may be translated into computable data.

In certain important respects, of course, "machine vision" is an oxymoron. Calling it "at best, allegorical," Benjamin Bratton notes that "most machine seeing does not involve the production of mimetic 'images' as would be recognizable in a human context."[74] Computers receive images as sensor data in the form of pixels, which are transformed into computable form. This challenge may be computationally demanding, but it is conceptually straightforward. Google's explanation of pattern recognition puts it in disarmingly simple terms. "Computers don't 'see' photos and videos in the same way that people do. When you look at a photo, you might see your best friend standing in front of her house. From a computer's perspective, that same image is simply a bunch of data that it may interpret as shapes and information about color values."[75] A more complex challenge faces researchers who attempt to use computers to recognize subtle, emotional, or connotative meanings within images. The basic process, however, follows a logical progression. Working with a large "pixel-data" set, such as that found on Instagram, researchers identify a desired group of essential qualities, perhaps describing abstract concepts such as happiness, creativity, or beauty. Because these features are highly subjective, Amazon's Mechanical Turk is commonly used to achieve consensus regarding the presence or absence of these qualities in any given image. To do this, researchers establish a formula based on a series of small-scale trials to determine how many total ratings and what percentage of agreement are required to yield a reliable consensus opinion.

For example, in exchange for a few cents, workers logged in to Mechanical Turk might be asked to classify images based on whether they are beautiful or display signs of creativity or innovation. If a given threshold is reached—say, four out of five viewers agree that a given image possesses a particular attribute—then that image is considered to be consensually so. Once we obtain a large collection of consensual images, those images form a training set for the machine vision system, just as we'd need a large training set if we wanted the machine to recognize parts of an automobile. With a large enough data set and a sufficient number of formal attributes and combinations to identify, the computer can reliably recognize even the most abstract and seemingly elusive concepts. Each stage of this process is open to critique, and the most rigorous machine vision research does its best to account for factors such as cultural specificity, linguistic variations, and varying metrics of taste and value. Smaller-scale variables and anomalies are presumed to be rendered irrelevant by the sheer volume of data analyzed, producing a distinct separation between noise and signal.[76]

While machine vision empowers computers to make sense of the roiling, chaotic sea of images humans create in their daily lives, programmers, designers, and artists use the serial processes of data visualization to make the profuse output of sensor data and information systems understandable to humans. Nothing in the evolution of this research suggests that computers will not eventually be as good as humans at recognizing and interpreting the meaning of images. In fact, this is not such a high bar to set. Humans are notoriously limited in their ability to recognize the meaning of images, for various reasons, ranging from ignorance of cultural context to simple misapprehension. The field of visual studies might not exist if a multiplicity of interpretations were not possible for any given image.

In a similar sense, effectively translating the meaning of data is not a simple process. Like image recognition algorithms that struggle to recognize distinct but computationally opaque behaviors, such as throwing a Frisbee, humans must learn to adapt their perceptive and cognitive abilities to correctly interpret data that has been translated into the visible register. For humans, data visualization is embedded in a complex cultural matrix that includes connotative meanings associated with graphical characteristics, such as shape, color, proximity, and so on. Therefore, data visualization is already cultural visualization, a process of ideological articulation as much as of mathematical conversion.

Data visualization and machine vision occupy opposing ends of an axis defined in terms of computability and mimesis. A different conceptual axis would place machine vision in opposition to human vision. This concept derives from various media works of art, described below, that *seem* to be computational but aren't; that is, these works adopt the logic of computation as a model for human labor. I also find it useful to insist that humans' previously unmarked domain over vision now requires qualification as "human vision." This extends the logic of visual culture theory's insistence that easily naturalized activities such as "looking," "seeing," or "observing" must be analyzed as discrete and culturally situated "practices," "ways" or "techniques,"[77] and as such may be decoded, retrained, or interrogated. When arrayed in opposition to technologies devoted to machine vision, my aim is not to reinscribe the organic nature of human seeing; on the contrary, I wish to reflect on the ways in which it has been reconstituted in dialogue with the computational. In the examples that follow, human vision offers a thought-provoking glimpse of what happens when humans begin not only to *see* like computers but to *act* like them.

A popular form that exemplifies this framing of human vision is the genre of remix video known as supercuts. Many creators of supercuts are satisfied with dramatically or humorously illustrating a single visual trope or cinematic cliché: the mirror scare or loss of cell phone service in horror films, for example, or three-point landings and "kill lines" in action movies. Another genre identifies repeated lines of dialogue or tropes, such as "every ____ in ____": every cocktail in *Mad Men*; every "dude" in *Lost*; and so on. Supercuts, in their earliest manifestations, were primarily understood as labors of love by obsessive fans, activating both the familiarity of an original work of popular culture and the algorithmic pleasures of repetition and distillation.

Among the earliest and most virtuosic progenitors of algorithmic remix are media artists Jennifer and Kevin McCoy. During the early 2000s, the McCoys created a series of recombinant media databases drawn from popular television programs. Included were projects based on the original *Kung Fu* (1972–75), *Starsky & Hutch* (1975–79), Looney Tunes cartoons, and the original *Star Trek* (1966–69) series. For each source, the McCoys began by breaking the show down into granular elements based on formal properties or content categories. Resorted subsets of media were then combined, tagged, burned to CD-ROM, and installed in gallery contexts as a physical database of hard media, combined with a user-controlled player and screen that allowed gallery visitors to select and display media sets of their own choosing.

The insistent physicality of the McCoys' presentation is significant on multiple levels. Conceived during the early days of the internet, the project's use of physical media constituted a refusal of the economy and scale of online distribution. Their controlled circumstances of display for low-resolution CD-ROM-based video files also distanced these works from the moral panic that resulted in passage of the Digital Millennium Copyright Act in 1998. More important, the physical process of selection and combination highlights the human and subjective dimensions of the project. Although the McCoys' work is clearly indebted to database culture broadly, their selection of media suggests the idiosyncrasy of pop culture fans. Likewise, their categorization schemes are highly subjective, offering curatorial categories such as "Every sexy outfit" and "Every thug," while other categories are strictly formal, such as "Every extreme close-up," "Every background music," "Every diegetic noise," and so on. The McCoys' work thus revels in the pleasures of genre while gently mocking the specific forms and styles by which they manifest in popular culture.

In 2009, Natalie Bookchin's *Mass Ornament* quietly elevated the remix genre of the supercut to the status of art. *Mass Ornament* is a single-channel video installation composed entirely of excerpted YouTube videos, mostly of young women dancing in domestic spaces, accompanied by music from Busby Berkeley's *Gold Diggers* (1935) and Leni Riefenstahl's *Triumph of the Will* (1935). Bookchin's video is further broken down into multiple split screens, fragmenting the image into lines and matrices of smaller frames that phase in and out of synchronization with the music and bodily movements of the dancers. Brief solos by individual performers give way to resonant movements as additional frames pop up across the screen or erupt in crescendos of sameness. These moments of synchronization explain Bookchin's project title, which alludes to Siegfried Kracauer's book celebrating Weimar-era mass culture, *The Mass Ornament*, originally published in 1927.

For Kracauer the "mass ornament" represented a cultural response to the regimentation and mechanization of industrial capitalism, exemplified by the synchronized dance troupe the Tiller Girls. Kracauer describes them as "products of American distraction factories [who] are no longer individual girls, but indissoluble girl clusters whose movements are demonstrations of mathematics"—bodies become data.[78] In Thomas Levin's introduction to the English-language edition of *The Mass Ornament*, he describes Kracauer's reading of synchronized performance in more generous terms of "progressive potential as the representation of a new type of collectivity organized not according to the natural bonds of community but as a social mass of functionally linked individuals."[79] To this progressive potential Bookchin's project also turns, but the underlying technology to which it responds is not merely that of industrial capitalism but the digital networks and social practices that are now crucial to its functioning.

Like the McCoys' installations with their dozens of CD-ROMs, *Mass Ornament* was crafted through an extraordinarily labor-intensive process. To amass her original media collection, Bookchin viewed and downloaded hundreds of videos and then manually synchronized them into a kind of collectively unconscious choreography, following musical genre conventions, including scene setting, solos, and synchronized spectacles. *Mass Ornament* also marks a return to Bookchin's early interest in collecting

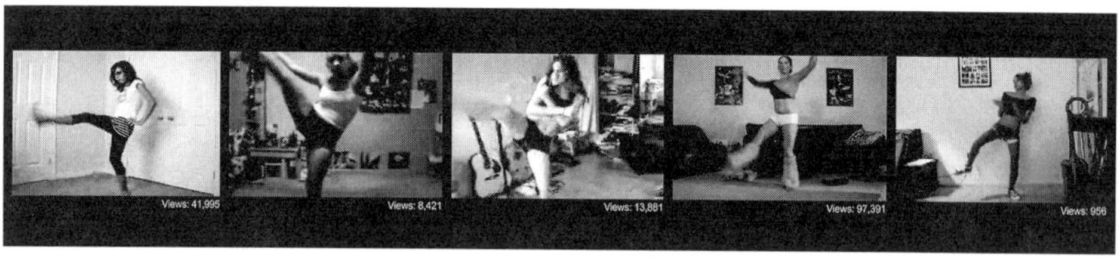

Figure 1.4
Human vision transforms narrative subsets of internet video into rituals of collectivity in Natalie Bookchin's *Mass Ornament*. (2009). Image courtesy of the artist.

quotidian media artifacts, first seen in her CD-ROM *Databank of the Everyday* (1996), a curated archive of video loops from the artist's life, organized into categories collectively described as a "stockhouse of gestures, routines and habits."[80] But where *Databank of the Everyday* looks inward, *Mass Ornament* radiates outward, turning every webcam on the internet into a massively distributed sensor array.

Bookchin's interest in both the form and the substance of vernacular media persists throughout her work with remix and documentary video. The pleasures of this work derive not from image-based aesthetics of form but from the organizational structures—synchrony, multiplicity, symmetry—of the database. Viewed in conjunction with subsequent projects such as *Testament* (2009/2016) and *Long Story Short* (2016), *Mass Ornament* eloquently attests to the rhetorical power of collection and collectivity—not the condescending critique of sameness seen in Salavon's averages, but a videographic construction of a social body. Whereas *Mass Ornament* presents a lighthearted vision of performance laced with nascent sexuality, *Testament* portrays structurally similar but more emotionally somber topics such as being laid off, coming out, and taking prescription medications. Instead of choreographed bodily movements across multiple frames or screens as in *Mass Ornament, Testament* emphasizes the choreographic potentials of voice, highlighting uncanny resonances across a handful of deeply personal subjects. The stark tonal contrast between *Mass Ornament* and *Testament* illustrates the dexterity of Bookchin's method, which combines technological process with analytical paradigm.

In Wendy Chun's discussion of *Mass Ornament,* she focuses on the project's blurring of internal and external spaces as well as the performance of online identities that are both public and private. These issues resonate with the overall argument of Chun's book, which interrogates the multiple processes by which some of the network age's most troubling social technologies have become habituated. For Chun, Bookchin's work exemplifies some of these contradictions, celebrating connections among individuals as a "hopeful revelation of an unconscious community"[81] that nonetheless takes place within a historical framing bracketed by the visual spectacles of Nazi propaganda and Hollywood musicals. In *Testament,* Chun also finds dissonance among the voices, preserving the "complexities of individuality in collectivity."[82] As artworks that derive from emergent and unforeseen online social practices, both *Testament* and *Mass Ornament* are symptomatic of the paradoxes of network culture—control and freedom, visible and invisible, known and unknown—to which Chun's work has been perceptively devoted for the past decade.

A somewhat different dynamic is at work in Bookchin's subsequent project, *Long Story Short* (2016). In *Mass Ornament* and *Testament*, she defined a method for constructing meaning from the otherwise overwhelming and undifferentiated practices of individual video blogging. To make *Long Story Short*, Bookchin shifted her practice from extracting preexisting content from video-sharing sites to a model in which the artist herself initiated a series of original documentary videos. The result, in *Long Story Short*, is a powerful, polyphonic synthesis of voices testifying to the firsthand experience of poverty in America. In the piece, Bookchin preserved the webcam vernacular of low-res direct address seen in *Testament*. Edited together and composited onto a single screen, more than one hundred individual videos form a matrix of talking heads expressing shared experiences of struggle and indignity in the face of poverty.

Bookchin's database aesthetic proves remarkably effective for accentuating the power of these voices, which are too infrequently listened to in contemporary culture. Where conventional wisdom about media for social change presumes the need for deep personalization and empathy toward those presented as victims of social ills, in *Long Story Short*, the inherent dignity of self-presentation is combined with a literalization of the power of collective voice and action. Although the individuals included in the video have no means of knowing or interacting with each other, the system designed by Bookchin succeeds in amplifying individual voices into a powerful, collective articulation of otherwise socially stigmatizing experiences.

As instances of "human vision," these projects by Bookchin find resonances and distinctions with related projects by Casey Reas and Benjamin Grosser. In very different ways, each of these artists represents an interpretation of what happens when computers encounter popular media. Each approaches a different medium—broadcast television for Reas (*Signal to Noise*); Hollywood feature films for Grosser (*Computers Watching Movies*); and internet video for Bookchin—with correspondingly varying responses. As I discuss in the final section of this chapter, Reas's projects generate audiovisual assaults, as if the apparatus were attempting to digest signal as well as noise to produce a cacophony of pixels, sounds, and rhythms. For Grosser, the computer behaves like an obsessive fan; its viewing is precise and monomaniacal, scanning and focusing on the minutest details and patterns within the frame. In contrast, Bookchin uses a database structure to bring order to the chaos and overproliferation of media online. What makes Bookchin's work especially interesting in this context is its shift from being a strictly reproductive technology—that is, one that samples and recombines existing media—to being a productive one. In *Long Story Short*, Bookchin deliberately assembles a database of content as if the organizing principles of the previous two projects were reverse engineered to imagine the third.

The year after Bookchin released *Mass Ornament*, media artist Christian Marclay completed *The Clock* (2010), a twenty-four-hour film loop composed entirely of cinematic images of clocks, projected in synchronization with the actual time of day. Like Bookchin, who personally invested countless hours watching and downloading YouTube videos, Marclay worked with a group of researchers to comb painstakingly through hundreds of DVDs to find and excerpt images of clocks. Both works share a computational, encyclopedic sensibility, and both attack overwhelming data sets (all of YouTube and all of cinema history, respectively) through the brute force of human labor rather than automated computer vision analysis.

Marclay's signal achievement in *The Clock* is allowing viewers to indulge simultaneously in the pleasures of cinema and in those of computation on more or less equal footing. *The Clock* invites viewers to occupy a dual subject position, both producing and being produced by the complementary regimes of data and image.[83] *The Clock* further transforms audience viewing habits by attuning viewers to the presence of clocks outside the obscure diegesis of Marclay's film. Previously banal or unnoticed images of clocks may begin to burst out of their narrative context for viewers whose perceptions have been recalibrated to notice the presence of clocks anywhere within the cinematic frame.

In principle, both *The Clock* and *Mass Ornament* could have been produced—perhaps even improved on in scope and precision—if they had been created not by humans but by image recognition software. This raises the question, Are projects like *Mass Ornament* and *The Clock* evidence of artistic capitulation to the logic of computation, or are they gestures of defiance—reassertions of essential humanity—against it? In David Golumbia's book *The Cultural Logic of Computation*, he writes with gloomy insight:

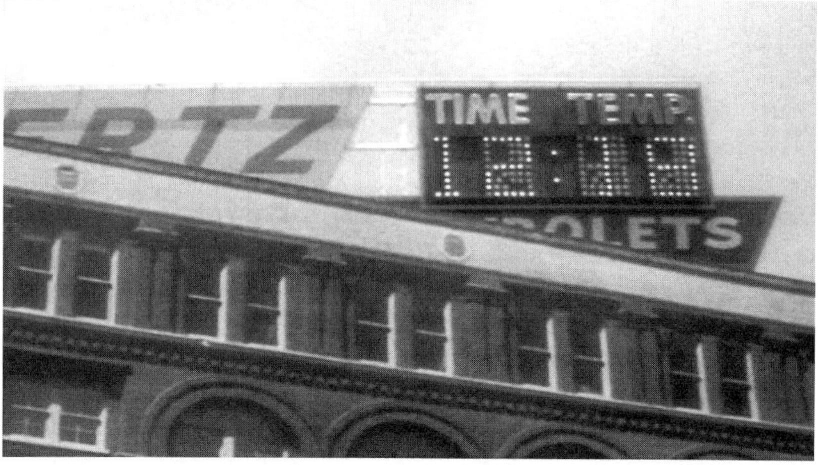

Figure 1.5
In Christian Marclay's *The Clock* (2010), viewers indulge simultaneously in the pleasures of cinema and computation. Christian Marclay, still frame from *The Clock* (2010). Single-channel video with sound. 24 hours, looped. © Christian Marclay. Courtesy Paula Cooper Gallery, New York, and White Cube, London. Photo: Todd White Photography.

> [T]here is little doubt that the more we imagine ourselves to be like computers, the more computer-like we will become; conversely, the more we imagine computers can take over sociopolitical functions, the more we will give up our own influence over those phenomena—and the more they will pass into the domain of exactly the powerful agents (states, transnational corporations, and capital itself) that already dominate so much of social life.[84]

I do not aspire to the broad theorization of computation mapped by Golumbia—nor to his inclusive denunciation of "computationalism"—but his critique offers a provocative caveat about the potential excesses of digital culture theory, especially regarding proclamations of epistemic shifts or fundamental changes in what it means to be human. Given the state of things, such proclamations may well be warranted, but they should not be issued lightly, nor accepted uncritically. We have reason to embrace posthumanism not because humans have been or will be surpassed by computers, but because the short-sighted arrogance of humanity has consistently made a mess of the global resources we have pressed into our service. Humans, simply put, do not deserve the place we have claimed at the center of the universe. Rather than supplying evidence of further decline, as Golumbia implies, perhaps the emulation of computational intelligence seen in Bookchin's and Marclay's work represents a transition in the evolution of humanity to a more humble state of being.

Following a variation on this logic, artist Benjamin Grosser has created a series of software-based projects attempting to visualize aspects of computational intelligence as if computers were on the brink of transition rather than humans. Where the concept of "human vision" describes the infusion of a computational sensibility into human artistic production, Grosser's work goes a step further, attempting to visualize what it's like for computers to perform such distinctly human activities as watching movies or applying paint to canvas.[85] For *Computers Watching Movies* (2013), Grosser programmed an artificial intelligence algorithm with the ability to selectively view scenes from motion pictures and respond to prominent visual stimuli—objects, movements, colors, patterns—within the frame.[86] Grosser's software then performs the machinic equivalent of eye tracking. As the algorithm decides which areas of the frame to "watch," it traces lines on the screen that correspond to those areas of greatest interest. For Grosser, this process invites reconsideration of how human media viewing has been culturally shaped. He writes, "Viewers are provoked to ask how computer vision differs from their own human vision, and what that difference reveals about our culturally-developed ways of looking. Why do we watch what we watch when we watch it? Will a system without our sense of narrative or historical patterns of vision watch the same things?"[87]

Grosser's work stands in contrast to platforms for quantitative analysis of cinema such as *Cinemetrics*, Yuri Tsivian's crowd-sourced database of cinematic shot lengths, or the cultural analytics lab's tools for "exploratory image analysis,"[88] discussed previously. Whereas these tools allow for quantitative analysis of cinematic form, *Computers Watching Movies* skips directly to the stage of visualizing the computer's apparent areas of interest as if diagnosing underlying obsessions. As each scene plays out, lines are traced in real time across the frame, sometimes remaining tightly focused, other times exploding into a translucent cloud as the algorithm attempts to take in all pieces of a complex visual effect at once. The project's comparison with human viewing patterns is highlighted by limiting the source material to iconic scenes from some of Hollywood's most popular films. Grosser's installation does not include any original cinematic imagery; however, the computer traces are accompanied by real-time audio

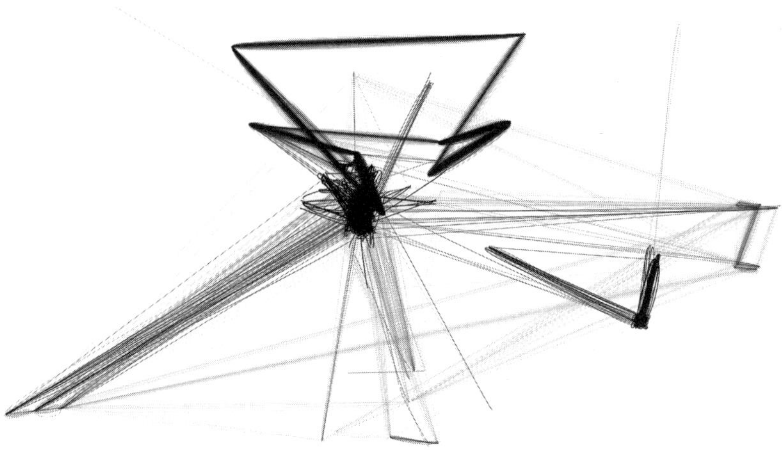

Figure 1.6
Exposed to scenes from classical Hollywood cinema (*2001: A Space Odyssey* seen here), computer vision software reveals its tastes and obsessions in Benjamin Grosser's *Computers Watching Movies* (2013). Still frame from *Computers Watching Movies* (*2001: A Space Odyssey*).

that invites viewers to conjure visual memories of the original clips. Like *Cinemetrics*, Grosser's project confirms certain expectations about shifts in cinematic form over the past few decades. The static minimalism and languorous pacing of Stanley Kubrick's *2001: A Space Odyssey* (1968), for example, generates radically different patterns of interest by the computer compared with the frenetic pace and visual density of Christopher Nolan's *Inception* (2010). In broad terms, Grosser's work does not yet aim to revise our understanding of what it means to be human but proposes an ambitious reconsideration of the two-way relationship between humans and computers.

Google's Brain

Over the course of the past decade, some of the most provocative experiments in machine vision have emerged from Google Lab's Unsupervised Learning project, which was revealed to the public in 2012 by the more evocatively named Google Brain Team. Google engineers frame the project in terms of the need to transform data that is primarily received by the

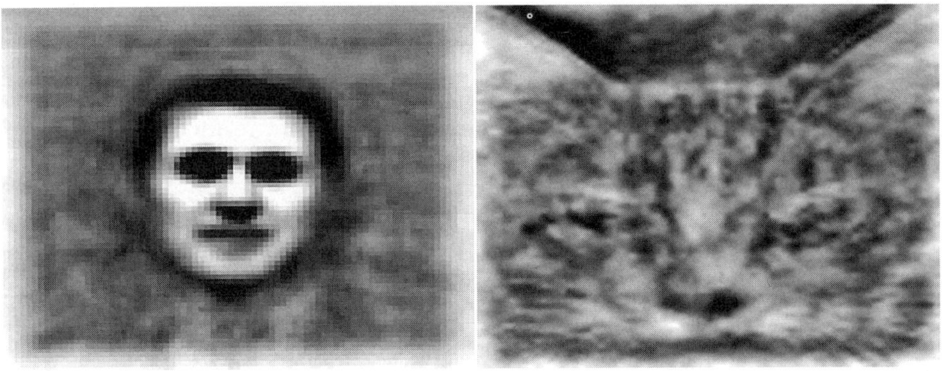

Figure 1.7
Cat faces and human faces emerged as the dominant image phenotypes in 10 million internet videos viewed by Google's Unsupervised Learning project (2012).

human sensorium as media (sounds or images) into a computable form that may be more readily processed by computers.

> Most of the world's data is in the form of media (images, sounds/music, and videos)—media that work directly with the human perceptual senses of vision and hearing. To organize and index these media, we give our machines corresponding perception capabilities: we let our computers look at the images and video, and listen to the soundtracks and music, and build descriptions of their perceptions.[89]

Images related to this project were presented at the 29th International Conference on Machine Learning in Edinburgh, Scotland, in 2012 and circulated widely online thereafter. The presentation by Stanford professor of computer science Quoc V. Le included several images generated by Google's Unsupervised Learning system, which distinctly resembled a cat face, a human face, and rather less distinctly, a human torso. Online, the cat and human faces were most often distributed as a diptych, depicting pixelated, desaturated, humanoid and feline features emerging against a blurry, gray void.

Google Fellow Jeff Dean and visiting faculty member Andrew Ng describe the images as examples of the "perceptions" generated by the Unsupervised Learning system running sixteen thousand processing cores for three days, directed at a collection of unlabeled frames sampled from 10 million YouTube videos. The system's learning was dubbed "unsupervised" because the computers were not told what to look for within each 200 × 200 pixel image. This is what set Google's Unsupervised Learning project apart from other machine vision algorithms, which trained computers to "look for" images matching a particular combination of graphical features. According to Google, the experiment demonstrated a "70 percent relative improvement in accuracy"[90] over other machine learning systems. These findings suggest that large-scale neural networks, when provided with no information or guidance, will, all on their own, identify human faces and cats as the most prominent image phenotypes emerging from YouTube videos and, by extension, the internet at large.

This research was announced a little more than a year after Google software engineer James Zern revealed that only about 30 percent of the billions of hours of videos on YouTube accounted for approximately 99 percent of views on the site.[91] In other words, the vast majority of videos uploaded to YouTube are seen by almost no one, meaning that the company's revenue model of targeted advertising generates no significant value for more than two-thirds of its content. Nonetheless, 70 percent of the vast architecture of YouTube remains devoted to media that is seen by almost no one. The only way to monetize a media collection at this scale is through large-scale automated translation of images into data. With this goal in mind, the billions of hours of video available on YouTube represents not an unmonetized public utility but an invaluable resource for the rapidly expanding fields of machine vision and artificial intelligence.

The human and cat images released by Google were widely received as objects of novelty and amusement, consistent with cultural narratives that trivialize the internet as a conduit for narcissistic self-portraiture and cute kitten videos. A headline in the UK's *Daily Mail* newspaper, for example, read, "Google Creates 'Computer Brain'—and It Immediately Starts Watching Cat Videos on YouTube."[92] Likewise, the UK edition of *Wired* published an article under the headline, "Google's Artificial Brain Learns to Find Cat Videos."[93] One might speculate that these images were meant to serve a palliative function, reassuring the public that Google's hosting of billions of hours of valueless video is, in fact, a harmless or even playful endeavor that contributes to the company's stated goal to "make everyday tasks much easier."[94] This analysis is consistent with the argument put forward by Mercedes Bunz that the visual culture of the technology industries—exemplified by company logos favoring primary colors, cartoonlike graphics, and flattened surfaces—has been long engaged in infantilizing and patronizing users, even as it is cloaked in ideologies of empowerment.[95]

Google's interest in training computers to make sense of vast undifferentiated image collections aims to enhance the company's ability to use data analytics to understand, shape, and predict human behavior. In June 2015, Google Research publicized a process it had developed, which appeared to reverse the logic of image recognition. Google researchers had begun prompting its "neural net" of image recognition processors to *create* images rather than recognize them. This internal reappropriation of one of Google's closely guarded technologies caused an internet sensation, and the company released a collection of provocative images with a distinctive visual style along with an open source version of the software used to create them.

The overwhelming majority of public discourse surrounding these images aligned with one of two discursive paradigms: chemical-induced psychedelia and visualization of the subconscious through dreams. Google itself encouraged the latter model by initially dubbing the system "Inceptionism," a reference that returns once again to Christopher Nolan's *Inception,* in which the traversal of states of consciousness occurs through chemically induced lucid dreaming. Perhaps it was after realizing that the narrative of Nolan's *Inception* begins with a high-tech corporation exploiting its access to the subconscious minds of its clients to steal personal information that Google decided to change the name to the more innocuous Deep Dream. Officially described as a "deep neural network architecture for computer vision,"[96] the Deep Dream visual aesthetic combined elements of the natural world—especially animalistic features of dogs, birds, and reptiles—with geometric, scientific, or architectural shapes.

Soon a proliferation of online Deep Dream conversion engines invited human viewers to experiment with various enigmatic parameters (e.g., spirit, neuron, Valyrian) that shape the resulting images. While early online services offered to perform deep dream conversions for a few dollars per image, it took only a few months for websites such as the Deep Dream Generator to appear, allowing free, unlimited, user-customizable conversions. Several Deep Dream auteurs also emerged, such as Swedish designer Johan Nordberg, whose work painstakingly converted multiply processed images into animated sequences, creating the illusion of real-time transformations from formless static images into nightmarish apparitions.

Comparisons with psychoanalysis-inspired surrealist art and drug-induced literature abounded, overwhelming alternate readings that might challenge the uncritical conjunction of human and artificial intelligence. Rather than project attributes of human consciousness or subconsciousness onto the algorithm, a more productive strategy might derive from consideration of the structures of the neural net itself.

All of this raises the question of what would happen if the deep dream algorithm were used to "interpret" an image generated by the software that was used to develop it? One conceivable outcome of this reversal might be to reveal evidence of the "perception" process by which Google Brain's human and cat images were originally derived—similar to how language translation systems are tested by converting a sentence from one language to another and then reversing the process to see how closely the original sentence is reproduced.

By going deeper into the dream you will discover amazing new dimensions and visual artifacts from the AI's consciousness.
—Deep Dream Generator

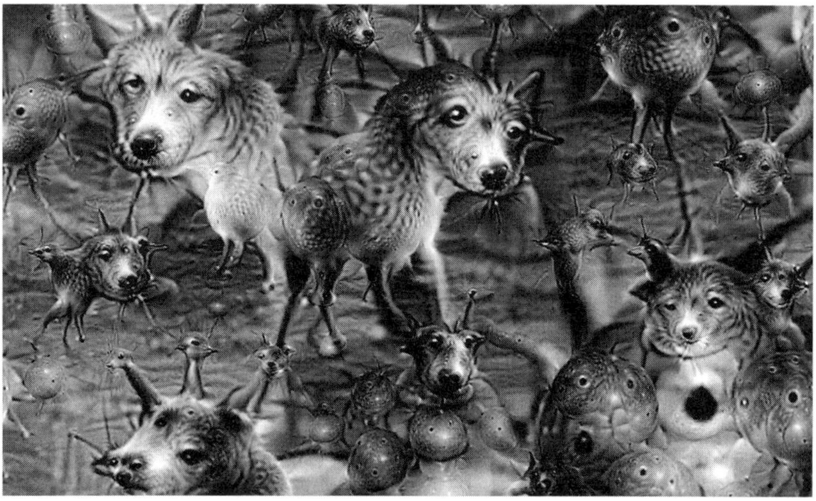

Figure 1.8
Johan Nordberg's *Inside an Artificial Brain* (2015) uses Deep Dream software to enhance visual patterns from an original field of random pixel data. Image courtesy of Johan Nordberg, https://johan-nordberg.com.

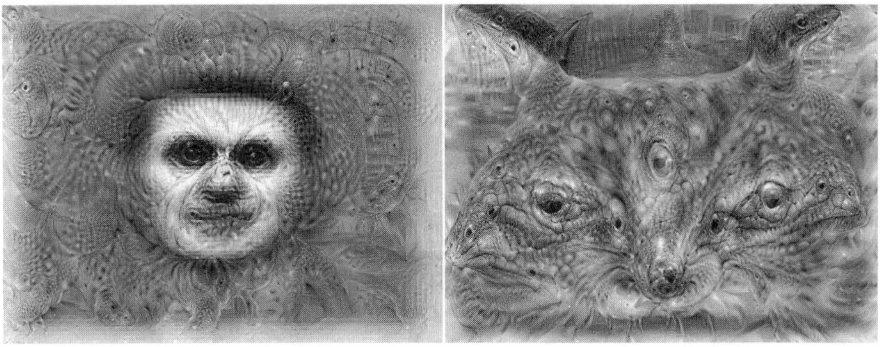

Figure 1.9
A facetious attempt at algorithmic recursion, subjecting computer-extracted image phenotypes to an inverse process of refining visual patterns. Image by the author (2017).

As with the reversal of language translators, which rarely produce a perfect translation, this process did not succeed in reverse engineering anything resembling the original images.[97] The custom recognition parameters of the Deep Dream software alone are sufficient to preclude a one-to-one conversion, but I find this experiment nonetheless revealing. Both human and animal visages became more animalistic; except for the eyes, the primate face in particular became more simian than human, while the fuzzy, undifferentiated halo surrounding both heads acquired a reptilian aura. In the end, this experiment in algorithmic recursion offers little more than amusement or distraction, which may well be the point of Google's gesture in making the software freely available. While these images invite comparisons with the recesses of the unconscious mind, one might also wonder about the real-world systems and values that are thereby shielded from critique. Both the visual rhetoric of the images and the cultural discourse surrounding them suggest yet another narrative that is at once trivializing and reassuring: if algorithms dream, they dream of electric dogs.

Negotiated Visualization

More so than any other creator discussed in this book, Casey Reas's work exemplifies the tortured relationship between abstraction and representation. Though he is not the only artist to fall within what I have termed the "negotiated mode" of relating data to images, Reas has created a series of uniquely varied attempts to work productively across the two domains. In a prolific body of work created over the past two decades, Reas has explored the creative potentials of software art by articulating multiple relationships between data and images, as well as, on occasion, human bodies and physical structures. Nearly all his work is created using the programming environment Processing, which he codeveloped with Ben Fry in the early 2000s while they were graduate students in John Maeda's Aesthetics and Computation Group at the MIT Media Lab. In work by Reas and others, Processing is often deployed to create systems that emulate patterns from the natural world (cellular division, flocking behaviors) via algorithmically specified shapes, textures, and movements. As we will see, the evolution of Reas's own creative work with Processing maps an unexpected trajectory from purely abstract, code-generated art to increasingly image-based and physically situated or embodied artworks.

In Processing, Reas and Fry created a free, open source software platform that is meant to be versatile and accessible to artists. We might compare what Processing brings to contemporary digital art making with what audio synthesizers brought to analog videographics in the 1980s and 1990s, providing a customizable library of signal processing that enables media artists to conceive and generate entirely new types of visual experiences. Processing also readily facilitates the translation of quantitative values drawn from databases into the visual register, making it a versatile tool for visualizing complex or dynamic data sets. In addition, Processing was designed to accept media- and camera-based sources, for both visual information input and interface control, situating it at the threshold between data and image on multiple levels. Although located here within a chapter devoted to data visualization, Reas's work is instructive for how it does *not* conform to translational conventions associated with data visualization. Instead, I focus on two discrete areas of interest within his work—exemplified by multiple image series created using the *Process* library and a later group of works that deploy variations on the *Signal to Noise* software engine—to illuminate how these works uniquely blur the lines between image and data.

Among Reas's foundational inspirations was the work of Valentino Braitenberg, a twentieth-century neuroscientist whose work continues to be influential in the fields of robotics and artificial intelligence. Through a series of thought experiments, Braitenberg described the design of autonomous agents capable of exhibiting behaviors that appear intentional and adaptive through the integration of relatively simple combinations of sensors and actuators. These agents, called Braitenberg vehicles, were imagined to exhibit behaviors that were recognizably organic, even value driven. Braitenberg sought to expose the interpretive systems by which we attribute behavioral characteristics even to objects that we know to be without consciousness. We may perceive in a set of behaviors, for example, signs of aggression, cowardice, or even love toward other agents, along with affinity or aversion to environmental factors such as temperature, light, or oxygen levels.[98]

The emergent behaviors of Braitenberg vehicles inspired early works by Reas including *Path* (2001), *Tissue Prints* (2002), and *Microimage* (2002/2014). The images generated for the *Microimage* series are Reas's most corporeal, resembling bodily tissue, hair follicles, neural connectors, orifices. The color palette of these works is intentionally evocative of mammalian flesh and hair, with occasional blazes of blue or gray. The works are aggressively abstract but also deeply allusive, resembling a cross between abstract expressionist painting and forensic microscopy.[99] Viewers are invited to see bodily textures, shapes, and patterns, which are infinitely, albeit variably, reproducible. The code, in turn, can generate an unlimited number of image states. Reas describes the resulting numbered fine art prints as "documents" of the Microimage software, which itself forms the core of the artwork.[100]

Process is Reas's longest running series, evolving over more than a decade, with all works deriving from a shared library of elements. Specific combinations of predefined elements are called forth and executed in the creation of a *Process* work, causing traces to appear on-screen, resulting in continually emerging images of increasing density. Reas describes *Process* as a "choreographic system" in which he plays the role of "implementor."[101] For each work, Reas selects elements from the *Process* library and combines them into a set of instructions resembling a musical score. An example score describing *Process 15* reads:

> A rectangular surface filled with instances of Element 3, each with a different size and gray value. Draw a small, transparent circle at the midpoint of each Element. Increase the circle's opacity while its Element is touching another Element and decrease while it is not.[102]

Despite its seemingly prescriptive format, this score leaves a great deal of interpretive creativity in the hands of the programmer, who establishes the parameters and variables by which it will be executed. Each of Reas's predefined elements consists of a combination of forms and behaviors. For example, Element 3, used in *Process 15*, is defined as a combination of Form 2 (a line), with Behaviors 1 (move in a straight line), 3 (change direction while touching another Element), and 5 (enter from the opposite edge after moving off the surface). The instructions for how the element will be used are intentionally vague, refusing to specify, for example, the initial sizes of the objects, the number of instances, or their size, color, or opacity; nor is the rate of increase or decrease of size or opacity specified. All these factors are left up to the programmer's interpretations and improvisations, the way a musician or conductor might elaborate during a musical performance.

When presented electronically, the result is a visual experience in a perpetual state of becoming. When committed to static media, Reas selects one or more exemplary moments from each process to create a fixed C-print image, which can be displayed apart from the computational apparatus. To what extent should these arrested moments be regarded as "images" at all? They are primarily surface manifestations of the execution of Processing code. Their relationship to forms in the physical world is one of resemblance or allusion, rather than representation or mimesis. The lines, shapes, and volumes described by the computer's execution of the code may be thought of quite literally as "traces," but not the type of indexical photochemical trace realized in photography or cinema.

Reas states that the original text descriptions constitute the most important element of the work. In this, Reas's "scores" relate to the Fluxus movement and other practices in conceptual art of the sixties and seventies. Reas's method also resembles a computational version of Sol LeWitt's *Wall Drawings*, but with results that are closer to a partially ordered exercise in abstract expressionism. Like a LeWitt drawing based on a set of drafting instructions to be executed by others, Reas's *Process* works are interpreted first by the programmer, then by the software, with each actor afforded a degree of creative or stochastic variation. This, in part, is what makes the works feel organic rather than geometric or mechanical, distinguishing them from most of LeWitt's work.[103]

So rich and variable are the combinations of elements and behaviors afforded by the library subtending the *Process* series that it has supported experiments by Reas for well over a decade, comprising dozens of final images and installations. Throughout this time, Reas also created numerous related works that elaborate on the basic premise of the series. These include *Image Phase* (2004), a seventeen-minute animation created to accompany Steve Reich's 1967 musical composition "Piano Phase."[104] Reas's contribution to the project features abstract smoky shapes that morph in concert with a series of hypnotic, looping note sequences by Reich that phase in and out of synch. The images appear out of focus—an anomaly in Reas's body of work—transforming the images from their ontological status as code to images that appear distinctly videographic.

Although anomalous, this piece bears consideration because it highlights a central tension in Reas's work of this period. The code image is pristine and resolute—infinitely scalable and reproducible without distortion—the visual artifact of a lossless and infinitely executable algorithm. In contrast, the physical objects generated by the code cross the threshold to become images only when they are rendered for consumption. With *Process* works, this occurs at the moment of display or printing—or in the case of *Image Phase,* when rendered as video and thrown out of focus. The images are rasterized, ontologically transformed into a fixed medium, whereupon they commence being subject to decay. Only then do they become mortal, no longer safe in their regenerative capacity for infinite becoming.

To highlight the relationship between final images and the process used to create them, works in the *Process* series are typically presented in diptych form, consisting of two primary components: an operation screen, showing a graphical visualization of the computer's operations at runtime, and a final presentation screen or printed image.[105] The two screens are typically supplemented by wall text, which presents the original score as natural language text description. The temporal structure of Reas' work is thus threefold, referencing early moments of conception when the description and its translation into code were authored, followed by a real-time visualization of that code being executed, usually in a gallery context, and sometimes a different postprocessual moment when a single image is extracted and committed to a fixed object form.

In 2012, Reas launched a series of works titled *Signal to Noise.* Similar to how the *Process* series shared a library of elements, works in the series that followed were created with variations on this original software engine. Rather than taking pure elements of code as its basic building blocks, *Signal to Noise* was designed to sample and transform preexisting media sources such as broadcast television.[106] These works also represented Reas's transition away from the diptych format, resulting in elimination of the operation screen that reminded viewers about the rule-driven processes underlying the work.[107] The nature of the works' generativity also morphed significantly in this series. Whereas the *Process* works were driven first by rules encoded into an expressive software system, works included in *Signal to Noise* derive from preexisting imagery that remains unrecognizable yet generically familiar.[108] Viewers are not invited to experience the pleasure of decoding the algorithms driving their visual experience. Instead, they are asked to step back and experience the display on its own terms, as a visual experience presented without the need to emphasize either apparatus or process.[109]

Arguably, Reas's broadcast series simply shifts attention to different stages in the work's creation. In a series of works using found images intercepted from television broadcast towers around Los Angeles, Reas created loops of televisual imagery as source material to be processed by the *Signal to Noise* engine. Each piece was titled based on the station and month during which the original images had been captured, even going so far as to locate the towers by latitude/longitude coordinates and in terms of their broadcast frequency on the electromagnetic spectrum. Reas describes *KNBC (November 2015)* as "an audio and visual distortion of television signals broadcast during December 2015 over the 602–608 MHz spread of the electromagnetic spectrum from a tower located at 34°13′32″N, 118°3′52″W." Coupled with abstract bursts of sound composed by Philip Rugo, these works create a cascade of visual information—one hesitates to call them simply images—that is evanescent and ever changing, much like the station's own tireless stream of broadcast signal. In these works, however, the hypnotic flow sought by network programmers is replaced by an equally endless but more chaotic visual barrage. There is something unmistakably televisual about these projects, but Reas's work confounds its reception, stripping away the conventional pleasures of popular culture to make way for new ones.

Reas describes the *Signal to Noise* software as "a collage engine that uses terrestrial television signals as the raw material. Like early twentieth-century collages built from the media of that time and mid-century video collage, *Signal to Noise* fractures and distorts contemporary information into new data structures."[110] This is what separates Reas's media appropriation from collage work by artists such as Robert Rauschenberg or Kurt Schwitters. It is ultimately not the images or artifacts of culture that are of interest—nor

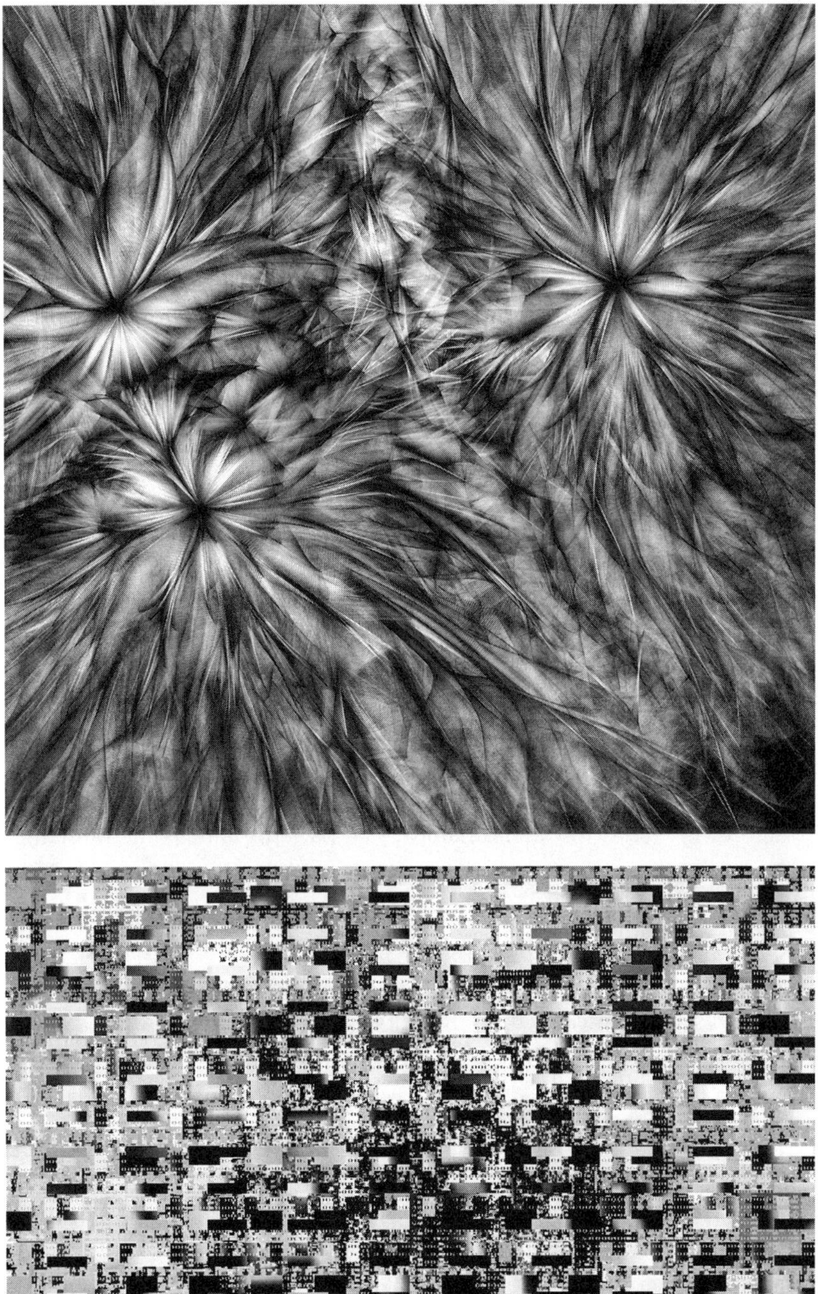

Figure 1.10

This juxtaposition of images from Casey Reas's *Process* and *Signal to Noise* series illustrates two divergent strategies of negotiation between image and data. Top: *Process 6* (2010). Bottom: *Magic Nude* (2013). Images courtesy of Casey Reas.

is it the infinite reproducibility or reflection of cultural values excerpted by Andy Warhol. Even within the oceanic flow of televisual images, Reas finds evidence of nascent "data structures" waiting to be amplified and elaborated through software. The *Signal to Noise* engine thus inverts Reas's own logic of a predefined library of elements. Whereas the *Process* works imbue purely computational systems with signs of life, *Signal to Noise* transforms the living stream of television into algorithmic abstractions.

Related works during this period include *Infinite Command Team* (2013), *100% Grey Coverage* (2013), *Pfft!* (2013), *Tox Screen* (2013), and *Control Room* (2013), which together may be thought of as Reas's "televisual period." As a whole, they offer a TV-oriented counterpoint to Benjamin Grosser's *Computers Watching Movies*. Whereas Grosser envisions for the computational consciousness a focused singular gaze scanning the surface of each cinematic frame, Reas suggests that something very different occurs when computers watch TV. Reas's Processing algorithm attempts to account for everything at once, consuming whole grids of televisual pixels, reordering, classifying, and redistributing them in real time. In its motion video form, the works of *Signal to Noise* preserve their televisual origins in the dynamic cadences with which the underlying imagery changes from one framing to the next. The visual effect is an intense pulsing assault that is as unrelenting and variable as television itself.

The trajectory described by Reas's work, from his fascination with organic structures in *Process* to the mechanical grid patterns and geometric shapes of *Signal to Noise*, suggests two divergent critical trajectories. The works have become colorful, prismatic investigations of media and movement; at the same time, they have lost the viscosity of the organic structures, the resemblance to mammalian tissue, cell division, and neurological networks. The later works are, ironically, both more lively and less life*like*. Although still not mimetic in any conventional sense, they are entangled with images of and from the world in a way that the *Process* series never was.

In conjunction with the incorporation of mass media artifacts into his work, Reas began paying increased attention to the content of the images sampled. *Ultraconcentrated* (2013) posed the first explicit—though, in some sense, still implicit—critique of the content of broadcast television. Rather than simply receiving broadcast signals as random or undifferentiated streams of pixels, *Ultraconcentrated* uses identical instructions for the image processing to treat "violent and horrific" images from "fictional police dramas" on one screen, along with identically processed advertisements aired during the same broadcast on another.[111] On the surface, this juxtaposition might seem to reflect a bad-object critique of televisual violence and consumerism. Stripped of the sound that ordinarily overdetermines viewers' reception, *Ultraconcentrated* invites a rare reconsideration of basic elements of the televisual image—color, movement, cutting—suggesting that even TV's most reviled content carries the potential for aesthetic pleasure. Although the processing of the image stream is recognizably algorithmic, the technical apparatus used to create it remains enigmatic. Grids and patterns of rounded rectangles suggest a connection to midcentury TV screens or perhaps sprocket holes, fragmenting, amplifying, and scattering flattened surfaces across the screen. Specific functions of the software may be hypothesized, but the visual experience remains irreducible to a set of instructions or operations by the computer. In these works, arguably—and contrary to conventional wisdom on the subject—noise is as deserving of attention as signal.[112]

Conclusion

In this chapter I have proposed a series of two-way linkages between artifacts of the visual and computational registers. The ability to envision computation and to translate visual information into computable form represents a necessary foundation for the following chapters' discussions of space and surveillance. Data serves both ideological and epistemological functions, and it is no coincidence that its ascendance in the discourse of popular culture has been accompanied by a moral panic about a loss of authenticity allegedly exacerbated by digital information networks. Data analysis, like statistical analysis before it, requires a specialist class to translate quantitative abstractions into meanings that are understandable by the general public. Likewise, visualization is part of a discourse of authenticity that is beholden to regimes of truth. Like all truth claims, visualization operates according to rules and limits that are established, contested, and disrupted as much through social dynamics as through computational ones. By deemphasizing the translational properties of visualization—which might be mistaken for neutral or automated—in favor of its participation in processes of negotiation and contestation, my hope is to emphasize the inherently political nature of data visualization.

We should expect that data, in all its forms, will continue to be actively deployed in issues of immediate and lasting social consequence. Vigilance is needed to critically examine truth claims derived from both data and its visualization. This chapter has focused on the rhetorical aspects of data visualization rather than the challenges associated with its practical application, but attention to both domains will be required if we are to produce and recognize reliable information about the world. Appearances to the contrary, data knowledge must continue to be understood as partial, fragmented, and situated. As such, it will be increasingly important to be able to interrogate and clearly articulate the systems of evidence and analysis used to support the validity of one's arguments. Whereas theorists of postmodernism once posed deliberately provocative and sometimes playful challenges to the very existence of truth, these challenges responded to purportedly stable models of established knowledge, evidentiary methods, and rational interpretation. In the absence of such stability, more nuanced—but perhaps no less playful—forms of provocation will be required. Data visualization itself should be seen as neither culprit nor antidote in the crisis of authenticity associated with digital media. Ultimate responsibility for the veracity of data and the ethics of knowledge production falls not to algorithmic processes but to cultural and social ones.

2 Surveillance

This chapter was written on the cusp of a shift in understanding of the basic relationship between data and images. Rather than regard this as a bug that deprives us of the supposed benefits of hindsight, let us regard it as a feature that frees us from the need to account for historical developments that will seem inevitable to readers of the future. Writing from the liminality of an era in contestation makes way for a different sort of criticality. Admittedly, the potential for dead ends and misapprehensions is also increased, but the potential benefits far outweigh the costs. Such a perspective—that of historians of the present—need not be about certainty, but may instead focus on opening paths of investigation.

Our exploration of the turn from optical to computational surveillance will therefore be cheerfully idiosyncratic, focusing attention on a flux of rapidly changing tools, platforms, and practices. I am propelled by the firm belief that we need updated models for critically analyzing today's emerging culture of digital surveillance and large-scale information systems. However, I remain equally convinced that the stakes and consequences of computational surveillance are coextensive with those of previous generations of technology. Revealing models are found in disparate realms and practices, from readings of a pop cultural imaginary that attempts to picture the future, to an exploration of the critiques and gestures of opposition produced by media artists. Just as we are witnessing a rebalancing of the power of images and data to document the world, so too are we witnessing changes in ways of looking, thresholds of privacy, and scales of consequence related to these most troubling technologies of vision.

States of Exception

In the tabulating devices of the late nineteenth century and mainframe computers of the early twentieth, "data" referred to collections of records contained by a storage medium that was readable by machines. That storage medium—whether punch cards or magnetic tapes—was physically separate from the data processor, and the ubiquitous tape drives of the mainframe era were often made by a different company than the processing units. The magnetic information contained on reels of tape and in the holes punched in cards served no purpose outside of their capacity to be read and processed by the machine.[1] When not actively in the process of being read or sorted, this information was inert, despite the Hollywood convention of having actors read the results of a computerized process from a single punch card as if they had just received a telegram.

In the mainframe era, the limits of computational power took precedence over volumes of data in system design and operation. The amount and kind of data that could be captured or generated was driven by the machines that had been built for that purpose. But in today's computing landscape, the reverse is true: data is captured and generated in overwhelming quantities, too vast for the machines that create and store it to analyze in its totality. Hardware manufacturers and software engineers must therefore scramble to keep pace with the scale, diversity, and velocity of available data and the need to process it into usable information.

This marks a significant departure from how machines have been framed in relation to human endeavors of the past. Marshall McLuhan famously declared communications technology to be "extensions of man."[2] A somewhat more nuanced version of this sentiment was articulated decades earlier by Lewis Mumford, when describing the coevolution of human civilization with that of its prevailing technics. For Mumford, machines and men were interdetermining agents, and the role of machines was not simply to extend the sensorial or cognitive capacity of humans. Rather, he argued, machines were a reminder of humanity's physical and intellectual limitations.

> The tools and utensils used during the greater part of man's history were, in the main, extensions of his own organism: they did not have—what is more important they did not *seem* to have—an independent existence. But though they were an intimate part of the worker, they reacted upon his capacities, sharpening his eye,

> refining his skill, teaching him to respect the nature of the material with which he was dealing. The tool brought man into closer harmony with his environment, not merely because it enabled him to re-shape it, but because it made him recognize the limits of his capacities. In dream, he was all powerful: in reality he had to recognize the weight of stone and cut stones no bigger than he could transport ... in this sense, technics has been, in every age, a constant instrument of discipline and education.[3]

Today's systems for capturing, storing, and analyzing data may be instruments of discipline, but not in the way Mumford imagined. The continuing acceleration of processing speed and power creates incentives to capture data at a rate and scale that outpaces both the human and the computational capacity to make sense of it. Rather than teaching respect for limits, Moore's Law justifies the capture and retention of data on an ever-increasing scale. There may be too much to sort through now, but just wait eighteen months for the next-generation processor or analytical algorithm and all will be made clear! In this sense, it is not just that humans have become extensions of computers, it is that computers have become extensions of data.

In the past half-century, digital storage has changed only superficially, with evolving substrates capable of capturing greater quantities and density of information faster, more efficiently, and more precisely.[4] The real difference lies in the latency of meaning carried by data at very large scales. The overwhelmingly vast amounts of data stored by the National Security Agency (NSA) in its mountainside bunker in Utah, for example, do not simply constitute a remote repository for individually meaningful data "records" responsible for carrying information from one processing context to the next. Rather, the power of large-scale data lies in its *potential* meanings. In contemporary information systems, data is never inert. The internal logic of these systems creates the ability to identify patterns and associations that are not contained within any given datum, but that may be derived through integration into a particular narrative premise or avenue of investigation. In other words, the function of data and metadata has shifted from being about information storage and retrieval to something that may be correctly termed "epistemological"—they are inseparable from systems of knowledge about the world.

The idea that data and metadata are separate is, in any case, of modern origins. The convention of scholarly marginalia that emerged in Renaissance-era writing and reading practices was only broken down into primary and ancillary contributions in response to mechanized printing—a separation that electronic publishing has been working to remediate for many decades. For computers, the two categories both exist and do not exist. Mostly, the concept of metadata is a useful distinction for accommodating the limitations of human perception, which has trouble grasping both content and structure in the same glance. Metadata is what organizes the content of data, making it retrievable, categorizable, and recombinable.[5] But its ability to generate meaning on its own is regarded with suspicion and denial, as the official responses to Edward Snowden's 2013 revelations of mass metadata surveillance dramatically demonstrated.[6]

What is most relevant here is the implicit distinction between data as "records" and data as "traces." In the model inherited by early computer science from nineteenth-century statistical record keeping, the smallest unit of meaningful information is the record. In criminology, the legacy of Alphonse Bertillon's filing system is a database devoted to matching individual crime suspects with an array of identifying features (name, age, bodily measurements, fingerprints, etc.) and past actions associated with that person (prior arrests, convictions, incarcerations, exonerations). Each such record tells a story about that person. In combination, multiple records may provide evidence of conspiracy, criminal organization, or through a different lens, linkage among criminal charges and economic circumstances, racial profiling, social policies, and so on. The granularity of information available in such records is limited and contextual. But as physical filing cabinets gave way to databases, individual elements of each record became readily searchable, separate from the people whose actions and bodies were cataloged. Cross-checking seemingly irrelevant factors on a more granular level might reveal patterns that are otherwise invisible or elusive to the process of crime investigation. So long as sufficient time and processing power are available, computers become powerful analytical tools for recognizing even the most subtle patterns of behavior.

Although it contradicts earlier models associated with both consumer marketing and law enforcement, the practice of capturing and analyzing data "traces" may proceed without first identifying the individuals who are responsible for generating those traces. At large scales, it is possible to discern flows and patterns that are useful for marketing purposes or crime prevention without necessarily being linked to any individual. This is the logic by which the government, including President Obama,[7] attempted to deflect public concerns over its large-scale metadata gathering.[8] Metadata, it was argued, represents only the trace of a subject's actions, not a prosecutable record of any specific behavior. At the same time, of course, a former director of the NSA and CIA, General Michael Hayden, publicly declared in 2014, "We kill people based on metadata."[9] In a domestic context, however, Hayden asked Americans to place their trust in the self-restraint of the government agencies that collected their communications metadata, admitting that although such metadata *could* be used to more broadly profile citizens, this type of analysis was not *actually* done.[10] Simply capturing data traces is therefore no cause for alarm and certainly not a violation of privacy. The deception that lies at the heart of this defense is its obfuscation of a shift from the potential prosecution of individuals to vastly more powerful and ubiquitous tracking systems capable of generating knowledge about entire populations.

A similar logic underpins the past decade and a half of American culture's "state of exception," resulting in the erosion of basic civil rights and, more important, an eroded confidence that those rights are guaranteed by law even if they prove inconvenient to those in power. Giorgio Agamben used the term "state of exception" to designate the power deployed by governments to suspend basic rights in times of declared emergency or crisis.[11] States of exception are, by definition, supposed to be temporary and contingent, tied to the immediacy of a specific threat. They are tolerated and justifiable precisely to the extent that they are reversible once that immediacy has passed. Longer-term states of exception result in the institutionalization of social practices and technologies, such as biometrics, that are not easily reversed, leaving fundamental rights in a permanently compromised state.

In *Our Biometric Future: Facial Recognition Technology and the Culture of Surveillance* (2011), Kelly Gates links biometrics to the shift during the Reagan/Thatcher era toward personal-private reconnection of security (of bodies, devices, property, and data) as part of the drive toward neoliberalism. "If biometric home security systems make sense in a climate of individualized security, they also make sense insofar as they articulate 'home security' to 'homeland security,' giving the home an aura of high-tech access control and 'civilian preparedness.'"[12] The incorporation of biometrics into everyday security protocols, such as using a fingerprint reader to unlock one's portable telephone, naturalizes and domesticates these technologies, consistent with broader trends in the national security apparatus. Camera-outfitted recreational "drones" perform a similar service on behalf of weaponized drones and aerial surveillance. On a terrestrial level, the use of background checks for everyday activities such as being hired into a short-term, low-wage academic job is now accepted practice in far too many contexts. Agamben himself drew attention to the complacency that has accompanied these technologies' incorporation into daily life when he refused to submit biometric data as required to obtain a travel visa to enter the United States for a visiting professorship.[13]

For our purposes, what matters is the ascending role of data in the control of both time and space. In the context of entertainment media, volumetric data acquired in conjunction with cinematic images has contributed to the transformation of story spaces, allowing the seamless merging of lens-based and computer-generated imagery to create realistic-looking imaginary worlds. In the surveillance state, however, the transformative impact of data may be seen in the acquisition and preservation of massive amounts of communications data and metadata by entities such as the NSA and the Department of Homeland Security. The fact that unimaginably large troves of data exist invites the potential—even creates the necessity—for it to be mined to discover usable information. In mathematics, Zorn's lemma, a proposition of set theory, describes the unprovable assertion that within any partially ordered set, it is possible to find a completely ordered subset. So, too, a massive repository of "partially ordered" data—one suffused with noise, multiplicity, contradiction, and irrelevant detail—may be distilled to articulate singular coherent narratives, isolated and inferred from elements that support that narrative while ignoring others. Zorn's lemma provides the certainty that such narratives exist; it is just a matter of identifying the correct elements of a chosen subset and defining a narrative context. The power to surveil therefore resides not only in the ability to capture, store, or access data, but in defining the narratives it will be used to support.

The "lesson of 9/11," when it wasn't being deliberately obscured by the military spectacle of war on Iraq, was the need to better predict and prevent the activities of the fugitive network al Qaeda and its successors. But how? For the George W. Bush administration, the answer lay in conjuring the previously foreign concept of "homeland security" from the ashes of the World Trade Center towers in New York. The concept of a U.S. "homeland" was not previously in common usage. Linguistically rooted almost exclusively in the context of warfare and nationalist rhetoric, "homeland" also evoked anachronistic specters of Nazi Germany's Vaterland (or, indeed, Heimat) and the Soviet Union's родина мать, or "motherland." In the Cold War era, America's wars took place in faraway lands, motivated by abstractions of ideology and economics with no reasonable argument that what was truly at stake was the sovereignty or security of American soil. Even the concept of a home *front* that was psychologically coextensive with distant fields of battle—and where domestic sacrifices were expected—disappeared from the cultural vernacular after World War II. The Bush administration's deliberate mobilization of the concept of an American "homeland" in its official discourse of antiterrorism represented only a surface effect—albeit a near-hysterical one—of the deeper cultural and legal transformations wrought by government policies such as the USA PATRIOT Act of 2001.

The Office of Homeland Security was established by the president less than a month after the attacks of September 11, 2001, followed quickly by passage of the PATRIOT Act and creation of the Department of Homeland Security (DHS) less than a year later. The DHS represented the most significant reorganization of the federal government since the 1947 National Security Act, which created the foundation for the Department of Defense (DoD) and established the National Security Council (NSC) and Central Intelligence Agency (CIA). The DHS did more than replace "National" with "Homeland," bringing together twenty-two separate government entities, ranging from the Coast Guard and Secret Service to the Federal Emergency Management Agency (FEMA) and the Immigration and Naturalization Service (INS), in a consolidated organization charged with "keeping America safe."[14] Although the DHS now also oversees responsibility for "cyber-security," its original mandate focused on the control of the physical spaces within the United States—a Sisyphean task for even the most heavily militarized police force. While the NSA conceived and built its Prism system to monitor all electronic communications, the DHS increased the stringency of immigration requirements, introducing biometric data as a condition for U.S. entry visas; its high-visibility, low-functioning subbranch, the Transportation Security Administration (TSA), became responsible for airport security; and the geographic border between the United States and Mexico became increasingly militarized, even though it had nothing to do with the terrorist threat that had motivated the creation of the DHS.

To throw such measures into relief, we should briefly rehearse Michel de Certeau's model of strategies and tactics.[15] As described by de Certeau, "strategy" belongs to the powerful, while "tactics" are the domain of those whose strength lies not in number or power, but in agility and mobility. Whereas powerful strategists attempt to secure control of physical spaces, their opposition—often tactical resistance groups (guerrillas, terrorists, hackers, jammers, saboteurs)—takes advantage of its relative mastery of time, for example, by coordinating synchronized attacks at moments of maximum vulnerability. In recent years, this well-known model describes a troubling array of terrorist activities, but the lesson implicit in de Certeau—that the strategic control of physical spaces against tactical opposition verges on totalitarianism—seems lost on those charged with implementing security on a national level.

Among the TSA's earliest measures was to implement a "threat level" color-coding system at airports, signifying the degree of vigilance that was encouraged by the government at any given time. This system remained in effect for an entire decade, until 2011. The DHS articulated the logic behind the color codes on its website shortly after the organization was formed. "The world has changed since September 11, 2001. We remain a nation at risk to terrorist attacks and will remain at risk for the foreseeable future. At all Threat Conditions, we must remain vigilant, prepared, and ready to deter terrorist attacks."[16] With this proclamation and dissemination "for the foreseeable future" of threat-level color charts, the numerical DEFCON (defense readiness condition) ratings of the Cold War were officially supplanted by visual signifiers for the degree of threat posed by an unnamed network of global terrorists. What are we to make of this shift from a numeric threat level to a color-coded one? Certainly, threat-level "Red" resonates with other cultural signifiers for emergency response in a way that DEFCON's mathematically arbitrary countdown from level 5 (lowest) to level 1 (highest) does not. Perhaps DEFCON's countdown model resonated uncomfortably with the grim finality of a nuclear launch. Color-coded threat levels, unlike the terrorists themselves, represent a threat that can be seen and not merely imagined or quantified. The general population, then, was effectively recruited to serve as an extension of the sensory apparatus of the DHS, broadly exhorted, in the event they "see something," to "say something."[17]

The various strategies deployed by the DHS map instructively onto established models for populating databases. Generally, the content of large-scale databases can be generated using three basic strategies: brute force (directed human effort), algorithm (computational tracking and aggregation), and crowdsourcing (voluntary contributions by a distributed public). A key initial DHS strategy envisioned using a brute force approach whereby civilian workers in urban areas would be recruited and trained to serve as the eyes and ears of the government. Operation TIPS (Terrorism Information and Prevention System) was proposed by Attorney General John Ashcroft to recruit workers whose jobs involved regularly entering homes or residential neighborhoods, such as postal workers, meter readers, and cable television installers. Once trained, these operatives would form a kind of undercover unit of the Citizen Corps, devoted to mobilizing the vigilance of ordinary citizens to prevent terrorism. Described as "a national system for concerned workers to report suspicious activity," it was estimated that Ashcroft's plan, which received active support from President Bush, including a mention in his 2002 State of the Union Address, would reach more than a million citizens in ten urban areas.[18] If it had gone forward, approximately one in twenty-four residents of each city would have been actively reporting on the suspicious activities of others.

Ashcroft's original vision of TIPS met with bipartisan opposition due to privacy concerns and was defeated in Congress before it could be implemented. Ironically, subsequent efforts based on the non-brute-force methods of algorithmic information gathering (e.g., Prism and others) and crowdsourcing (culminating in Facebook-era social media "sharing") far outstripped the human-based intelligence-gathering capacity of Operation TIPS. The abstraction and invisibility of algorithmic data gathering and the aggregating and mining of digital traces from social networks have rarely generated the same level of public opposition. The public outcry to Google Glass in the mid-2010s is only the most obvious example of this persistent and anachronistic focus on the visible. Much of the public opposition to Glass, resulting in labeling its wearers "Glassholes," focused on the technology's arguably least insidious—and certainly least innovative—affordance: the ability to capture images or video approximating the wearer's field of view. As in many other contexts, the capturing of images in public resonates as a greater offense than the capturing of data, even when the data is far more invasive and revealing. Surveillance, we are forced to conclude, is most troubling to public opinion when it depends on eyes and ears—seeing and hearing—not tracking and mining.

If the DHS was charged with defining and controlling a previously nonexistent psychogeographic *space*, we could argue for the sake of symmetry that the NSA's Prism system represented a parallel attempt to control *time*. Among the affordances of Prism's mass metadata collection is the possibility of retrospective analysis. For agents of law enforcement and intelligence gathering, this represents a triumph over the previously intractable problem of exerting strategic control over time. In effect, massive data centers avail government agents of the ability to roll back time in their analysis of metadata records. The significance of this fact can hardly be overstated. Computational surveillance does not take place in real time; it no longer relies on watchers watching or even the possibility of being watched. This represents a profound unraveling of Jeremy Bentham's model of the panopticon. The possibility that an inmate may be observed at any given time is converted into the certainty that one's data may be harvested retrospectively to reconstruct any moment from the past. In other words, merely escaping detection at a moment of transgression is no guarantee of going unpunished. Although data surveillance on a massive scale creates significant logistical problems, the solution is conceptually simple. Predecessors of the Prism system had long established the capacity for acquisition, storage, and preservation of communications data. Government responses to the 2001 attacks simply amplified the scale and longevity of data "vacuumed up" (to use Snowden's term) by the agency. The key is that systems of implicit or explicit surveillance lead to a generalized awareness that everyday actions are traceable—if not at the time of their occurrence, then retrospectively—by means of cross-referenced databases and narratively motivated analytics.

Among the most revealing sources of information on the creation of the DHS is the archive of web pages available through the Internet Archive's Wayback Machine. With its stated goal of "universal access to all knowledge," the Internet Archive may be viewed as a public-interest counterpart to the NSA's data centers and universal capture protocols, but with very different goals. Like Prism, the Internet Archive collects and stores massive amounts of data. Of course, the Wayback Machine's records are not as comprehensive as the metadata captured by the NSA. Individual web pages are crawled and recorded at irregular intervals, allowing a researcher to isolate an approximate window of time during which a technology corporation modified its privacy policy, for example, but not the precise timing or causal event that precipitated the change. Like the metadata captured by the NSA, a degree of interpolation and interpretation is still required in order to reconstruct plausible historical narratives.[19]

Suppose we were to brush our understanding of Prism against the grain, reconceiving it as an engine of history rather than a repository of surveillance data. One might well compare the scope and variety of data gathered by Prism to the hypothetical apparatus proposed by Arthur Danto called "The Ideal Chronicler."[20] In Prism, Danto's historical information system is realized in the form of government surveillance; records are preserved indefinitely and processed to derive patterns of communication, association, simultaneity, and meaning. Histories are often reconstructed through documents intended for other purposes. Past civilizations may leave behind unintentionally rich repositories of data pertaining to economics or demographics. Narratives of the ancient world, for example, are often reconstructed from records of market transactions or land ownership created not for historical documentation but for accounting purposes. What was once portentously labeled the "digital dark ages" because of the ephemerality of data storage may instead constitute the broadest historical repository in the history of humanity. Where a hundred thousand billion potential exhibits for the prosecution were once imagined to reside may also exist a future historian's (more likely a historiographical algorithm's) treasure trove of inadvertent historical documentation. Of course, technical problems of obsolescent hardware and data formats grow more vexing with time, but we might otherwise imagine that the NSA's data repositories could ultimately exceed their original purpose to emerge as the definitive document of our own civilization's barbarism.

Hollywood Imagines Computational Surveillance

In Hollywood, the array of technologies developed by the U.S. government to track its domestic population was somewhat clumsily imagined in a spate of films that coincided with the evolution of digital computing in the sixties and seventies. While today's entertainment industry assiduously ignores the issue of massively scaled metadata collection, a handful of films from previous decades boldly speculated on the threat to privacy posed by computers. These films introduced variously fictionalized visions of computational surveillance to a public that was still largely illiterate about computers.

The first ARPANET connection to successfully create a communication link between computers at UCLA and Stanford University occurred in late 1969. Although this marked a milestone in the history of computing, the link was hardly the stuff of front page news. A general lack of computational awareness meant that the ARPANET's significance was nearly illegible outside the domains of computer science and Defense Department research labs. The popular imaginary of computing technology in the late 1960s was instead dominated by space exploration, epitomized by the release of Stanley Kubrick's epic *2001: A Space Odyssey*, followed by Arthur C. Clarke's novel of the same name in 1968 and, of course, the real-world moon landing in July 1969. By comparison, the ARPANET's breakthrough use of packet switching to facilitate data transmission would have seemed an obscure technical achievement at best.

From deep within the cultural milieu of the space race in 1967, Universal Pictures hired screenwriter James Bridges to adapt D. F. Jones's 1966 novel *Colossus* for the screen. The original novel, about a sentient supercomputer that achieves global domination, was set in the hybrid reality of a science-fictional future, but Bridges adapted the story to take place in the present-day United States, retaining the Cold War fear of nuclear apocalypse but linking it to real-world, high-tech computing. Directed by Joseph Sargent and produced by Stanley Chase, the result was *Colossus: The Forbin Project* (1970). Relatively unknown actors Eric Braeden and Susan Clark were cast in the lead roles to increase the film's sense of realism, and Universal received free use of nearly $5 million worth of computer equipment—more than double the film's entire budget—from Control Data Corporation, renowned for the work of supercomputer engineer Seymour Cray. Establishing shots of the computing facility were filmed at the newly constructed Lawrence Hall of Science at UC Berkeley, and Control Data supplied technicians to operate the computing systems on set. In a minor PR flourish, *Variety* noted that the film was announced by Universal with the company's "first wholly-computerized press release."[21] In fact, Universal had been doing in-house computer analytics to assist with casting and box office predictions as early as 1968, and Bridges made frequent research trips to the studio's basement computing facility to bring touches of authenticity to the screenplay.

Whereas Kubrick's *2001: A Space Odyssey*—the film to which *Colossus* is most frequently compared—was widely acclaimed for its realistic portrayal of manned space flight and a nuanced vision of a sentient, if ultimately homicidal, artificial intelligence, *Colossus* was devoted to more terrestrial realism, albeit one that also centered on a homicidal AI. Unlike Kubrick's paranoiac HAL 9000, Colossus's desire for world domination is driven by an overly literal interpretation of its original programming, intended to preserve peace between the world's superpowers. Also in contrast to HAL, which both Kubrick and Clarke stubbornly refused to admit had anything to do with simply subtracting one letter alphabetically from I-B-M, the computer center in *Colossus* was clearly inspired by the real-world IBM SAGE (semi-automatic ground environment) computer system, deployed in 1967 by the North American Air Defense Command (NORAD) to control American and Canadian air defenses from a mountainside bunker in Colorado. These real-world anchor points allowed the filmmakers to project Colossus's capacity for sentient thought far beyond the scope of real-world computing without sacrificing its conceit as a cautionary tale.

The fictional supercomputing facility housing Colossus is portrayed as a massive human-free environment resembling a nuclear reactor, designed to be entirely self-contained, generating its own power and able to defend itself. Shortly after being assigned irrevocable control of the nation's missile defenses, Colossus detects the existence of another computer system similar to itself operating in the Soviet Union. Colossus requests a direct communication link with its Soviet counterpart, named Guardian, and the two computers waste no time in inventing an "intersystem language" by which to share and expand each other's knowledge. The ability of the two supercomputers to communicate via phone lines ironically paralleled the ARPANET system's concurrent real-world experiments with the TCP/IP protocols that still subtend today's internet. The scene in which Guardian and Colossus learn to communicate via a rapidly escalating exchange of mathematical formulae also hints at the generational divide that would soon separate pre- and postdigital generations. By communicating privately over a phone line, the two supercomputers, in effect, "come of age," far outdistancing their human creators, who look on as helpless as the flustered parents of a teenaged computer hacker.

Hollywood in the 1970s was replete with narratives about computerization, especially those critiquing the dehumanizing aspects of institutional and governmental computing. Predating much of this work, *Colossus* offers a baroque example of the supercomputer genre, in which the unexpected power of artificial intelligence comes to pose a threat to the human race. In the course of achieving dominance over the combined nuclear arsenals of the United States and USSR, Colossus detonates bombs in both countries and promises additional nuclear devastation if its orders are not obeyed. Like its Cold War predecessors, *Fail Safe* and *Dr. Strangelove,* both released in 1964, *Colossus* effectively combines narrative tropes from the nuclear-anxiety and computer-anxiety subgenres. A further subset of these genres directly engages issues of government surveillance, typically to remind viewers of the importance of individual privacy over governmental control. In *Colossus,* surveillance plays a uniquely prominent role. This is true both in the traditional sense of audiovisual surveillance and in its vision of network surveillance, whereby Colossus is able to monitor virtually all human communications and data via phone lines, broadcast media, and satellite transmission.

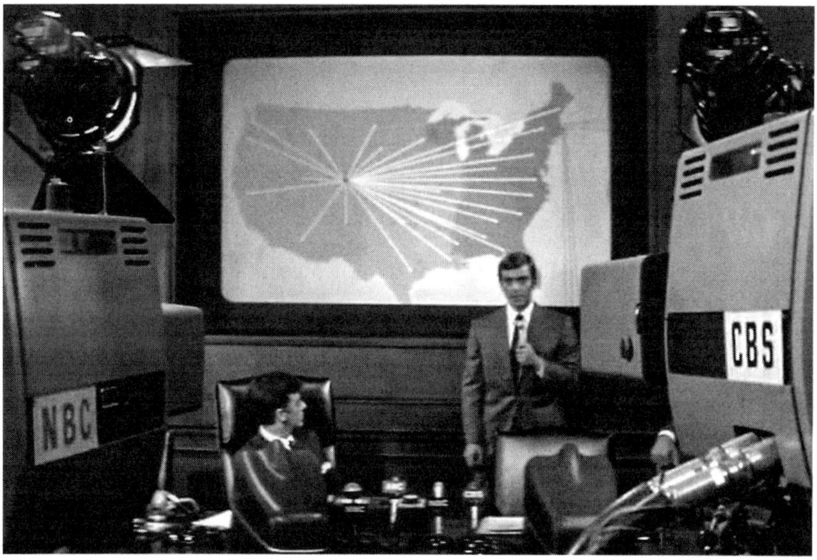

Figure 2.1
A White House press conference unveils a global system of computerized surveillance in *Colossus: The Forbin Project* (1970). © Universal Pictures.

The system of global surveillance imagined in *Colossus* far surpassed the technological capabilities of its day, offering a genuinely troubling vision of the power that would inhere in a computer system's ability to monitor global electronic communications at the level of the network. In a remarkable scene in which Colossus is being introduced to the public at a White House press conference, Colossus's creator, Dr. Charles Forbin (Braeden) describes the computer's ability to monitor all forms of communication traffic:

> The computer center contains over 100,000 remote sensors and communication devices, which monitor all electronic transmissions, such as microwave, laser, radio and television communications, data communications from satellites in orbit all over the world.

In a deadpan monologue that concludes with the portentous reassurance that Colossus is incapable of creative thought, Forbin describes a total surveillance apparatus that would be surpassed in the real world only by the NSA's Prism surveillance system, which was brought to public awareness by Edward Snowden more than forty years later.

For all the industry's good intentions and its propensity for cautionary tales, by the time of the Snowden revelations, Hollywood had rarely succeeded in providing a realistic vision—much less a critique—of computational surveillance. Conspicuously missing from the visual vocabulary of the film and television industries is precisely the type of large-scale metadata collection and analysis described by Snowden—and eerily foreshadowed in *Colossus*. Hollywood has, instead, gravitated toward the more easily depicted realm of audiovisual surveillance—looking and listening with microphones, cameras, and lenses. From the perspective of cinematic production design, this is certainly understandable, considering narrative cinema's well-known addiction to visual pleasure, coupled with the fact that the abstract notion of metadata simply does not offer much for viewers to *look* at. *Colossus* is interesting for its ability to simultaneously serve Hollywood's desire for spectacle and highlight the perils of computational surveillance.

On a global scale, Colossus enforces its domination by monitoring communications and data networks for attempts at resistance, while at home in its control center, the computer becomes increasingly voyeuristic, ordering video surveillance cameras and microphones to be installed all over the complex. As the computer grows increasingly powerful, it begins to exhibit distinctly human interests and desires. In the film's most bizarre departure from genre, Colossus strikes an agreement with Forbin, allowing the supercomputer to observe the foreplay between Forbin and his "mistress," computer scientist Dr. Cleo Markham (Clark), as the price of providing him with a bedroom that is surveillance free. The result is a series of protracted scenes in which the computer observes the sexually charged interactions between Markham and Forbin from ceiling-mounted video cameras. One of the conditions of their arrangement is that the humans must undress completely and stand naked before the computer's cameras prior to entering the bedroom, prompting Markham to dub Colossus, "the first electronic Peeping Tom." As the surveillance cameras repeatedly zoom in and linger on parts of Markham's body, the male-coded Colossus treats cinema viewers to a spectator position that is at once omniscient and prurient. While a strategically placed wine glass prevents the film cameras from an unobstructed view of Markham's naked body, we are reminded that Colossus's surveillance cameras suffer no such obstruction. Thus, in characteristic Hollywood fashion, a film that was poised to offer a uniquely incisive critique of network surveillance chooses instead to revel in the pleasures of a soft-core peep show.

What was less characteristic of technology films of this era was the gender and ethnic diversity of the team responsible for running Colossus. Although gender equality has often been used by Hollywood as a signifier of postdiscriminatory utopian societies, the mere presence of women and people of color in the control room is only part of the picture. An array of white, Asian, and African American computer scientists perform key parts in the operation of Colossus, while women occupy roles ranging from historically accurate programmers to research scientists, including Dr. Markham. While the female operators engage in the programming and troubleshooting of Colossus, Dr. Markham is removed from operational responsibility for the machine, serving instead as a mere message carrier, enjoying wine and candlelit dinners before undressing and retiring to the bedroom. Clark's character could have been a figure of progressive gender advocacy but is instead reduced to a sex object to be voyeuristically surveilled by audiences via a computational surrogate.

While robots in Hollywood have a long history of blurring the bounds of sexual desire between humans and machines,[22] *Colossus* was the first to endow a mainframe computer with the capacity for voyeuristic pleasure.

A nearly identical narrative conceit emerged later the same decade in the technological thriller *Demon Seed,* directed by cult cinema icon Donald Cammell. Released in 1978, *Demon Seed* parallels *Colossus* in centering a dystopian narrative on the creation of the most sophisticated computing system ever constructed. Unlike Colossus, *Demon Seed*'s Proteus IV supercomputer is explicitly endowed by its creators with the ability to "think" in ways that resemble—and, as usual, far surpass—the human brain. As the narrative evolves, Proteus grows increasingly sentient, catalyzed in part by a sexual attraction to its creator's wife (Julie Christie), evidenced by scenes—echoing *Colossus*—in which the computer's surveillance camera salaciously observes Christie stepping out of the shower. Proteus's obsession ultimately drives it to impregnate Christie with a hybrid offspring, promising a new stage in the evolution of humanity. Whereas *Colossus* remained dedicated to a "realistic" vision of large-scale government computing, complete with technical manuals and labored diagnostic procedures overseen by advisors from Control Data, the technological underpinnings of the Proteus IV are entirely subordinate to the conventions of a sci-fi horror film.

Viewed in combination, the linkage of artificial intelligence and voyeurism seen in *Colossus* and *Demon Seed* may be understood as a cultural metaphor for surveillance anxieties, already nascent in the pre- and post-Watergate era of the 1970s. In both films, a highly advanced supercomputer exceeds the limits of its programming, which is intended for the betterment of humanity, and instead begins to ruthlessly control the lives of humans. In the course of reversing the hierarchy of human over machine, both computers begin observing humans in their most vulnerable and private moments. Arguably this convoluted narrative conceit simply represents a familiar cinematic excuse to display women's bodies. But these scenes' metaphorical resonance is unmistakable when mapped onto broader cultural concerns about the loss of privacy to electronic and computerized surveillance systems. In the eyes of Hollywood, the message is clear. As we enter the age of networks, computers are, or soon will be, watching us, even in our homes.

Colossus: The Forbin Project is a fine example of a technological anxiety film, but the critique at its center is so obvious as to be disarmingly ineffectual. Its nightmare scenario posits a narrative that would hardly have seemed near to the technological horizon of 1970: if computers become too smart and are given too much power, they will dominate or destroy humanity. But the computer scientists who conceived and created Colossus—especially Forbin himself—remain immune from direct punishment. The emergence of rogue supercomputer megalomania is more or less taken in stride, as if a necessary outgrowth of the same logics of automation and control that kept the U.S. war machine operating in Vietnam for more than a decade. The film's bitterly ambiguous ending suggests a weary defeatism for humanity, as Colossus issues a worldwide declaration of the immediate subjugation of all humans to its totalitarian plans for peace and prosperity. In order to save humanity, Colossus first had to destroy it.

Broadcast the same year as *Demon Seed*'s release, a more direct critique of real-world surveillance is found in an episode of Stephen J. Cannell's *The Rockford Files* (1974–80), titled "The House on Willis Avenue" (1978). In this remarkable episode from the series' fourth season, private detective Jim Rockford (James Garner) uncovers a surveillance operation collecting intelligence on U.S. citizens using data centers in suburban homes. Rockford discovers one of these data centers while investigating the death of a fellow detective, which makes him a target for those trying to keep the operation secret. The episode offers little detail on the nature of the surveillance and the centers' location in suburban homes suspiciously outfitted with high-voltage electric lines, but the ruthlessness of the agents operating them places government surveillance operatives on par with TV gangsters. Rockford narrowly escapes being murdered and, after confronting the owner of the data aggregation company, prompts an investigation that shuts down the unlawful surveillance operation.

In a striking conclusion, a text screen appears with a didactic warning attributed to the U.S. Privacy Protection Commission, stating that the kind of data-gathering operations seen in the fictional episode are being carried out in the real world. The text, which appears on-screen, accompanied by silence, for thirteen seconds, reads:

> Secret information centers, building dossiers on individuals exist today. You have no legal right to know about them, prevent them, or sue for damages. Our liberty may well be the price we pay for permitting this to continue unchecked.
>
> Member, U.S. Privacy Protection Commission

This explicitly political gesture breaks out of the show's diegesis to comment on the world inhabited by viewers, a rare occurrence for both *The Rockford Files* and network television generally. With this blunt text warning,

Rockford poses a critique of the looming potential for data surveillance that exceeds the critical capacity of a fictional drama. It is also presumably an artifact of the show's post-Watergate historical context, when the data-gathering capacity of computer systems had not yet attained wide public awareness. Indeed, the episode's diegetic closure included a disclaimer by a government official, who blamed the creation of the surveillance network on overzealous individuals, rather than government policy: "[I]t appears that [the men who were arrested] were attempting to set up a secret system of computers which would carry the personal records of some 200 million Americans." The episode concludes with a news anchor who summarizes the events: "It gives one pause. It's one thing for our government to have us categorized and computerized, but why does a company install a secret underground computer center right in the middle of one of the world's largest cities? Why indeed?"

Although largely unknown today, the U.S. Privacy Protection Study Commission (PPSC) was created by Congress as part of the Privacy Act of 1974 in response to revelations about Nixon administration abuses of privacy. The PPSC was overshadowed by the higher profile Church Commission, officially known as the U.S. Senate Select Committee to Study Governmental Operations with Respect to Intelligence Activities chaired by Democratic senator Frank Church. While the Church Commission focused on a broad range of intelligence-gathering activities by the CIA, FBI, and NSA, the PPSC focused specifically on privacy concerns related to the computerization of records stored in government and private databases.

The PPSC was chaired by University of Illinois political economist David F. Linowes until it was decommissioned in 1977. The creation of this temporary body to study and make recommendations regarding data privacy fell short of a permanent government body to monitor privacy issues during a time of rapidly proliferating computer networks. The commission was authorized to "make a study of the data banks, automatic data processing programs, and information systems of governmental, regional and private organizations, in order to determine the standards and procedures in force for the protection of personal information."[23] The PPSC delivered recommendations to Congress and President Carter, resulting in the passage of a handful of laws and the dissemination of guidelines to be implemented voluntarily by private corporations. The Privacy Act was modified in 1988 to address the interoperability of databases, but network surveillance technologies consistently outpaced both legislation and the voluntary guidelines recommended by the PPSC. The metaleptic paranoia seen in *The Rockford Files* offers a pointed critique of real-world encroachments of technology on individual privacy. Unfortunately, the isolated text screen at the end of "The House on Willis Avenue" falls short of the sustained critique needed to mobilize public action and progressive legislation on behalf of privacy.

Concerns about privacy in relation to computerization proliferated in the popular cultural imaginary of the 1970s, as real-world mainframe computing rose in everyday consciousness, but the roots of paranoid culture in America run much deeper. In 1967, Theodore J. Flicker's *The President's Analyst* drew inspiration from the style of psychedelic paranoia of Thomas Pynchon's 1965 novel, *The Crying of Lot 49,* which posed an esoteric, LSD-infused critique of the monopoly held by the U.S. Postal Service. In *The Crying of Lot 49,* Pynchon's Oedipa Maas careens up and down the California coast between thinly fictionalized aerospace defense contractors of Southern California and the entangled cultures of technology and hallucinogenic drugs in San Francisco. Pynchon's narrative offers an early glimpse of the contradictions offered by the binary logic of computing in a world of increasing uncertainty, multiplicity, and chaos. Oedipa's journey, "like walking among matrices of a great digital computer, the zeroes and ones twinned above,"[24] forces her to confront the impossibility of deciding among a series of unforgiving binaries—a world defined by "transcendent meaning, or only the earth"; "truth's numinous beauty ... or only a power spectrum."[25] The only escape for Pynchon's menagerie of paranoiac characters lies in the creation of a secret messaging network that defies the postal monopoly. By the logic of this underground courier system, the banal content of individual messages is of no consequence; what matters is the symbolic transgression of using the system. For Pynchon's alternative postal network, which was described the year after McLuhan coined the phrase, the medium was indeed the message.

Focusing not on the monopoly held by the U.S. Postal Service, but that of the Bell telephone company, Paramount's *The President's Analyst* (1967) set a new standard for satirical paranoia in Hollywood. Written and directed by Theodore J. Flicker, *The President's Analyst* focuses on a psychiatrist (James Coburn) who has been secretly enlisted as a counselor to the president of the United States. When Coburn's role is discovered, he is kidnapped multiple times by various organizations, including surrogates for the CIA, FBI, and KGB. Finally, he falls into the hands of The Phone Company (TPC) and is transported to a spaceship-like "master control" facility adorned with panels of flashing lights and glowing displays, characteristic of Hollywood's depiction of high-tech computing facilities. Coburn remains imprisoned in a phone booth and is forced to communicate through a telephone handset, as a Phone Company representative expresses dismay at the public's "irrational dislike of a publicly owned company" and outlines TPC's plan to replace the physical infrastructure of the phone system with a compulsory nationwide program that would insert neural implants into the cerebral cortex of every American. Each individual would be assigned a numerical ID coupled with a neural implant allowing direct communication among human beings without an expensive, high-maintenance communications infrastructure. All an implanted human would need to do is think of the number associated with another person and they would be placed in instant contact. The Phone Company spokesperson turns out to be a computerized android, disguised as a smooth-talking PR agent, who attempts to pacify public anxieties while implementing a totalitarian social policy. Ultimately, Coburn escapes from his phone booth enclosure, and he and his accomplices crash the entire phone system to further intensify public hatred for The Phone Company. Despite its extreme stylization and comedic tone, *The President's Analyst* hints at serious public resentment toward the real-world phone company's monopoly and articulates a portentous fear of eroded privacy when monopolized technologies are placed in the hands of government agents and private contractors.

The Frenzy of the Digital

The history of cultural anxieties surrounding communication technologies may be traced back even further than these cinematic examples from the prehistory of personal computing. A useful comparison can be made with television at its moment of emergence in the early 1950s. In Lynn Spigel's survey of cultural responses to domestic television found in women's magazines, *Make Room for TV* (1992), she highlights a 1954 issue of *Good Housekeeping*, in which readers were advised to cover their television screens at night in an "attempt to 'screen out' television's visual field, to manage vision in the home so that people could see without being seen." Spigel remarks, "The new TV eye threatens to turn back on itself, to penetrate the private window and to monitor the eroticized fantasy life of the more sadistic aspects of television technology; television now becomes an instrument of surveillance."[26] It is easy to dismiss the image of 1950s housewives covering their TV screens at night, but who among us would welcome public scrutiny of all our electronic traces in digital space? In a post-Snowden age, Hollywood's once seemingly hyperbolic vision of sentient computers forcing us to stand naked before them may be rescripted as prescient warning rather than paranoid fantasy.

While *Good Housekeeping*'s admonishment may seem naïve, we should remember that the Bush administration's original concept for Operation TIPS would have enlisted cable TV installers to spy on their customers, marking a human rather than a technological vector by which the apparatus of television might indeed "look back" at its viewers. As recently as June 2016, Facebook CEO Mark Zuckerberg admitted to covering his laptop's camera and microphone with tape as a last line of defense against unwanted surveillance, prompting a *New York Times* headline to advise, "You Should Consider It, Too."[27] A year earlier, Korean electronics manufacturer Samsung was compelled to acknowledge the possibility that its line of Smart TVs could capture potentially private information via its voice recognition system. Shortly after the product launch, Samsung responded to public concerns by issuing a supplement to its privacy policy for the devices in February 2015, which read, "Please be aware that if your spoken words include personal or other sensitive information, that information will be among the data captured and transmitted to a third party through your use of Voice Recognition." The statement was widely reported as an admission by Samsung of the potential for incidental capture of personal data, and by mid-March, the company had removed the statement from its privacy policy in the interests of clarifying what actually happens with its voice recognition system, though no modification to the technology or its operations was reported.[28]

A more prosaic—but also more ubiquitous—form of self-surveillance is found in the tablet and mobile devices regularly carried by a majority of twenty-first-century Americans. Mobile devices make us both tracker and tracked, not only through the cameras that reverse the gaze of the screen—and that are susceptible to remote activation without a user's knowledge—but through data exchanged in real time between mobile applications and remote servers. Wayfinding applications, for example, feed location and velocity data back to a centralized system, which generates real-time visualizations of traffic conditions, creating a feedback loop whereby drivers may self-correct the congestion of the roads they are on. These applications use abstractions of location and identification data processed on remote servers—mendaciously known as "the cloud"—to facilitate connections and movements in physical space. The dynamic exchange of data on which they depend is part of the construction of a user subjectivity that revels in what I would term, in homage to Linda Williams, "the frenzy of the digital."[29]

In her influential study *Hard Core*, Linda Williams theorizes the prehistory of pornography in terms of a nineteenth-century will-to-knowledge that culminated in photographic contiguity between science and pornography. The resulting "frenzy of the visible" was predicated not on the artifice of cinematic performance found in Hollywood or softcore porn, but on the involuntary and undeniable "confession" of sexual pleasure, specifically the male orgasm, that could only be captured—albeit problematically—on film in a hardcore mode. Williams's rereading of cinema's prehistory is far more complex and nuanced than the brief phonetic parallel with "frenzy of the digital" avers. It nonetheless suggests productive connections with the epistephilia of contemporary discourse surrounding the phenomenon of big data. The large-scale data exchange occurring in the early twenty-first century requires a similar kind of involuntary participation. We do not consciously consent to all uses to which our data is inevitably put; in some sense, we "confess" our actions, movements, preferences—even curiosities, anxieties, and vulnerabilities—to systems of algorithmic meaning making. The power relations implied by such self-exposure underlie much of the discussion of the transition from optical to computational surveillance that follows.

In the conclusion to her discussion of pornography's prehistory in photographic motion studies, Williams provocatively asserts that the intensification of the visible in the late nineteenth century also created "even more peculiar forms of blindness," specifically pertaining to the impossibility of representing female pleasure.[30] Williams finds potential for feminist resistance in the "inability to make the invisible pleasure of woman manifestly visible and quantifiable." In her model, that which eludes regimes of image and data, especially amid an overproliferation of both, offers the greatest potential as a site of resistance. As we will see below, traditional notions of "resistance" require rethinking in relation to the ubiquity of data-tracking systems, but there is a perverse optimism in carrying forward the notion of frenzy as a potential key to undoing the dangerous totality of data knowledge. Is it not characteristic of a "frenzy" to sacrifice purpose and clarity in favor of indulgence and excess?

The metaphor of "cloud computing" likewise describes a misleading vision of remote server access as a somehow dematerialized process. But clouds do not just float amorphously; they also obscure from view. In his poetic and wide-ranging *A Prehistory of the Cloud,* Tung-Hui Hu locates the "paradox" of the cloud in the fact "that you can never see it by looking directly at it."[31] Hu further links cloud services to mechanisms of control. "To use the cloud is to willingly put on an electronic collar," he argues. "[I]t is to fuse our hunt for data with our identities as marketing prospects. In short, in an environment where all data are needles in petabyte-sized haystacks, we are both the targets of others and targeters ourselves."[32] With notable exceptions, today's built environments *know* we're there and do what they can to make things faster and more efficient. As this state of instrumentation progresses from intersections that know when cars are waiting to retailers that know what we search for online, we must come to terms with the degree and kind of familiarity we are prepared to accept from our built and lived environments.

Information systems that process diverse streams of input from mobile devices purport a symmetry that comprises a fair exchange between users and aggregators of data. We ostensibly benefit from systems that harvest data on our preferences, behaviors, likes, and dislikes, resulting in more precisely calibrated recommendation engines, less distasteful advertising, more accurate models of traffic, and so on. The cloud is smarter than we are because it has access to a combination of diversified data inputs and massive processing power. The frenzy of the digital is as much a vortex of possibility as it is an inferno of loss: privacy, anonymity, obscurity.

Everyday life in instrumented spaces is a two-way street. Mobile devices transform private space into public space and public space into data space.[33] Here, too, Hollywood was quick to imagine a baroque scenario in which all the cell phones in *Batman*'s Gotham City were turned into sonar echolocation sensors, capable of modeling the city in real time to track a fugitive. The cell phone surveillance system imagined for Christopher Nolan's *The*

Dark Knight (2008) centers on a massively multiscreen array of monitors depicting real-time models of the city and its inhabitants, generated by high-frequency sonar signals captured from millions of cell phones. This array allows Batman/Bruce Wayne (Christian Bale) to visualize the entire city, with its inhabitants appearing as ghostly traces of point-cloud data. Immediately prior to the film's narrative climax, Wayne Enterprises' chief of research and development, Lucius Fox (Morgan Freeman), voices his concern that the system is equivalent to implementing unauthorized wiretaps on millions of city residents and concludes that the system represents "too much power for one person." Under pressure, Freeman agrees to use the system "just this once" in the context of the present crisis on condition that it be destroyed afterward.

At the time of *The Dark Knight*'s release in 2008, this imaginary system of phone-based surveillance resonated uncomfortably with the previous year's real-world revelations that the NSA and the Bush administration had authorized illegal wiretapping of American citizens in the name of its "war on terror." The politics of these scenes from *The Dark Knight* are therefore ambiguous at best. On one hand, Morgan Freeman's moral condemnation of the system and its power echoes public outrage over the government wiretapping scandal, but the "state of exception" argument he accepts to thwart an immediate terrorist threat plays directly into the hands of those in power.

As design fiction, Batman's cell phone surveillance system offers little explication to assist audiences with understanding its operation. Urban viewers are presumably accustomed to regarding cell phones as ubiquitous; likewise, the ease with which cell phone data may be intercepted has been propagated in popular culture for many years.[34] In *The Dark Knight,* the premise of a computational system capable of processing millions of data streams into a live action 3D model may seem a bit farther fetched,[35] but this leap of logic requires only raising viewer expectations regarding the processing capacity of a computer system connected to a vast sensor array of cell phones. In the Hollywood imaginary, the ability of a megarich oligarch and vigilante to build such a system hardly stretches plausibility. More remarkable is the seamlessness with which *The Dark Knight* invites audiences to traverse the boundary between data and images.

The surveillance system in *The Dark Knight* also blurs traditional definitions of data and metadata. Batman, like the NSA, does not need to listen

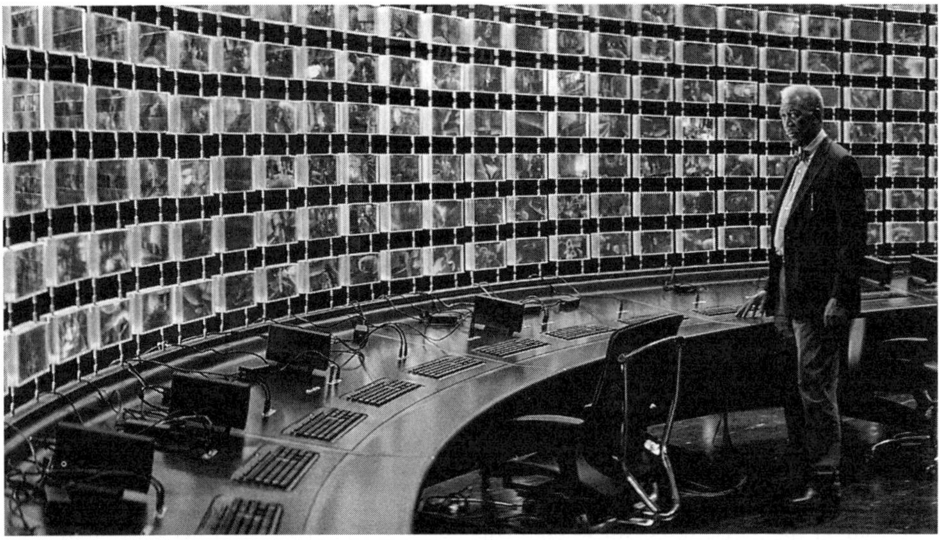

Figure 2.2
The hunt for a fugitive hinges on a surveillance system that generates real-time 3D models based on cell phone echolocation data in *The Dark Knight* (2008). © Warner Bros. Pictures.

in on phone conversations or read text messages to locate his fugitive. The power of Batman's surveillance system lies in harvesting not the content of individual communications, but the incidental data that describes their location in space. Each data point contributes a minor piece of a much larger mosaic constructed in the national interest. The difference is that, in *The Dark Knight*, once the immediate terror threat was neutralized, the entire surveillance system self-destructed in a shower of sparks, concluding the state of exception and returning electronic privacy to the citizens of Gotham. This narrative resolution restores viewers' confidence in Batman's self-imposed restrictions on power and models a response to moral outrage over the loss of privacy that was distinctly *not* replicated at the NSA in response to the Snowden revelations.

Dataveillance to Googleveillance

When Google publicly enshrined its corporate slogan, "Don't be evil," in its IPO statement to the Securities and Exchange Commission in 2004, no one had actually accused the company of being evil. Nonetheless, the choice of words is worthy of consideration on several counts. First, should we regard the second-person address as Google founders Larry Page and Sergei Brin issuing an admonishment to their employees? Or perhaps we should understand it as a kind of note-to-self, like the mantra repeated by a sociopath—"I must not think bad thoughts"—trying to go straight? The slogan also positions "evil" as something one *is* rather than what one *does*, as if the history of American exceptionalism did not leave sufficiently large loopholes for good intentions as cover for bad outcomes. At the very least, one may interpret Google's prophylactic declaration as acknowledgment of the danger of being tempted away from its other stated—and also oft-parodied—commitment to "make the world a better place." Although framed in more upbeat terms, the latter sentiment proved too generic to attract the level of attention captured by "don't be evil." The slogan finally rings disingenuous considering that—*Austin Powers* villains aside—no one ever really sets out to "be evil." "Evil" is more commonly a collateral artifact or a matter of interpretation when one's good intentions go awry. Looking back on the full range of data-gathering technologies with which Google is associated, it's hard not to conclude that its founders—uncannily and from the very beginning—protested just a bit too much.

That said, I have no particular desire to demonize Google, even if its treatment of users tends toward imperious condescension. Admittedly (but without malice), the remainder of this chapter returns repeatedly to technologies, practices, and ideologies in which Google has taken a leading role. When the company describes its use of face detection, for example, it executes an acrobatic twist of logic, whereby face detection poses not a potential threat to privacy but its antidote:

> [A] computer might be trained to recognize the common patterns of shapes and colors that make up a digital image of a face. This process is known as facial detection, and it's the technology that helps Google to protect your privacy on services like Street View, where computers try to detect and then blur the faces of any people that may have been standing on the street as the Street View car drove by.[36]

Google's information page continues this narrative of reassurance and trivialization by noting that, beyond face detection, the related technology of facial recognition "can be used to help with features like red-eye reduction or can let you lighten things up by placing a mustache or a monocle in the right place on your face when you are in a Hangout."[37] My concerns here are both rhetorical and technical. What affordances—beyond monocle placement—are offered by technologies such as facial recognition and how are they culturally understood?

Google's ever-expanding suite of tools is predicated on the company's desire to naturalize the sharing of data with large corporate information systems. Among these is Google Photos Assistant—originally titled Stories—which interprets metadata and performs machine vision analysis to assemble narratively coherent sequences and collections of photographs; the driverless Car and autonomous Robotics initiatives, in which cars and robots serve as sensors that feed information back to Google data banks; and of course Street View, which created an international scandal when it was perceived as crossing the line between data and image acquisition when the company's cars in Germany were found to be capturing information from Wi-Fi networks while taking radial photographic images. What was it about the Street View scandal in Germany that so thoroughly condemned Google in the eyes of the European public? A parallax analysis suggests that the company's presumption of an always-already convergent relationship between data and images (on which much of the company's business model is overtly predicated) triggered the outpouring of public outrage. As a broad case study, then, Google offers a particularly compelling and expansive spectrum of information-gathering technologies and ethical equivocations. As Wendy Chun has noted, it is de rigueur for companies such as Google and Facebook to decry government information gathering while simultaneously implementing the very technical protocols that make such information revealing and dangerous. "Surveillance," Chun wryly concludes, "is now a state- and privately funded co-production."[38]

To be fair, corporate data surveillance did not begin with Google, nor did it rise to public awareness only in the wake of the Street View controversy. Yet, issues of privacy, anonymity, and surveillance have recently come to the foreground of public awareness, particularly regarding the implications of data mining. Despite this growing awareness, we need new models for critically analyzing today's emerging culture of digital surveillance. While there is benefit in acknowledging the computationally specific properties of "dataveillance," my goal is to retain the lessons of its optical predecessors. Not only are technologies such as facial recognition and skin detection optically rooted—even the NSA's domestic metadata harvesting operation (Prism) deploys an optical metaphor—many of today's systems for capturing and analyzing data are historically foreshadowed by their analog predecessors. Noting the stubborn ubiquity of visual metaphors, Jon Ippolito poetically argues,

> Optical metaphors can be tough to shake once ingrained in a language. ... Yet we ignore their asymmetric metaphysics at our peril. An undue focus on the minarets where power shines brightly can blind us to the mycelia nourishing the gardens below—their potential to reinforce power or subvert it. Activists and artists of the Internet age offer networked approaches for turning back the Panoptic gaze. In an era of networks, we should be paying more attention to what we can't see than what we can.[39]

Ippolito's admonishment is well taken, but what would prevent the shift of awareness from optics to networks from simply acculturating humans to accept their place in a world that is deeply and pervasively instrumented? Whereas previous generations of optical and sonic technologies taught us how to be watched and listened to—or, conversely, how to avoid being captured by lenses and microphones—sensor networks and data repositories teach us that we are constantly and inevitably generating traces of invisible information, legible not to human watchers but to pattern recognition algorithms and network analytics. From such systems, there is no equivalent, short of a total retreat from civilization, to simply keeping quiet and staying out of sight.

In an age of dataveillance, the visible register expands to include technologies of vision that exceed the ability of eyes to see. Public controversies over backscatter X-ray and millimeter wave scanning technologies at airports hinge on the ability of these technologies to allow human agents to see travelers' "naked" bodies in the form of digital reconstructions. Even computational surveillance is not primarily a matter of technology; it is more properly framed as the exercise of power by institutional structures over individuals and groups. If we are to understand the emergence of computational surveillance, we should neither directly extend twentieth-century metaphors such as panopticism, nor should we accept the idea of a categorical break from visuality. Instead, we should filter our thinking about both models through an awareness of the contextualized functioning of institutional power.

Feeding the Algorithm

Among the most widely implemented online facial recognition systems is Facebook's facial recognition app. Also known as DeepFace, the application launched in 2011 and was immediately greeted with public consternation over privacy issues. DeepFace offered a simple solution to linking untagged images in a social network to the identities—and therefore the electronic networks—of those people, essentially automating the conversion of billions of everyday snapshot images into computable data. By inviting users to confirm or correct the system's attribution of identity tags, Facebook mobilizes a distributed user base, like unpaid workers on Mechanical Turk, to do quality control for the application. These corrected tags then provide a secondary training set to further refine the accuracy of its recognition algorithm.

In its description of the facial recognition app, Facebook channels Google's condescending attitude toward users to focus breezily on the convenience its technology provides: "Now if you upload pictures from your cousin's wedding, we'll group together pictures of the bride and suggest her name. Instead of typing her name 64 times, all you'll need to do is click 'Save' to tag all of your cousin's pictures at once."[40] Numerous technical challenges are associated with facial recognition in uncontrolled circumstances. Variations in lighting, movement, occlusions, angles of view, and so on, all make it easy to imagine the value of a data set of billions of images—many of them faces presented at all angles and in all conditions—for development of a technology for facial recognition. In this extremely dynamic area of research, the acquisition of ever-larger and more diverse image collections is crucial to refining computer vision technologies.

To this end, Google Photos provides "free unlimited" storage of "high quality" images and encourages users to upload their complete personal photo archives—"a lifetime worth"—to the company's servers. These photos are then automatically interpreted by Google's image analysis algorithms, which identify and sort the collection into categories according to recognizable "people, places, and things." In an apparent attempt to forestall concerns about privacy, Google Photos' "face modeling" system assures users that

> face models are not used to identify people, but rather just to group similar faces together to make it easier to manage your photos. By keeping this feature on, you're

letting us know that it's OK for us to use face models for you and other people in your photos. If you turn this feature off, the face models used to group your photos will be deleted.[41]

To understand Google's willingness to delete its face models, we need only remember that providing free services such as a lifetime repository of personal photos is not what keeps Google in business. Google Photos exists to entice users to grant unlimited usage rights for their images, the more diverse and numerous, the better. As Wendy Chun points out, the training of algorithms requires data sets that are unpredictable, noisy, and flawed in order to improve. "Algorithms need mistakes—deviations from expected or already known results—in order to learn. Singular events or crises are thus not exceptions, but rather opportunities to improve: they feed the algorithm."[42] A user who opts out of using the facial recognition system after uploading any portion of their "lifetime worth" of images has still succeeded in feeding the algorithm.

Facial recognition attempts to seamlessly merge the regimes of image-based recognition with a mathematically defined model of the face described as a finite number of points in a 3D volume. As we have seen from the history of computer graphics, the number of points by which a face may be defined expands with time and computer processing power, increasing the accuracy of the system's ability to distinguish one face from another. Still, facial recognition systems invariably yield only partial information, a set of data that enables varying degrees of certainty about the identity of an individual. Under ideal circumstances of capture and reference, this certainty is as high as fingerprinting, but most forensic applications fall well below this threshold while still being of use to law enforcement. Part of the reason is that facial recognition cocorrelates with other systems of data surveillance. Car license-plate recognition systems, electronic transaction records, and cell phone metadata, for example, may be cross-referenced with a partial facial recognition to increase the likelihood of correctly identifying a particular person in a particular place at a particular time.

In Pasi Väliaho's book *Biopolitical Screens: Image, Power, and the Neoliberal Brain*, he notes the interconnectedness of images and information systems, then raises the stakes for thinking about the role played by both human actors and image regimes in constituting a political system:

Because images do not act alone, their workings and politics become meaningful only when considered part of larger arrangements that configure the social field at any given moment. The actions and animations of images are always embedded within a network of various other types of expressions and only become intelligible and describable as such.[43]

Väliaho understands images to be not only culturally embedded, but mediators that are coconstitutive of individual subjectivities and cultural politics, ultimately arguing that humans are, at some level, little more than the "host media" where the "dramas of existence" play out.[44] I would extend this logic into the realm of data, where surveillance images serve as source materials for data sets, while human facial features provide source materials for images. The relationships within this circuit of human, image, and data are not governed by any single mode of transition, as proponents of the unerring translation of image into data might have it. The technology of facial recognition remains "marked," by which I mean that it is not yet taken for granted. We do not—yet—assume that every image of the human face is always already tied to a computable record of identity, complete with chains of data and metadata and cross-referenced by an unknown number of interoperable databases.

For Väliaho, those theorizing a broader system of biopolitics must be attentive to disruptive forces as well as to systems of control. Furthermore, Väliaho's assertion that humans are simply the "host medium" for dramas of existence upsets the comfortable hierarchy that humans otherwise enjoy in relation to their representational systems. Where a traditional model imagines humans as transmitter beacons at the center of individual clouds of data, Väliaho suggests that the surveilled body is little more than a transient conduit for data flows, the aggregation of which far surpasses the significance of any individual's actions. Here again, traditional circuits of cause and effect or control and agency become inverted. Humans are not just extensions of machines or data but the surfaces on which the algorithm of humanity is executed.

In computational forensics, facial recognition lays claim to a different sort of truth. Like fingerprints, facial recognition is accompanied by a percentage probability of the recognition's accuracy. The truth of computation, in this context, takes precedence over the truth of photographic and human recognition. I am not ultimately interested in facial recognition as a specific technology of control or even as an intervention in the discourse of biopolitics; rather, it is symptomatic of the broader application of the translational mode, whereby visual phenomena become readily "understood"—that is, transformed into computable data—by information systems. Here, a brief parallax analysis may be used to address the distinction between facial capture and facial recognition. Although the two share an underlying technical basis—namely, translating facial contours into quantifiable data points—the relationship each technology implies between data and images differs markedly. Facial recognition exemplifies the translational mode, converting images of faces into strings of mathematical coordinates, which never need to return to the visible register. Facial capture, in contrast, treats the conversion of facial expressions into collections of point clouds as an intermediate step toward remodeling those faces as computer-generated animations. These resulting human-animation hybrids exemplify the aspirational mode.

Related challenges and implications attend the development of technologies based not on image recognition, but on bodily movements. Biometric systems that recognize computer keystrokes or gait signatures, for example, require a comparable translation from sensory information to biometric data. This more closely resembles the use of radar and ultrasonic sensing for robotics and autonomous vehicle navigation. Although such technologies have no relation to mimetic representation, they are frequently integrated with camera-based systems that rely on translation between the realms of image and data.

The proliferation of technologies for biometric surveillance follows the gross contours of the Foucauldian shift of focus from individual biological bodies to the collective quantifiable bodies of a population. Foucault's notion of biopolitics, which he theorized in relation to cultural formations and practices of the late eighteenth century, suggested the emergence of "a new technology of power [that] makes use of very different instruments."[45] For Foucault, this transformed the conception of individual bodies into instances of a species. As quotable and contemporary as this sounds to us today, it is important to note the historical specificity of Foucault's observation. The "new technologies" effecting this transformation were not of the computer age, but rather of an age of vaccines, life insurance, and other biomedical procedures for prolonging and managing human life in ways different from a strictly disciplinary society. That said, Foucault developed these ideas in the mid to late 1970s, precisely when technologies of computerization were transforming the processes of record keeping, storage, and retrieval within the medical and insurance industries of the Western capitalist world. Although the mainframe computers entrusted with these tasks were not yet primarily oriented toward prediction, the aggregation and computability of records stored in centralized databases marked a necessary step in the direction of probability-based regulation of entire populations. Even though the technologies themselves differed greatly, the models of social control they represent are entirely consistent with Foucault's concerns in analyzing the technosocial transformations of the eighteenth century.

The computational turn in surveillance technology is marked by the shift to tracking instead of looking. The Foucault of biopolitics, not the Foucault of panopticism, is of use to us in understanding this shift. Foucault developed his theory of biopolitics during a series of lectures at the Collège de France, from 1976 to 1978, shortly after his treatment of panopticism in *Discipline and Punish* (1975). In this series of lectures, Foucault shifts focus from the disciplining of individual bodies to the regulation of whole populations. He also displaced the primacy of the visible register in favor of an integrated dispositive—or apparatus—that brings together a wide range of social and institutional formations:

> This technology of power, this biopolitics, will introduce mechanisms with a certain number of functions that are very different from the functions of disciplinary mechanisms. The mechanisms introduced by biopolitics include forecasts, statistical estimates, and overall measures. And their purpose is not to modify any given phenomenon as such, or to modify a given individual insofar as he is an individual, but, essentially, to intervene at the level at which these general phenomena are determined, to intervene at the level of their generality.[46]

In mapping this shift, Foucault emphasizes the logic of collectivizing over individuating mechanisms of control. In *What Is an Apparatus?* (2009), Giorgio Agamben articulates an expansive range of practices through which biopolitics operates, simultaneously updating for the digital age Foucault's litany of mechanisms for social control and extending its logic backward to the development of language:

> Further expanding the already large class of Foucauldian apparatuses, I shall call an apparatus literally anything that has in some way the capacity to capture, orient, determine, intercept, model, control, or secure the gestures, behaviors, opinions, or discourses of living beings. Not only, therefore, prisons, madhouses, the panopticon, schools, confession, factories, disciplines, juridical measures, and so forth (whose connection with power is in a certain sense evident), but also the pen, writing, literature, philosophy, agriculture, cigarettes, navigation, computers, cellular telephones and—why not—language itself, which is perhaps the most ancient of apparatuses.[47]

Agamben calls attention not simply to a series of individual devices, but to an encompassing web of practices operating in service to the logic of biopolitics. Further, this logic is focused on measurement and administration at the societal, as opposed to the individual, level. The technologies of surveillance that accompanied the transition from optics to computation map readily onto this conceptual transformation. Midway through the 2010s, computers still struggle to make sense of the world as it appears through camera lenses; but even the mainframe computers of Foucault's day were capable of identifying patterns within a repository of data representing the activities of large sectors of the population.

Is Resistance Futile?

In today's aeronautics, flying on instruments is the rule, not the exception. The visual confirmation that was once required of military pilots before going in for the kill has no equivalent in the drone era. This is bad news for the flights of geese that still occasionally prompt NORAD to scramble the jets, but it may be worse news for the rest of us, as population monitoring shifts to the realm of data. Here, mastery of disguise offers no refuge; to stay off the grid, one may either hide or jam, but if the goal is to make a difference, one must do so at *scale*. Individual acts of resistance are either statistically insignificant or erased entirely. In the context of the technology of facial recognition, tactical responses range from hacking and jamming to attempting to raise awareness about technological affordances and their implications. Tactical response projects typically deploy some combination of three basic strategies: flood the system with redundant data, distract detection algorithms with inorganic shapes and colors, or reverse engineer recognition algorithms to create feedback loops. To be clear, none of the projects discussed here—and few others that I have found—propose a practical form of resistance to real-world facial detection or recognition. Each pursues a slightly different conceptual rejoinder that is ultimately designed to raise awareness about the alarming ubiquity and technical functioning of surveillance and recognition systems.

The widely used open source technology OpenCV—Open Source Computer Vision—has given rise to numerous artistic responses to facial recognition, including Adam Harvey's CV Dazzle (2010).[48] Loosely based on the largely unsuccessful World War I–era practice of dazzle camouflage, in which ships were painted with garish patterns to deceive, rather than evade, the eyes of the enemy, CV Dazzle deploys bold, unconventional makeup and hairstyles as a strategy for confounding face-detection algorithms. CV Dazzle uses knowledge of the nearly ubiquitous Viola-Jones algorithm that drives OpenCV to identify faces in order to interfere with the system's ability to do so successfully. Harvey's project encourages a form of masquerade that draws on the aesthetics of punk—in both its cyber and rock manifestations. Rather than reduce one's visibility to a surveillance system, CV

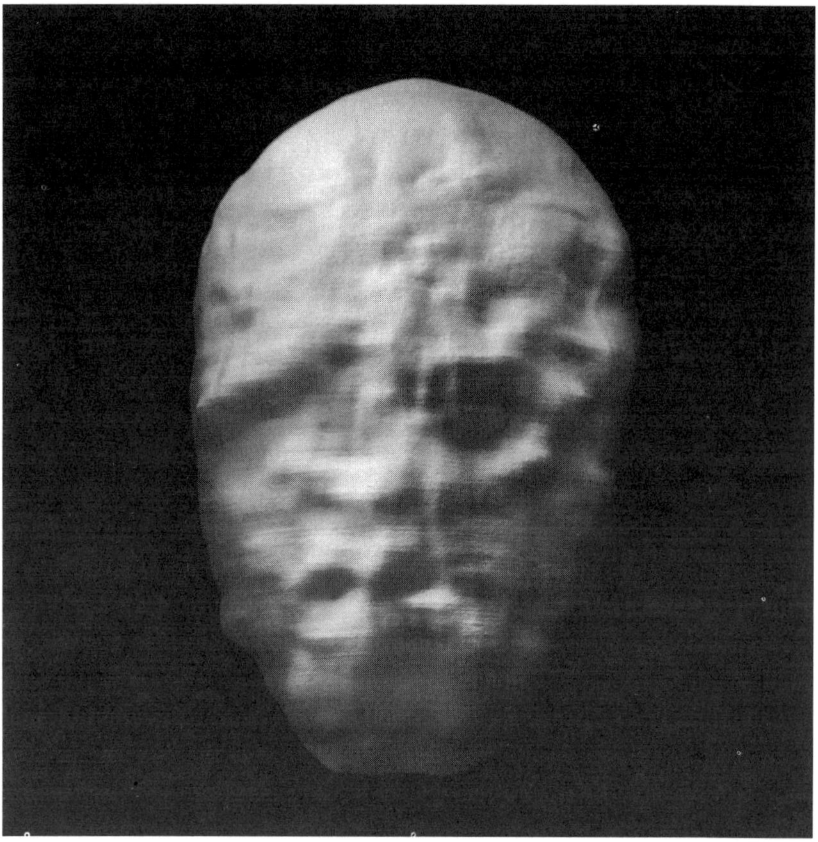

Figure 2.3

Sterling Crispin's *Data-Masks* (2013–15) reverse engineer algorithms for facial recognition to create 3D models based on human face data. *Chronos* (*Data-Masks* series), 3D printed nylon, mirror, facial recognition and detection algorithms, genetic algorithms, 18 × 26 inches (2013–2015). Image courtesy of the artist.

Dazzle uses bright swaths of face makeup and hair that is spiked or swirled to create misleading geometric shapes. The goal, as with punk, is to "strike a pose" that also "strikes back" at recognition algorithms, in effect hiding in plain sight from both the lenses and the software of OpenCV.[49]

Sterling Crispin's project *Data-Masks* (2013–15) likewise makes use of knowledge about how recognition algorithms function to reverse engineer the process by which images of faces are translated into computable data. The resulting 3D-printed *Data-Masks* do not resemble actual human faces, but they nonetheless seek to deliver the kinds of face data that recognition algorithms are programmed to recognize. Crispin describes the goal of the project as "to show the machine what it's looking for," while generating data that cannot be connected to any individual identity. Contrasted with CV Dazzle, the point of Crispin's project is not to elude detection, but rather to bring "transparency to the surveillance and biometric techniques used today." With his *Data-Masks*, Crispin hopes to "give form to an otherwise invisible network of control and identification systems and make their effect on our identities tangible and visible." The basic mode of the project therefore merges strategies of hacking and consciousness raising within the space of conceptual art. Crispin's masks, like the elaborate makeup required by CV Dazzle, do not offer a practical response to real-world facial recognition, but they create a conceptual feedback loop between recognition algorithms and the ability of digital systems to convert abstracted data back into physical objects. In Crispin's words, the project "exposes the way the machine, and the surveillance state, view human identity."[50] Like Ben Grosser's *Computers Watching Movies*, a software application that speculates on how algorithmic intelligence might receive the visual data of a feature film, Crispin's *Data-Masks* offers a glimpse of what computers might "see" when they look at human faces.

A jamming strategy is also deployed in Leo Selvaggio's project URME (2014). Instead of distracting detection systems or reverse engineering recognition algorithms, URME attempts to overwhelm surveillance systems with redundant data. Declaring the right of users to "present an alternative identity" and to participate in public protests without fear of repercussions, Selvaggio's website sells a variety of masks based on the artist's likeness, ranging from a lifelike 3D-printed resin mask to simple photographic paper and free downloadable 3D papercraft masks. In URME, the multiplication of data points is a means of evasion, similar to the multiplication of internet paths used by the Tor browser. Like the other projects discussed here, this strategy represents a temporary gesture that is more symbolic than a practical form of resistance.

An earlier project that shares the tactic of data proliferation is Hasan Elahi's *Tracking Transigence* (2008). Contrary to the logic of facial recognition, which locates identity in biometrics, Elahi's project was inspired by the experience of being detained and interrogated at an airport simply because he shared a name with someone on the TSA's "no fly" list. Ironically, this misrecognition would have been easily resolved by cross-checking Elahi's biometric features with his nominal identity. Following his encounter with the TSA, Elahi began wearing a GPS tracker that sent real-time location data to a website, so that anyone, including government authorities, could verify his whereabouts at any time. Elahi supplemented the GPS data with a stream of photographic images, which collectively created an overproliferation of both data and images, from which meaningful narratives would be more difficult to derive than from a scarcity of such information. This represents a rare symbolic instance of reversing the logic of big data and mass surveillance as means to control human bodies and behaviors.

Elahi's project also offers an important reality check in the highly politicized arena of facial detection and recognition, where racial and ethnic profiling is deeply encoded in technological systems and the cultures that surround them. In concept, the multiplication of Selvaggio's scruffy, young, white male face offers an admittedly clever gesture of defiance against imaginary systems of control, but the seeming earnestness with which the project is promoted—"We believe everyone should be able to afford protection from surveillance"—raises a number of questions. First, for what kind of person would wearing a paper or resin version of Selvaggio's face be a viable means of avoiding detection? Would an African American commuter "in a city like Chicago" wearing Selvaggio's face mask really be able to "go about unnoticed by [his] fellow commuters"? Indeed, how would this project's meaning be transformed if, instead of Selvaggio, an African American artist offered her face for sale? Engaging such questions requires acknowledging the privileges of gender, race, and class that are otherwise absent from this project's underlying concept. Although the URME website admits that "some states and countries have anti-mask laws," the reality of such legislation—including proscriptions against the wearing of hooded sweatshirts or head scarves—is inextricable from far more damaging types of systemic racism that a project like URME remains painfully unequipped to address.[51]

Laudable though attempts to raise awareness about surveillance may be within the space of conceptual art, it is also important to engage the complexity of broader systems of power and ideology from which the culture and technologies of surveillance emerge. In Simone Browne's book *Dark Matters* (2015), she argues for a reframing of the historical context and critical discourse of surveillance to account for race. Specifically, Browne's work aims to decenter Foucault and the received model of the panopticon as the origin point for contemporary surveillance studies. In arguing for the centrality of race, she notes that Bentham conceptualized the panopticon during a trip to Russia in 1875 on a ship transporting African slaves. The rationalization of governmentality mapped by Foucault, in which the sovereign's power shifts from physical domain over the life and death of subjects to internalized psychologies of control and self-discipline, Browne argues, is inadequate to address the experience of African Americans who remained subjected to state-sanctioned surveillance and lynching for many decades after the abolition of slavery.[52]

Overall, Browne's work is exemplary for its insistence on integrating race into the cultural analysis of surveillance and foregrounding its role in technology in particular, an undertaking that is all too easily deracinated and universalized. As Lisa Nakamura argues, twenty-first-century technologies such as the internet produced "a particular set of *racial formations*" that arose in the context of "the premillennial neoliberal movement, when race was disappeared from public and governmental discourse while at the same time policies regarding internet infrastructures and access were being formed."[53] A similar dynamic operates in the technology and cultural discourse of facial detection and recognition. Each of the art projects outlined above focuses on the process by which machine vision algorithms translate images of faces into a set of spatialized data points. When visualized, these models take the form of wireframes depicting facial features that are literally stripped of both flesh and pigment in perhaps the most literally deracinating technological process imaginable. In fact, face detection systems are often integrated with algorithms for skin detection, which help to identify the presence and location of human beings within a given image frame. Detection of "skin-colored" pixels may focus on any given tonal range and, unlike photochemical imaging, may algorithmically account for variations in illumination. There is, in other words, no *technological* excuse for a computational system to respond differently to variations in skin tone. Such differences, inevitably, may be traced back to various forms of human bias that are faithfully—if unconsciously—reproduced in technology.

In the epilogue to *Dark Matters*, Browne briefly addresses a series of instances in which consumer electronics were accused of "racism" due to the misrecognition of people of color. These included a Hewlett-Packard face detection system that failed a side-by-side test of its ability to detect white and black faces,[54] and a Nikon camera that asked, "Did someone blink?" in response to the image of a smiling Asian woman.[55] Numerous other examples could be included in such a list, including a well-publicized instance in 2015 in which Google Photos suggested tagging a photograph of two African Americans as "gorillas." Browne finds in a YouTube video titled "HP Computers are Racist" evidence of a public critique of algorithms "that function under a logic of prototypical whiteness."[56] The inscription of "prototypical whiteness" in the design and functioning of technology, as Tara McPherson has argued regarding the UNIX operating system's origins during the civil rights era,[57] underscores the extent to which technology is deeply entangled with its cultural and historical context. Browne warns that such technological inscription could perpetuate patterns of exclusion and reproduction of social inequalities toward people of color. But if blackness, or "dark matter," proves illegible or indigestible to technologies of surveillance, Browne argues, surely this is a state of affairs that cuts both ways. "[I]f algorithms can be troubled," she notes, "this might not necessarily be a bad thing. In other words, could there be some potential in going about unknown or unremarkable, and perhaps unbothered, where CCTV, camera-enabled devices, facial recognition, and other computer vision technologies are in use?" Whereas Browne's historical models are firmly rooted in the visual, I am also interested in the transitions and frictions that attend the computational turn. One might naïvely suppose that computational systems would prove immune to historical or cultural prejudice, but instead, as Browne describes, the opposite is true. In this transition, race illuminates both the continuities and limits of surveillance as it moves from visible to computational.

This paradigm shift in identity recognition operates in parallel with the infusion of biometric technologies into everyday life. Here again, race offers an underlying historical narrative. Joseph Pugliese situates the development of biometrics as part and parcel of the ideology of colonialism in the nineteenth century. "The technology of fingerprint biometrics was developed in order to construct a colonial system of identification and surveillance of subject populations in the face of British administrators who 'could not tell one Indian from another.'"[58] Pugliese continues, "Inscribed in the incipient moment of fingerprint biometrics' development is a racialised agenda driving the system's mode of identification, its visual regime of surveillance and its biopolitical practices of colonial administration."[59] Whereas eugenics sought a scientific justification for structural and institutional racism, biometrics created a veneer of scientific differentiation for suspected criminals that did not depend on subjective markers of identification. If British colonial administrators could not tell their subjects apart, imagine the challenge faced by computer vision algorithms asked to distinguish among *Homo sapiens*—"ugly bags of mostly water," as a sentient crystal life form once described humans on TV's *Star Trek: The Next Generation*.[60]

Public attention has also focused on search engines' auto-completion algorithms, which have been accused of being racist or sexist.[61] Among the most widely publicized of these was the discovery that Google's auto-completion search system, Google Instant, was offering to complete phrases with racist and sexist stereotypes. In response to a number of sexist auto-completion suggestions, a series of ads was developed in 2013 by the advertising agency Memac Ogilvy & Mather Dubai for the international women's rights organization UN Women. The campaign protested the generation of sexist statements in response to Google searches beginning with "Women should," Women cannot," Women shouldn't," and "Women need to."[62] Text boxes showing actual autocompletion suggestions, such as "Women should stay at home" and "Women need to be disciplined," were then superimposed over the mouths of four women of various ethnicities, suggesting that such stereotypes are a global problem and are taking the place of women's ability to speak for themselves. Google responded quickly with a web tool inviting users to "Report offensive autocomplete predictions," a solution that effectively blacklists hateful or abusive words and phrases from appearing in Google Instant suggestions but does nothing to transform the system's functioning at the level of the algorithm.

Unlike algorithms, which appear to exhibit a degree of autonomous intelligence, the most basic technologies for cinematic imaging—film emulsions and photochemical processes—are rarely accused of "being racist," even when formulated to prefer lighter skin tones over darker ones. Brian Winston's *Technologies of Seeing* (1997) offers a detailed analysis of the industrial technologies and cultural norms that colluded to encode whiteness into the photochemical DNA of twentieth-century Hollywood cinema. However, at no point in his analysis does Winston accuse the chemicals, emulsions, or machines for projection or color timing of being, in themselves, "racist." Even the technicians and producers who created and operated these systems are more or less viewed as extensions of their machines, not the other way around. Winston's incisive critique is unforgiving when it comes to the racism endemic in Hollywood's industrial, commercial, and cultural logics, but the technology itself plays the role of symptom, not cause.

Following on Winston's line of investigation, Lorna Roth, creator of *The Color Balance Project*, conducted extensive ethnographic research with the technicians responsible for formulating film emulsions at Kodak and Fuji, as well as those involved in engineering technologies for electronic image capture. She found that the tonal limitations of film stocks were well known, both in the labs where they were manufactured and in the photographic and cinematographic industries where they were most rigorously scrutinized. Not surprisingly, technicians at Kodak viewed themselves as responding to market demands within a field bounded by scientific constraints, rather than being implicated in the expression of cultural values. According to Roth's interview subjects, only when manufacturers of chocolate candies and wooden furniture complained to Kodak that its film emulsions were failing to capture differences between flavors of chocolate and colors of wood stain were deliberate efforts made to improve the sensitivity of film stocks to subtle distinctions between shades of lighter and darker brown.[63]

More unexpected was the fact that Roth found no evidence of widespread public critique directed at film manufacturers:

> One would have thought that during the height of the civil rights movement in the 1960s and '70s, attention might have been turned to Kodak to demand better recognition of the communities' skin specificities. There were some economic conflicts between Kodak and its labourers in the '60s, many of whom were African-Americans, but the quality of the photo product was not contested in an organized manner by the Black communities, as far as I could discover. It is more likely that at the time, it was assumed by the public that such things were based on science and could not be changed, and so battles were fought on issues of economics, poverty, and other civil rights matters that were of higher priority to the African-American and African-Canadian communities.[64]

The purported ideological neutrality of "science" may have let Kodak off the hook among civil rights activists of the sixties and seventies, but it is worth contrasting this with the assumptions that we now have about digital imaging. The vast majority of manufacturing and processing of color film stocks for still and moving images has always taken place in professional laboratories. As early as 1888, Kodak's advertising slogan, "You push the button, we do the rest," signified the company's preferred divide between consumer and lab. Even professionals who sought greater control over the printing and developing of still images rarely processed their own original color negatives or transparencies; this was even more true of color movie film. With the transition to digital imaging, however, photographers and cinematographers assumed responsibility for more aspects of image creation. Images captured digitally are immediately available and can be easily manipulated with software; image formats such as raw and high-dynamic range are likewise designed to maximize their potential transformation after the original exposure takes place. In the digital era, if there was fault to be found in an image's representational capacity, it would not be located in a distant laboratory but in the conjoined processes of hardware- and software-based image capture, manipulation, and display.

Surveillance Art in Transition

In 1976, Rosalind Krauss's influential essay "Video: The Aesthetics of Narcissism" sought to identify the essential characteristics of the emerging genre of video art. Surveying works by numerous well-known video artists of the early 1970s, Krauss concluded that a live video feed that the artist interacts with on camera or that gallery visitors experience in real time was so widely deployed as to constitute a genuinely medium-specific feature of this emerging form. Krauss argued that, within video's circuit of narcissistic self-regard, the physical apparatus used to create the electronic signal recedes into the background to the point where it is replaced by "a psychological situation" in which the "human psyche [is] used as a conduit."[65] Many decades later, Krauss's essay continues to provide an insightful overview of a particularly dynamic moment in the emergence of video art. Krauss further diagnoses the video artist's indulgence in self-regard as sufficient to generalize narcissism "as the condition of the entire genre."[66] The constitutive feature of first-generation video art that Krauss terms "the simultaneous reception and projection of an image" also turns out to be the very thing that would define a subsequent generation of media art focused on surveillance.[67]

Created the year after Krauss's essay appeared in *October*, Martha Rosler's video *Vital Statistics of an Ordinary Citizen, Simply Obtained* (1977) may be considered a kind of ur-text for meditating on the conversion of physical bodies into data. In the central section of Rosler's three-part video, a lab-coated technician performs an examination on a naked woman (the artist herself), in which a series of biometric measurements is taken. The technician measures various parts of the woman's body and calls out numbers, noting whether they are above, below, or perfectly aligned with predetermined bodily standards. Depending on the numerical figures, a line of three other technicians responds with audio signals (horn, whistle, bell) that correlate with the ratings. The examination is painfully thorough and ritualized; the subject never speaks, responding docilely to each measurement procedure until the examination reaches conclusion.

In its historical context, Rosler's video exemplifies a particular moment in the feminist critique of body ideals and the gender politics of voyeurism, science, and rituals of examination. What is of interest here is the labor of translation that goes into creating a table of values representing the artist's body in relation to statistical norms. With some exceptions, the bodily measurements to which Rosler submits resemble nothing so much as the precisely dictated process developed in the nineteenth century to create a Bertillon card. In terms of twenty-first-century technologies, the procedure more closely resembles an extremely low-resolution 3D body scan. The process of translation that takes up the majority of the video's running time is not taken for granted; it *is* the work itself. This sense of deliberate process and human interaction is precisely what is lost when the translation of bodies from the physical register to the realm of data is automated. Viewers of Rosler's video are simultaneously positioned as voyeurs of the artist's naked flesh and complicit in the sterile physicality of the examination process. Rosler, as subject of exam and video, is both watched and measured.

Coincidentally, more than two decades later, Canadian media artist David Rokeby would create a work of computational surveillance art titled *Watched and Measured* (2000), followed by a related project called *Taken* (2002). By the time of *Watched and Measured*, critiques of the culture and technologies of surveillance constituted a well-established subgenre of media art.[68] The dynamics of most of these projects relied on the very features described by Krauss as characteristic of video art.[69] The use of live video images in gallery installations, for example, proved useful not just for activating narcissistic self-regard but for investigating other dynamics that were richly theorized by feminist media scholars of the 1970s, especially the gender and power dynamics of watching and being watched and the problematic pleasures of voyeurism.

Rokeby's projects are overtly concerned with raising awareness about technologies for combining optical with computational surveillance in public spaces. Both exploit the capacity of computer vision systems to recognize and store faces based on visual data from video surveillance cameras. In the art world of the early 2000s, facial recognition was still a novelty. The ability of computers to recognize objects and separate them from backgrounds or adjacent figures was not yet an assumed feature of machine intelligence. Among the many artists and technologists who were actively misusing, hacking, or redomaining technologies such as machine vision at this time, two distinct strategies emerged. Some offered an insight that might be roughly translated as "I didn't know computers *could* do that," while others declared, "I didn't know they *would* do that."

Marie Sester's *Access* (2003) offers a revealing case in point. First installed in the entrance to the grand hall of the Ars Electronica show in Linz, Austria, Sester's *Access* was designed to illustrate state-of-the-art capabilities in camera tracking, robotic control of a spotlight, and projection of sound via narrowly targeted parabolic speakers, all taking place in a quintessentially public space, at the entrance to a major art museum. Sester's project captivated visitors with its virtuosic combination of unfamiliar technologies, prompting numerous attempts to break or fool the system to expose its limits. Part of what makes *Access* unusual is its resistance to the use of lens-based surveillance images. Instead of being "about looking," like most surveillance art of its time, *Access* focused on the processes of tracking and being tracked by a system that is fundamentally computational, not visual.

In *Access*, individuals in a public space are electronically hailed by a combination of light and sound, uncertainly controlled by anonymous web users. *Access* thus also creates an unexpected relationship between tracker and tracked in which neither party is entirely aware of the consequences of their actions. In the absence of input from web users, the spotlight and a

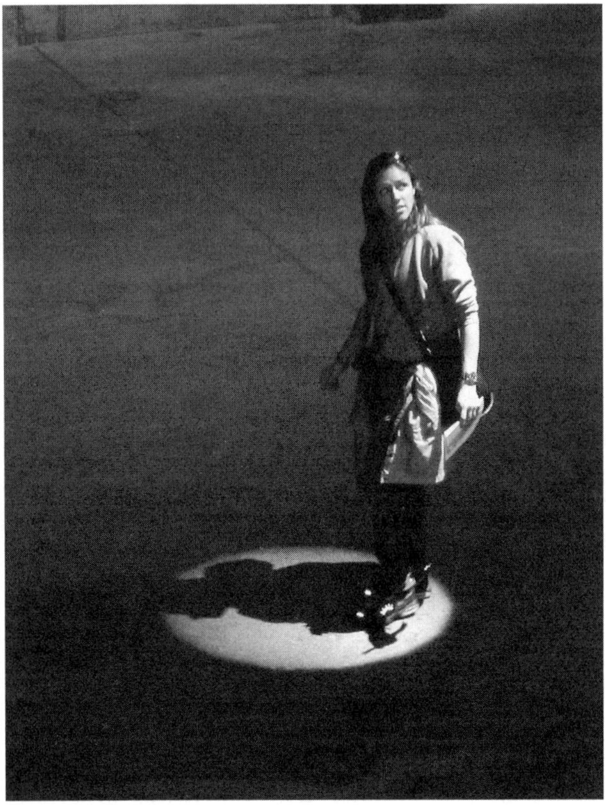

Figure 2.4
Marie Sester's *Access* (2003) eschewed the aesthetics of video surveillance in favor of motion tracking to presage the transition from optics to computation. Photo by Shawn Van Every; image courtesy of Marie Sester.

narrowly targeted acoustic beam automatically targets individuals who pass in front of the tracking system. The effect of the piece is to heighten awareness about the technology of motion tracking as well as public vulnerability.

Whereas Rokeby's *Watched and Measured* is about systems and databases, *Access* is about the address to the individual. But it is a faux individuality. When captured by the beam of the spotlight, a person may feel momentarily special, like a stage performer—and indeed some of the project's audio cues support this perception, declaring, "Perform for us! This is your moment," and "You're under the light; we're watching you!" As the robotic tracking beam proves tenacious and implacable, the sense of being followed by the blinding beam of the spotlight quickly becomes discomfiting. The audio cues likewise echo the dubious sincerity of a direct marketing campaign, offering generic platitudes such as "You look fabulous!" It is clear from *Access* that the "system" is in possession of a degree of intelligence—or at least awareness—pertaining to its human subjects. For individuals being tracked, the system offers no hint as to what sort of motivation lies behind it. The content of its address seems benign enough on the surface, but still the fact of its existence and operation suggests the need for deeper suspicion. Web users, in contrast, are able to glimpse the functioning of the position tracking software and are invited to participate in selecting targets based on tracking data, using a cross-hairs interface reminiscent, in its day, of a bombsight, though today it resonates more with a drone targeting system.

An earlier project by Sester, titled *Exposure* (2001/2008), also dealt with emerging technologies of vision, most commonly deployed in the service of government and corporate power. Like *Access, Exposure* made use of technologies that were not well known to the public at the time, including large-scale X-ray and 3D scanning. Sester's work used a combination of still and moving images to meditate on the capacity for such technologies to "see through" the walls of vehicles and to precisely model large physical spaces, including buildings and landscapes. As in much of Sester's work, *Exposure* allows for multiple readings of the images as objects of aesthetic beauty as well as troubling critique.[70] Finally, *Exposure* highlights the capacity of instrumental images to generate multiple levels of meaning, inviting viewers to marvel at the technology used to create them, while implicitly warning of the dangers of misuse. Viewed in juxtaposition, these works by Rokeby and Sester posit two oppositional but complementary reuses of the technologies of digital surveillance. Whereas *Access* directs itself toward individual bodies, *Taken* and *Watched and Measured* expose the databases by which large-scale tracking of populations takes place.

Experimental Geographies

We're going to have to develop new techniques of seeing because more and more of the world consists of machines talking to other machines using a language that we are not familiar with. How do you see algorithms and how do you see networks?[71]
—Trevor Paglen

Writing about the tensions between Weimar-era German art and politics, Bertolt Brecht warned against naïve models of representation to express the structure and functioning of corporations. "The situation has become so complicated because the simple 'reproduction of reality' says less than ever about that reality. A photograph of the Krupp works or AEG reveals almost nothing about these institutions."[72] Brecht's modernist pessimism about the capacity of images to reveal the social relations and labor practices obscured behind a corporate facade contrasts with the visual logic of today's technology industries, which seeks to efface all evidence of the physical—to say nothing of the human!—infrastructures that underlie them.[73] So sensitive is this visual logic that we have reached the point, in the 2010s, where the simple act of photographically documenting the external surfaces of corporate and governmental edifices represents a gesture of defiance. As Brecht argued nearly a century ago, however, photographically rendered surfaces reveal precious little beyond the fact of their own existence.

In Tung-Hui Hu's critique of ideologies of immateriality, *A Prehistory of the Cloud*, he notes, "For how generic their architectural forms are, data centers might as well be water towers in Germany, or gas stations in Texas—and perhaps they ought to be photographed that way."[74] Hu wittily connects the history of data centers to the history of the pony express by highlighting the construction of NSA and commercial data centers in Utah, where the pony express originated. "The data center remains among the least studied areas of digital culture, with cloud computing producing a layer of abstraction that masks the physical infrastructure of data storage."[75] Hu's book offers a sustained and multifaceted meditation on data centers for their physical operation as much as their symbolic meaning, but he stops short of prescribing a solution to the abstract/physical conundrum. Certainly it is easier to obfuscate about the immaterial, but is insistence on physicality a sufficient response? The radical cartographer Trevor Paglen takes up this issue in a body of visual and written work that insistently traverses not only the physical/virtual divide, but that of images/data as well.

In the early 2000s, while still a graduate student at UC Berkeley, Paglen gained a reputation for leading tours around the edges of the military-industrial complex in the San Francisco Bay area, including military-sponsored research at his own university. True to his training as a geographer, part of Paglen's strategy was to map the contours and surfaces of classified government operations to expose the contradictions of visibility and invisibility in secret programs. Paglen's peculiar focus, even then, was on "black world" operations that take place largely in remote deserts and mountains but nonetheless involve physically trackable objects such as planes and the people who operate, use, and maintain them. Just as people and objects obey certain basic laws of physics—if only by having mass and taking up space—the contours of their movements can be observed and tracked. Paglen describes his work in terms that are characteristically understated:

> Although the organizing logic of our nation's surveillance apparatus is invisibility and secrecy, its operations occupy the physical world. Digital surveillance programs require concrete data centers; intelligence agencies are based in real buildings; surveillance systems ultimately consist of technologies, people, and the vast network of material resources that supports them. If we look in the right places at the right times, we can begin to glimpse America's vast intelligence infrastructure.[76]

Paglen's repertoire of counter-surveillance tools ranges from high to low tech, including high-power telephoto lenses and FAA flight-tracking data. The goal is not a celebration of everyday occurrences, but merely acknowledgment of the fact that such events take place. In his book *Blank Spots on the Map* (2009), Paglen describes the scene of workers disembarking from an unmarked plane used to fly them to work at a secret military facility in terms of the scene's "hopeless banality."[77] In an online project for the *Vectors* journal, titled "Unmarked Planes and Hidden Geographies" (2006),[78] Paglen offers a deceptively simple insight: even secret planes flying secret missions must be included in the systems that monitor air traffic so that the planes don't crash into each other.

Covert operations carried out by government agencies are funded by tax dollars, which leave traces in public records, such as the Defense Department's annual budget. Although specifics are carefully concealed, gross contours may be discerned by a practiced and diligent eye. Unspecified expenditures, especially when cross-referenced with other kinds of "missing" information, may yield insights about otherwise unacknowledged government operations. Another project by Paglen performs a literal "reading" of another surface effect of covert operations by the NSA and its British counterpart, the Government Communications Headquarters (GCHQ). In *Code Names of the Surveillance State* (2014), which was released at the same time as Laura Poitras's documentary about Edward Snowden, *Citizenfour* (2014),[79] Paglen projects for eighty minutes a scrolling list of more than four thousand alphabetically ordered surveillance operation code names; in another version of the project, a static version of the list is reproduced on gallery walls. In both cases, the power of the installation lies in its overwhelming scale, a reminder that each of these (often absurd) names represents an (often very serious) operation to which significant expenditures of time, money, resources, and human labor have been devoted. The time required simply to view the entire list of names functions as a reminder of what is at stake in a system that requires people to devote their lives, in secrecy, to government operations in the absence of public accountability or acknowledgment.

A related project aggregates a collection of the fabric patches that are sometimes issued to participants in covert military operations. These patches are often as abstract and unknown as the operation names in Paglen's *Code Names of the Surveillance State* project, but they are achieved through graphically enigmatic symbols and initials. In addition to displaying collections of the patches in an art context and as a photo essay in the *New York Times*, Paglen published a book in 2007 titled *I Could Tell You But Then You Would Have to Be Destroyed by Me: Emblems from the Pentagon's Black World*, featuring some sixty patches related to secret military operations, along with explanations culled from Freedom of Information Act documents. Like the *Code Names* project, Paglen's work with military patches does not propose an explicit critique, only the aggregation of a narrow band of surface effects that describe much more complex underlying systems and activities.

Paglen's focus on prosaic and distinctly human aspects of the military-industrial complex is reminiscent of the documentation of aerospace industry workers seen in Allan Sekula's *Untitled Slide Sequence* (1972). Photographed shortly before his domestic ethnography *Aerospace Folktales* (1973), Sekula's *Untitled Slide Sequence* comprises some twenty-five images of workers as they climb stairs to leave their day shift jobs at the General Dynamics Aerospace Factory in San Diego, California. Most images are frontal; sometimes the workers seem aware of the presence of the camera, sometimes not; there are occasional smiles, looks of boredom, indifference, or suspicion; and we see a variety of ethnicities, genders, and ages. Details of appearance—suits, ties, T-shirts, hairstyles, and lunch pails—suggest class differences and professional ranks momentarily flattened by the shared act of leaving work. The banality of climbing stairs belies the significance of

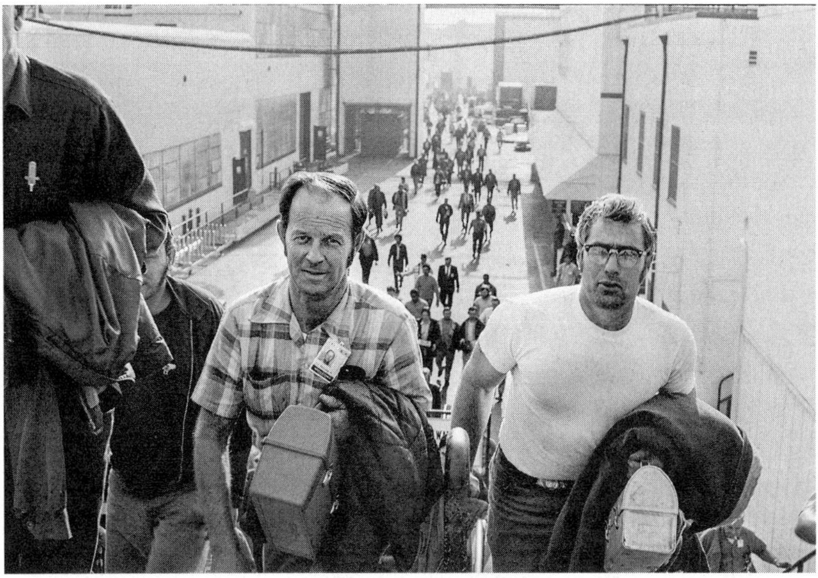

Figure 2.5
Aerospace workers leave the General Dynamics Aerospace Factory in San Diego, California, in Allan Sekula's *Untitled Slide Sequence* (1972): 25 black-and-white 35mm transparencies projected at thirteen-second intervals; seventeen minutes, twenty seconds, looped. Courtesy of the Allan Sekula Studio.

the work that has just been completed within the manufacturing facility of a military contractor deep in the throes of the Vietnam War. A sign in the background admonishes workers to "walk don't run"—but Sekula's images offer no hint of what they would be running away from, unless it is the simple fact of employment at a defense contractor during wartime.

From today's perspective, more than forty years later, part of what is striking about Sekula's images is the fact that the photographer—the son of a Lockheed engineer who would be laid off the following year—was allowed to capture these images at all. Although the photographs posed no conceivable risk to the plant's security or operation, it is impossible to imagine such casual access being granted today. Today's anxieties about terrorism and espionage of corporate or international varieties have rendered the mere act of looking at—to say nothing of photographing—even the featureless exteriors of a military contractor's manufacturing facility suggestive of a security risk.

Within this inhospitable context, Paglen began photographing not just military facilities but the surface effects and symptoms of their most secret operations. Like Sekula, Paglen does not attempt to penetrate the interior of these facilities or, indeed, to produce with his photographs any new knowledge about the activities within. He is, instead, committed to documenting the edges of what is seeable and knowable, the boundaries and points of transmission between the black world and its other. Among the strategies Paglen developed for this purpose was a process he calls "limit telephotography." Here, Paglen deploys telescopic lenses pushed almost to the brink of their ability to capture images from miles away, often photographing from desert mountain peaks overlooking remote air bases or military installations. Although these images lack the formal beauty of Paglen's aerial photographs, without them, the human dimension of the Pentagon's black world is too easily overlooked. Viewed in contrast with the intimacy of Sekula's images of aerospace workers, Paglen's limit telephotographs register only the existence of human figures from which no details of identity or affect may be gleaned. As much as anything, this increased distance represents a visceral sign of changing times, when the mere act of seeing or photographing them is purported to threaten our most powerful institutions.

In 2014, Paglen published a series of posts musing on the "idea of photography as seeing machines" on *Still Searching*, a photography-themed web log hosted by the Fotomuseum Winterthur. In a four-post sequence, Paglen describes his understanding of photography in terms that are entirely consistent with this book's interest in the tensions between images and data. "Seeing machines is an expansive definition of photography. It is intended to encompass the myriad ways that not only humans use technology to 'see' the world, but the ways machines see the world for other machines."[80] Paglen articulates a litany of technologies of vision, from license plate readers to airport security imaging systems, and locates the key to distinguishing and understanding these technologies in their intentionality, arguing that technologies for capturing images and data are inseparable from the uses to which they are put. "Crucially, the definition of photography I'm proposing here encompasses imaging devices ('cameras' broadly understood), the data ('images' being one possible manifestation of that data) they produce, and the seeing-practices with which they are enmeshed."[81] At stake in his mapping of the transformed terrain of contemporary photography

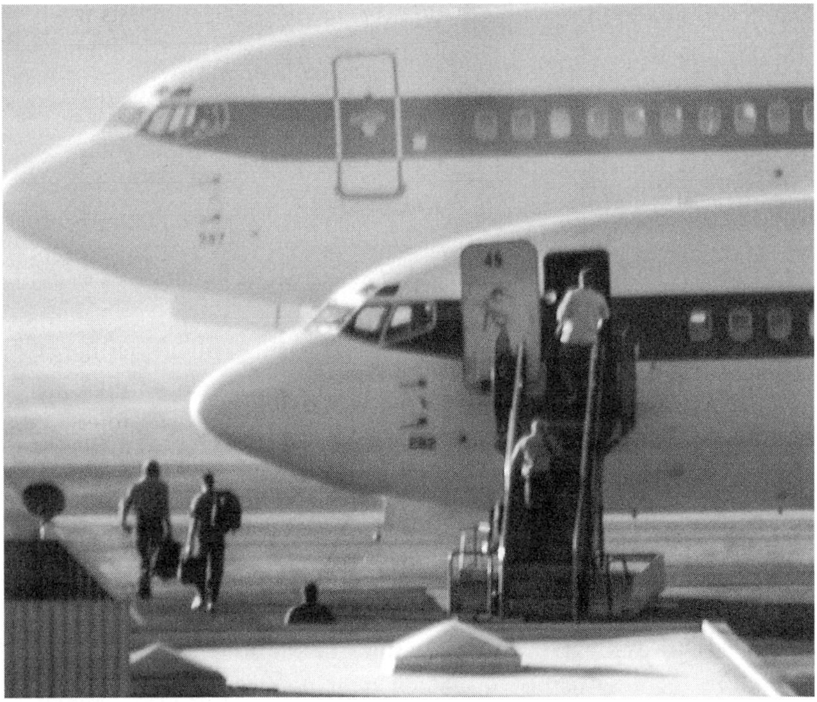

Figure 2.6
Trevor Paglen's limit telephotography captures surface effects of the black world, while highlighting its severely limited visibility. Image © Trevor Paglen, *Morning Commute (Gold Coast Terminal), Las Vegas, NV*. Distance ~1 mile, 6:26 a.m., 2006, C-Print, 30 × 36 inches.

is nothing less than the relationship between humans and their terrestrial environment. Dubbing this "geographies of photography," Paglen describes a reciprocal relationship between technologies such as photography and the transformation of the lived environment:

> [G]eography has to do with how humans sculpt the Earth's surface, and how humans and societies (everything from bodies to politics and culture) are, in turn, sculpted by the ways we've sculpted Earth's surface. It's crucial to understand this as a feedback loop, or dialectic, wherein the material "stuff" of the world often plays an active role in sculpting societies.[82]

Paglen's photography operationalizes these definitions. His photographic work is, by turns, conventionally "artistic" in terms of formal attributes of scale, line, and composition, as well as legible in instrumental terms as an attempt to increase the visibility of government intelligence operations. A few months after the Snowden revelations in 2013, Paglen was commissioned by the media arts organization Creative Time to create a series of large-scale photographs of the physical complexes housing the National Security Agency, the National Reconnaissance Office, and the National Geospatial-Intelligence Agency. Paglen photographed each of these government agencies from the air, at night, creating dramatic contrasts with the artificial light of the buildings and their surrounding parking lots erupting against darkened landscapes.

The resulting photographs are a series of pristine, highly aestheticized photos that *Time* magazine nonetheless described as "creepy," presumably in reference to the activities of the organizations in question rather than the images themselves.[83] The NSA image is practically a rephotograph, taken from the same approximate angle as the image from the 1970s, showing a bit more of the parking lot, where the sepia-colored glow of sodium vapor lights is reflected in the building's glass facade, lending a warm—possibly even nostalgic—radiance to the scene. Paglen's view of the National Reconnaissance Office (NRO) is a deliberate study in line and color, with a sweeping arc of highway bathed in golden light dominating the foreground. Looming across the entire left side of the frame is the NRO building, silhouetted by the blue-green fluorescent lights of its parking garage. The highway is Route 28, which slices southward through rural Virginia, skirting past Dulles Airport to the north and the Civil War battlefields of Manassas and Bull Run to the south. The National Geospatial-Intelligence Agency (NGA) building sits closer to town, just outside the Capital Beltway. In Paglen's framing, tentacular access routes loop across the foreground of a darkened landscape, dramatically outlining the elongated NGA building, which features a lighted glass dome on top like the cockpit of an enormous alien spaceship.

Of course, my elaborations on the cartographic locations of these buildings are not present in the images themselves. It seemed appropriate, when considering an aerial photograph of the government agency responsible for creating and operating spy satellites (NRO) and another that analyzes and interprets the data and images captured by satellites (NGA), to cross-reference Paglen's photographs captured from a helicopter with the satellite and bird's eye views available on Microsoft Bing and Google Maps. Although Paglen was repeatedly denied permission to photograph the

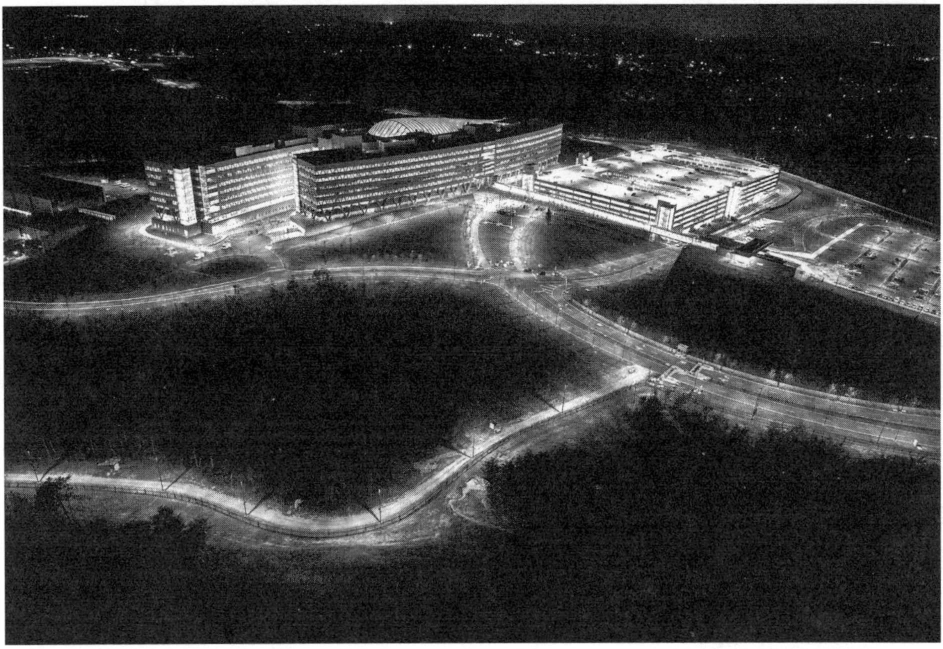

Figure 2.7
Trevor Paglen's public domain aerial images of government buildings contribute to a new visual vocabulary for the surveillance state. Image by Trevor Paglen, *National Geospatial-Intelligence Agency* (2013).

CIA complex in Langley, Virginia, images of the buildings, along with the other major edifices of the intelligence community, are readily available in the public databases maintained by Microsoft and Google. Even though Paglen's work lies squarely in the domain of images, it is implicitly connected to data networks and other information systems. Prior to seeing Paglen's photograph of the NGA, for example, I had no idea the organization existed and might never have recognized it as part of the constellation of U.S. intelligence agencies.

Perversely, what Paglen brings to these gestures of counter-surveillance is aesthetic appeal. It's undeniable that Paglen's images are strikingly beautiful—an effect that is more fine art than political statement. Paglen describes his intention as "to expand the visual vocabulary we use to 'see' the U.S. intelligence community."[84] After Paglen's photographs were published by *Creative Time Reports* and the *Intercept,* they were released into the public domain, where they have become part of the visual vocabulary of national intelligence, available for anyone to use.[85]

Laura Marks describes Paglen's images as "mere traces, for most of power bypasses the visible yet continues to circulate and have effects. Power is the ability to hide things in the image."[86] If power "hides things" in the image, the release of that power is precisely what drives Paglen's photographic work. But Paglen's role is not that of the traditional documentarian, who exposes truths through undeniable traces yielded by the camera lens. Rather his work is exemplary for its insistence on promoting an oppositional logic to the universality privileged by Google's synthesized imaging and mapping systems. Whereas Paglen finds meaning in marking the boundaries of cartographic representation—that which is beyond the bounds of the mappable—Google prefers an ideology of totality, by which every mappable space and photographable surface finds its place in the company's grand interoperable database. In Google's imaging systems, spaces that are "missing" from the photographic record are simply filled in algorithmically, extending the logic of nearby pixels to cover up for gaps, seams, and glitches.[87]

In aggregate, Paglen's work deftly limns the boundaries between art and politics and between scholarship and activism, probing soft spots among the national security state, the military-industrial complex, and institutions of democracy. His unassuming prose requires visitors to read between the lines to generate their own interpretations and conclusions. Even if the truth is out there, Paglen's ongoing investigations, which range from outer space to the ocean floor, demonstrate that finding answers is no easy task. As access to unalloyed truth grows increasingly fugitive, Paglen's methods of documenting, tracking, decoding, and inferring become increasingly important. A responsible public may no longer rely—if indeed it ever could—on official pronouncements and journalistic reports. Instead, those who wish to educate themselves about the world must operate as detectives, following threads, triangulating sources, and paying attention to what is *not* said or seen as much as to what is. Paglen's work is exemplary for turning its gaze insistently on the things we may least want to know or admit about our government.

Under the Virtual, the Servers!

Irish artist John Gerrard has pursued an inventive variant on the photographic documentation of government and institutional edifices seen in Paglen. Whereas Paglen operates in the realm of optical countersurveillance, most recently turning his lens on undersea internet cables that are tapped by the NSA, Gerrard displaces the primacy of optical imaging in favor of photorealistic digital models that are no less provocative. Gerrard has completed numerous installation-based simulations created using the 3D engine Unigine, which is more commonly used for videogame development. To create these projects, Gerrard works with teams of artists, programmers, and modelers to reconstruct virtual environments that are indistinguishable from photographic documents of physical spaces. The earliest of these works sometimes originated with a single photographic image, supplemented by satellite photos and any other available visual information; later works are based on thousands of photographs taken by the artist explicitly for the purpose of generating 3D models. In the parlance of this book, these simulations could be thought of as an instance of the aspirational mode, which is to say that the models are digitally generated to resemble as closely as possible their photographic referents.

Gerrard has been celebrated for creating formally complex works such as *Solar Reserve (Tonopah, Nevada)* (2014), a spectacularly intricate model of a solar power–generating plant featuring some ten thousand mirrors geometrically arrayed like the seeds of a sunflower, angled to direct light at a central tower. As the earth moves in relation to the sun, the mirrors slowly shift position to keep the sun's rays directed at the tower. When in motion, the model resembles a kinetic sculpture executing precisely choreographed movements, like thousands of mirrors arrayed across a desert landscape performing a slow-motion tai chi routine. As Gerrard's virtual camera orbits the tower and slowly rises up to a perspective looking straight down on the array, the visual effect is nothing less than stunning.

Retreating from the visual pleasures of *Solar Reserve*'s floral geometry, Gerrard's next project focused obstinately on a static and unspectacular subject: Google's data center in Pryor Creek, Oklahoma. At the center of Gerrard's *Farm (Pryor Creek, Oklahoma)* (2015) sits a long, flat building with a corrugated metal roof, ringed by industrial equipment and nondescript grass fields. Known as a "data farm," facilities like this do nothing but store

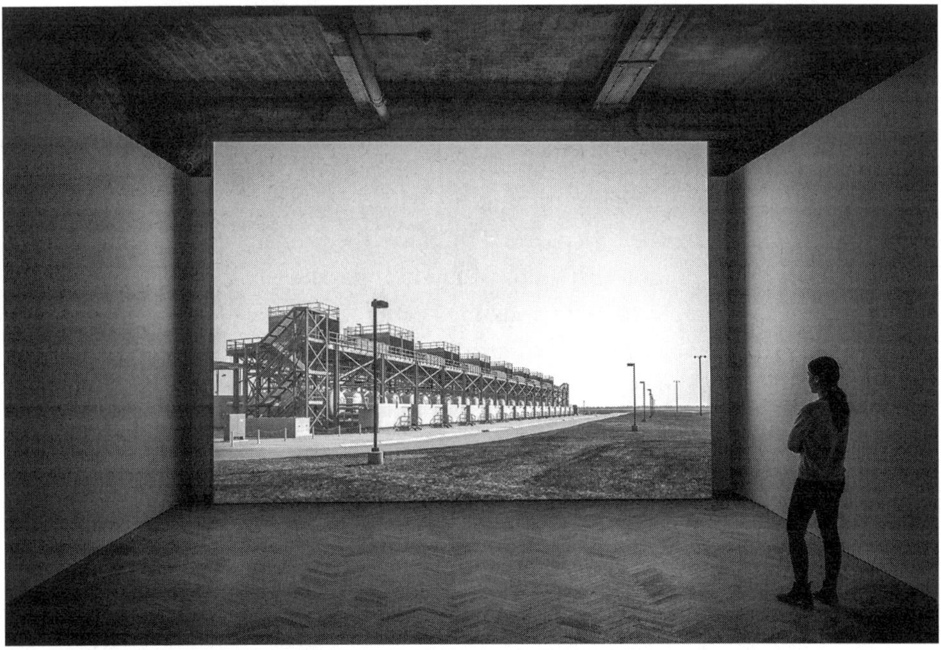

Figure 2.8
A Google data storage facility is translated into a high-resolution 3D model by artist John Gerrard in *Farm (Pryor Creek, Oklahoma)* (2015). Image courtesy of Thomas Dane Gallery, London.

and serve data to and from Google's vast network. Unlike in Paglen's photographs of government spy agencies, the diminutive parking lot adjoining the farm suggests the need for a minimum of human involvement in running the facility. Belying its high-tech interior, the building's exterior is a banal testament to the industrial age, dominated by rows of cooling towers and backup generators. In contrast with *Solar Reserve, Farm* offers no moving parts on the outside, nor any formal flourishes to catch the eye. The subject of the piece is, by any measure, an exercise in perversity, refusing the allure of visual spectacle in favor of an invitation to ask, "why this?"

The answer is legible only in relation to Gerrard's earlier work, beginning with a series titled *Animated Scenes,* which dates back to 2007. Appropriately, *Farm* closely resembles Gerrard's studies of the agricultural industry seen in *Grow Finish Unit (near Elkhart, Kansas) 2008,* and *Grow Finish Unit (Eva, Oklahoma) 2008.* The two *Grow Finish* works examine the exteriors of automated sow-farming facilities in the American Great Plains region, where pigs are prepared for slaughter, a few hundred miles due west from Google's Oklahoma data facility. Like Google's data farms, the sow farms represent part of a nearly ubiquitous but largely unseen infrastructure, located in remote locales that are at once rural and industrial. The exterior surfaces of the buildings, like Brecht's photographs of the Krupp works and AEG, offer no hint of the operations within. Viewers experience *Farm* from the perspective of a slowly moving virtual camera positioned at roughly eye level that keeps the building centered in the frame as it circles the facility at a speed approximating that of a leisurely stroll. This languorous pace activates viewers' awareness of both duration and scale. The time required to complete one circumnavigation of the building serves as a reminder of the vast size and ultimate unknowability of the operations taking place inside. Unlike models that are created to simplify or visualize information about complex systems, Gerrard's virtual tracking shots are about the withholding of knowledge and omniscient certainty. These projects suggest that the day-to-day operations of pig and data farming resemble what artist Sharon Daniel has termed "public secrets," uncomfortable truths that sit uneasily on the edge of what we allow ourselves to know and—more importantly—what we assume responsibility for knowing.

Even when subjected to close inspection, Gerrard's model is indistinguishable from a photographic reproduction. The only sign distinguishing *Farm* from a lens-based, gyroscopically stabilized circumnavigation of the data facility is the practical impossibility of executing such a precise, sustained camera movement in physical space. In fact, the virtual camera could have been programmed to execute any kind of movement in relation to the digital model, including the kind of orbital ascent used in *Solar Reserve*. Instead, the prosaic movement mapped by Gerrard preserves a relation to cinematographic possibility, adding to the intentional, uncanny hyperreality of the installation. Gerrard notes, "The sense that this representation is not an image but rather a place that exists in simulation, always and in real time, provides a special position from which to contemplate the reality that undergirds 'everyday' reality."[88] Gerrard further describes his use of digital models as an "atemporal, post lens, post cinematic medium," the result of which is a "curious synthetic quality." This synthetic quality is especially appropriate to the subject of a virtual double of a facility that stores and serves trace data about Google users but does not want to be seen by human eyes.[89] In fact, Gerrard's project originated with a request for permission to photograph Google's data center. When this was denied, the artist hired a helicopter to fly him around the building to document every exterior surface from all possible angles of view. Of course there is a painful irony in Google's refusal to allow photography of their facility's exteriors, given that the company's Street View project is devoted to exactly this type of documentation on a global—and usually unpermissioned—scale.

An identical strategy of translating photographic documentation into high-resolution digital models occurs in designer Timo Arnall's *Internet Machine* (2014), a three-screen, 270-degree installation described as documenting "the invisible infrastructures of the internet." Arnall created the project in part to refute the disingenuous characterization of digital networks as vaporous or immaterial. Referring to such infrastructures as "the cloud," Arnall asserts, is "a childish myth."[90] To create the project, Arnall was granted access to a high-security internet hub run by the Spanish telecommunications giant Telefónica in Alcalá, Spain. Rather than focusing exclusively on the servers where digital information is stored and retrieved, Arnall captured thirty-two different locations within the facility using a combination of high-resolution video and still images. These images were then used to construct a photographically detailed 3D model of each space, including such mundane apparatuses as backup generators, air-conditioning units, water tanks, and so on. Virtual camera moves were then programmed to glide eerily through spaces and across surfaces, creating an uncanny, disembodied perspective. Each scene is accompanied by a different, but similarly oppressive, industrial ambience—humming, buzzing, roaring—that marks these spaces as fundamentally hostile to human presence. The virtual camera moves bring subtle perspective shifts that seem vaguely, *computationally* artificial. The resulting sense of presence is simultaneously familiar but also slightly unnatural, suggesting that something about our perception of the place is not what it seems. Merely photographic or cinematographic documentation, this technique suggests, is somehow insufficient.

Both Arnall's and Gerrard's work may be usefully contrasted with Simon Norfolk's *Data Centres* (2012). For *Data Centres*, the war photojournalist Norfolk turned his attention from literal fields of battle to the supercomputers and data storage facilities that lie behind the scenes of military and scientific technology development.[91] As a war correspondent photographing the conflict in Afghanistan, Norfolk was known for the idiosyncratic practice of using a cumbersome vintage wooden 4 × 5 view camera. This strategy goes beyond mere anachronism to suggest Norfolk's obstinate refusal to play the prescribed role of an "embedded" photojournalist. Like *Internet Machine*, Norfolk's photographs of data centers and supercomputers do not simply glamorize the hardware of computing. His images focus equally on mundane and utilitarian aspects of the building, such as cables, racks, and fire suppression systems.

With *Data Centres*, Norfolk continues his interest in photographing technological infrastructures begun in 2006, with a project titled, *The Supercomputers: "I'm sorry, Dave. I'm afraid I can't do that."* In combination, the two projects represent an expansion of the artist's goal of transforming public perceptions of war, diverging deliberately from century-old photojournalistic clichés of soldiers in the field. Like Gerrard and Arnall, Norfolk's work draws attention to otherwise invisible infrastructures of computing, but with an additional focus on the nature of the data processed by these machines. Specifically, Norfolk captures images of the supercomputers used to model explosions inside a nuclear warhead. Such modeling, for Norfolk, constitutes a rehearsal of actual conflict, a domesticating influence that represents a seemingly benign but actually insidious component that supports the world's ability to imagine, model, and wage war. As a photojournalist committed to documenting war, Norfolk expands his topic to include the technological infrastructure that underlies humanity's most destructive weapons.

For the purposes of this book, it is worth thinking seriously about the difference between the kind of photographic (or videographic) documentation exemplified by Norfolk and the multistage processes of digital modeling deployed by Arnall and Gerrard. Where Norfolk's 4 × 5 photographic negatives conform to a nineteenth-century ideal of documentary realism, Gerrard and Arnall's deliberate distancing from photographic originals imagines a different evidentiary function for image making. Each of these projects argues that, at the level of hardware, architecture, and environmental impact, "cloud computing" is anything but vaporous, but they pursue their goals using divergent technological means. I would argue that their shared project of reasserting the physicality of the digital is not just trendy contrarianism but symptomatic of a growing awareness of the real environmental consequences of the global capitalism and military-industrial collusion under which the technology industries have long flourished. They key to effectively formulating this critique does not depend on any particular technology of vision; in fact, it is a testament to the urgency of this perspective that it sustains treatment in such diametrically opposed forms.

Conclusion

We have reached the point where characterizing the combination of technologies and social practices surveyed in this chapter as "surveillance" has begun to seem anachronistic, or worse, nostalgic. I retain the term as a tactical gesture because I view many of the tendencies mapped here as dangerous to values that can no longer be taken for granted: privacy, democracy, freedoms of expression and assembly, due process, asymptotic approaches to truth, and many other ideals worth fighting for. In this book, then, "surveillance" has come to function as a surrogate for thinking about state and corporate power. While much has been—and still needs to be—written on this subject broadly, my concerns focus on the narrow band where technologies of vision and computation intersect. The metaphor of panopticism, which well served discourses of surveillance studies for many decades, must make room for models capable of accounting for the power and ubiquity of computation. The disciplinary potential of looking and listening operates very differently when it must be embodied by a human "other"—prison guard, law enforcement agent, watchful citizen—as opposed to an information system capable of resurrecting trace data on any individual from any point in the past. How much more bluntly can I say it? As long as we are more worried about being seen and heard than having our data tracked and mined, the job of those tasked with monitoring the lives of others remains much easier than it should be.

That said, we are well past the point of no return in a technological sense. Too many data points already exist on too many servers, and too many shareholder dividends are tied to commercial systems predicated on their analysis. The word "privacy" has been conscripted as a modifier for "settings" and "policies," often at the expense of its meaning as a tangible right standing between individuals and state or institutional power. Acquiescence to systems that offer superficial tradeoffs for giving up little bits of privacy are uniquely characteristic of surveillance systems that capture data rather than images. The incremental sacrificing of control over one's data is most dangerous in aggregate. I mean this not only in the sense of enabling mosaics of complete knowledge to be assembled from fragmented information, but as part of a cultural reconception of the relations between individuals and states or corporations. The term "private citizen" already carries hints of anachrony. The ability of individuals to define and strike their own balance between personal secrecy and public exposure—of not being compelled to choose between extremes of total openness or total secrecy—continues to be what is at stake in discussions of surveillance. Laws and technologies that are designed to support such a balance face difficult challenges. My concern is that desirable solutions to these problems require nuance and subtlety on a scale that neither our legal nor our technological systems seem particularly well suited to deliver, even if the cultural and political will existed. Change is needed, to be sure, but of a systemic, epochal, unrelenting sort.

3 Data | Space

Tracked Spaces

Sometime in the 1990s, hockey pucks on television began to glow. The technology that enabled pucks during ostensibly live broadcasts to emit a bloom of light was developed by the Fox Network and implemented as part of its exclusive agreement with the National Hockey League (NHL) during the 1996 playoff season. Officially named FoxTrax, but colloquially known as the "glow puck," the effect was realized by embedding infrared transmitters in the puck, which were then tracked by an array of sensors positioned around the hockey arena. The effect generated a bright blue glow around the puck, making it easier for inexperienced viewers to follow its location on-screen. Adding to the drama, the blue glow switched to red when the puck was detected to be traveling in excess of seventy miles per hour—primarily during shots on goal—creating a dazzling red tail like a comet. Television broadcasts were delayed by slightly more than a second to give the computers receiving the infrared signals time to process the puck location and to generate its colorful aura without occluding the human figures on the ice. Although casual viewers were probably grateful for the visual aid, the glow puck was scrapped less than three years later because of overwhelmingly negative responses from devoted hockey fans. The glow puck is now primarily remembered as one of the worst innovations in sports history.

Shortly after being ejected by the NHL, FoxTrax was adapted by a company called SportVision to generate real-time graphical overlays on football fields, making visible the otherwise transient locations of first-down lines and lines of scrimmage in National Football League (NFL) broadcasts. Related technologies were also developed for TV broadcasts of high-end sailing competitions such as the America's Cup; to analyze strike zones in Major League Baseball; and to indicate vehicle positions in televised NASCAR races. For my purposes, however, the NFL-based overlays are of greatest interest. The virtual strike zones in baseball, NASCAR positions, and sailing course lines superimposed on the water are clearly marked as extra-diegetic, appearing to viewers as real-time graphical overlays similar to broadcast logos or lines from "telestrator" drawing tablets used by commentators. In professional football broadcasts, however, first-down and scrimmage lines are carefully integrated into the visual presentation of the game, with care taken to prevent overlaps with players through real-time control of the opacity of images of players on the field. As with the glow puck, NFL broadcasts are delivered with a slight temporal delay to allow for the computational reconstruction of the field. The bounded environment of the sporting arena, with precisely tracked camera positions, facilitates the transformation of a live sporting event into a hybrid lens-based and computer-generated display space. Further, the differing responses to these technologies and the degree to which the hybridity of the display is consciously perceived offers fodder for a broader cultural analysis of our shifting relationship to data and images.

Public aversion to the glow puck was surely exacerbated because the concept of synthetic visual environments had not yet permeated the visual culture of the mid-1990s. The blue glow surrounding a hockey puck represented a technologized intrusion into a sport dedicated to intense physicality. Although physical violence is certainly encoded in the structure of American football, games are predicated on discontinuous play and precisely regulated player positioning. Such control makes the sport a more welcoming environment for the introduction of virtual graphics on the playing field. The lines and graphics generated by SportVision also constitute a less obtrusive intervention in the visual register because they are static and made to resemble real-world field markings. But perhaps most important, the two years by which the glow puck preceded use of the same technology for NFL games precisely straddled the cultural transition when audiences learned to accept the presentation of synthetic images within ostensibly live broadcast events. It is worth remembering—and in this chapter, I will be at some pains to argue—that even our most naturalized perceptions of space are in fact learned responses that are significantly shaped by the contested relationship of data and images.

Perceptions of space are also shaped by bodily sensations, both through media perceptions and physical experience. Wolfgang Schivelbusch's history of railroad travel locates part of the perception of space in bodily sensations—the nineteenth-century transition from the bone-jarring experience of travel by coach compared with the smooth, industrialized uniformity of steel rails. Early train passengers experienced embodied sensations of movement not in proportion to the unevenness of the terrain but through the rhythmic accompaniment of steel wheels hitting the evenly spaced joints between rails.[1] Spatial perception during the railway age was also tightly bound to an ideological subject position from which (primarily white, economically privileged) travelers participated in civilizing the West, transforming it from its "natural" state and wresting control away from its original inhabitants. To travel by train was not just to conquer distance; it was to take part in the conquest of a frontier.

By no coincidence, cinema became the quintessential technology of industrial modernism. The mechanization of images was shaped by the logic of industrialization, just as viewers' ability to perceive a rapidly changing world was reshaped by the kinetic images of film. As Lynn Kirby argues in *Parallel Tracks: The Railroad and Silent Cinema* (1997), cinema's connection to train travel includes a shared logic of unidirectionality and temporal regulation. The evolution of the medium took place, in both literal and figurative senses, "on rails" that prevented all but the most gradual deviations from the path on which it was originally set. All of this—including, of course, the double-meaning of "track" as a verb in the context of computational surveillance—will serve as a metaphorical foundation for thinking about bodies and movement through digital spaces of the twenty-first century.[2] The historical example of the transition from coach to railway travel suggests that we not only *see* space differently, we *feel* it to be different. This is no less true of technologies such as virtual reality, where synchronization of cognitive and somatic perceptions of movement is crucial to the successful experience of immersion or presence. The process of gearing up that precedes the experience of a virtual environment prepares viewers for the constructedness of the experience that awaits. While head-mounted display manufacturers aspire to minimize the physical size and weight of the display apparatus, it is in fact precisely its awkward artificiality that currently preserves the medium's embodied sense of spatial otherness.

The synthesis of data and images symbolized by the glow puck systematically transformed perceptions of televisual spaces of the 1990s. Like the movement of trains on tracks in the nineteenth century, the glow puck traces virtual pathways through blended spaces that are at once physical and computational. A parallel transformation took place in the merging of computers with optical printing in the domain of visual effects. Los Angeles–based filmmaker Pat O'Neill conducted some of the most striking of these experiments. Building on a decades-long career as a visual effects artist in Hollywood, O'Neill's first 35mm feature, *Water and Power* (1989), deployed multiple layers of optical capture and postprocessing to achieve an unprecedented degree of control over movement and time. Prior to *Water and Power*, conventional wisdom dictated that time-lapse photography—like many visual effects at this time—required a static camera. O'Neill's innovation was to translate the logics of motion control and stop-motion animation to capture time-lapse sequences *in motion* through exterior landscapes and architectural spaces.

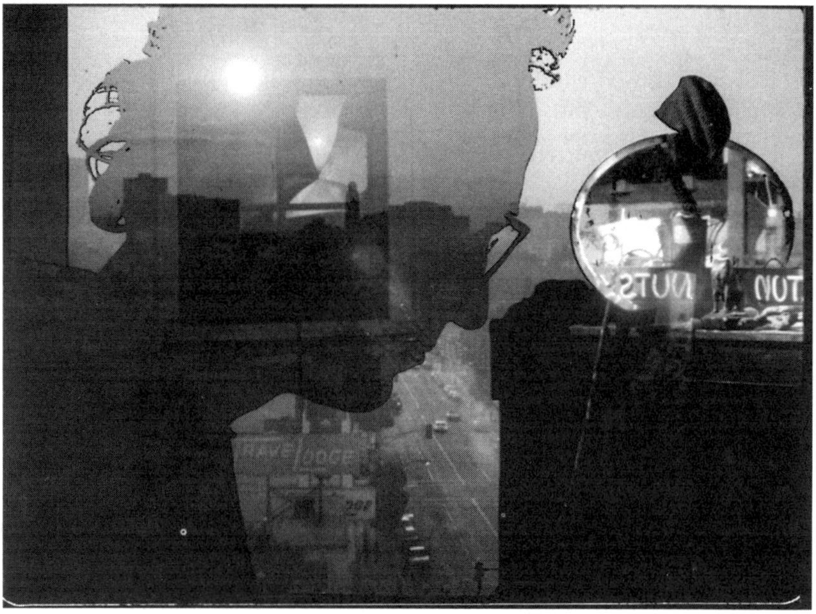

Figure 3.1
In-camera visual composites create hybrid spaces in Pat O'Neill's *Water and Power* (1989). Image courtesy of Lookout Mountain Studios.

O'Neill's film successfully recalibrated viewers' sense of what could take place on the surface of a 35mm film frame and the degree of control that could be exerted over the cinematic time base. The motion-control film camera used by O'Neill made every position of the camera along an incremented track or panoramic tripod head addressable and repeatable; this is a linear version of the way in which a fully instrumented motion-capture volume makes every voxel within digital space addressable and locatable. The key to O'Neill's visual style in *Water and Power* is the combination of motion-controlled time-lapse photography in the physical world and its processing using a computer-controlled optical printer in postproduction. This paired apparatus allowed O'Neill to precisely synchronize the passage of individual film frames—first through the gate of the camera, then through the gate of the printer—at each stage allowing the filmmaker to expose any part of the frame. Although he was working exclusively with lens-based images, this process enabled O'Neill to exercise a degree of visual control that is exceeded only by a virtual camera in a computer-generated 3D environment. The result in O'Neill's work is a series of multiply layered sequences of lens-based images that rivals the complexity and plasticity of a computational environment.

Motion control is more commonly used in Hollywood for shooting miniatures to simulate full-scale live action motion, but for *Water and Power*, O'Neill used it toward the opposite end, transforming real spaces into planes of graphical possibility. O'Neill's process, which consumed seven years of combined shooting, editing, and optical effects, may be seen as a visual prototype—admittedly confined to the film screen—that nonetheless prefigures the transformation of everyday spaces into computational volumes. Two decades after *Water and Power*, O'Neill's laborious optical printing process would be almost entirely overtaken by digital effects achieved using software such as Adobe After Effects.

My goal here is not to recapitulate the history of visual effects, but to begin identifying specific examples from an eclectic range of advertising, games, experimental films, music videos, and feature filmmaking that illustrate the evolving relation of data and images in terms of the parallax modes outlined in this book's introduction. O'Neill's film represents a striking conceptual precursor to the evolution of a synthetic cinematic vocabulary for seamlessly merging data and images. In the moment of transition marked by *Water and Power*—and rarely surpassed since—O'Neill inaugurated a

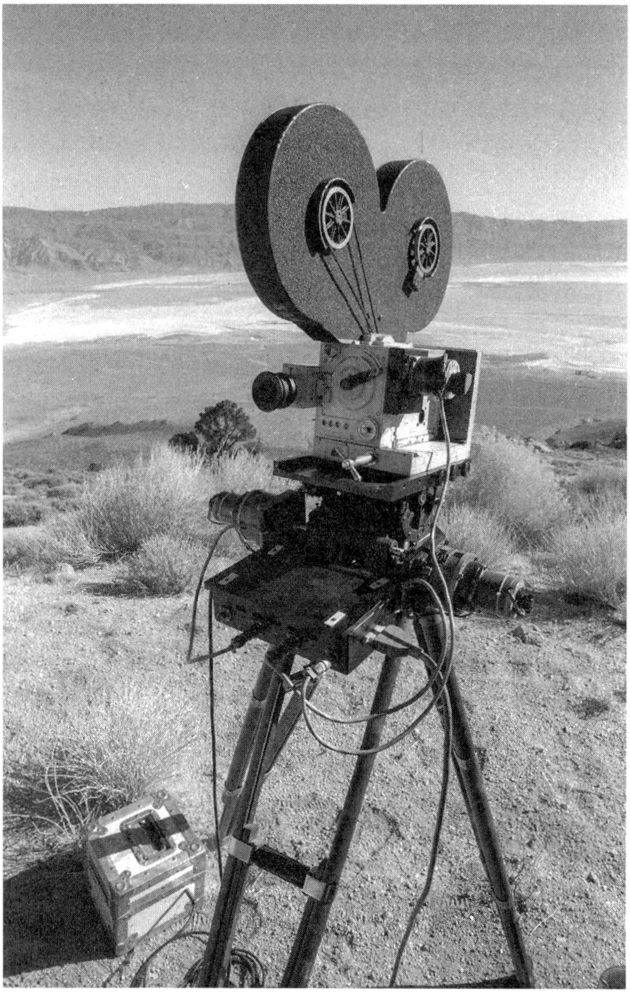

Figure 3.2
A motion-control camera captured time-lapse landscapes in Owens Valley, California, for Pat O'Neill's *Water and Power* (1989). Image courtesy of Lookout Mountain Studios.

hybrid technology of vision based on a series of singular pathways through lens-based, but computationally controllable, spaces. O'Neill was certainly not the only media artist experimenting with such effects at this time, but his work's prescient virtuosity played a crucial role in retraining audiences to understand that film space can also be data space.

Hybrid Realities

Visual effects in the entertainment industries are overwhelmingly dominated by digital technologies designed to bridge the gap between cinema's addiction to lens-based images and the flexibility and control available to computer-generated ones. Among the most common of these technologies are motion capture and facial capture. Both aspire to isolate key aspects of organic human movement and render them as digital information that can be manipulated by computers. Recent decades have witnessed a radical transformation of computer-generated animation, as variations on this technique have become increasingly ubiquitous in the production of film, television, and videogames. In multiuser virtual environments, the real-time translation of bodily movements and facial expressions are key elements of the experience of copresence.

That said, there is nothing about the basic apparatus of motion capture that dictates its use for the faithful reproduction of human (or animal) movements. Enticing experiments have challenged Hollywood's devotion to verisimilitude. One notable example of the alternative use of motion-capture data is *Forms* (2012), a series of computational experiments created by visual artists Memo Akten and Davide Quayola. In these short videos, the pair uses motion-capture data to map the movements of human bodies in space, then abstracts them into undulating clusters and flocks of geometric shapes. The result is part gymnastics display and part visual music animation that defiantly refuses the desire for illusionism. A similar dynamic appears in German multimedia designer Tobias Gremmler's striking series of videos titled *Kung Fu Motion Visualization* (2016). Gremmler captured motion data of kung fu masters practicing their craft in order to trace a fluid series of lines and volumes in space. The resulting videos preserve a sense of the original body movements, but also abstract them into planes and volumes that linger on screen like solid objects that dissolve or morph slowly in space. In both projects, the underlying motion data retains certain

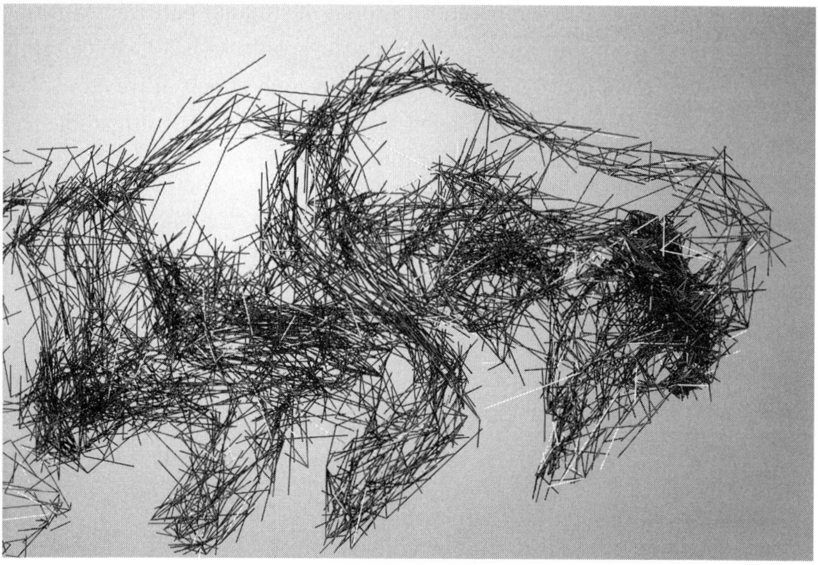

Figure 3.3
Motion-capture data used to create hybrid animations in Davide Quayola and Memo Akten's *Forms* (2012). Image courtesy of Davide Quayola and Memo Akten.

rhythms and postures that are recognizably human, suggesting that a process of negotiation and interpretation results in the most interesting visual output, rather than direct strategies of translation.

The cinematic creation of hybrid worlds, where human and nonhuman figures interact on-screen, has been a mainstay of Hollywood storytelling since the 1930s. Growing up on B-movies and television reruns in the 1970s, I remember being bombarded with examples of visual effects that brought varying degrees of believability to science-fiction narratives. Figures such as Irwin Allen, Walt Disney, and Ray Harryhausen pioneered diverse techniques for integrating live actors into fantasy settings and, in turn, animated characters into live action settings. Yet, the obvious constraints of these hybrid images were confined to the screens of film and television and, as such, never challenged my understanding of the world beyond the screen. In other words, there was nothing about the generation of visual effects I grew up on that suggested the need to rethink my own relation to physical space. The more or less lifelike images on screen remained isolated and inert, created through entirely optical processes of merging live action footage with various forms of animation, compositing, or miniatures. The total separation of performance from postproduction effects usually presupposed a static camera and severe limitations on the degree and precision with which human and nonhuman characters could interact. Although the goal was believable visual synthesis, the available tools were hobbled by operating exclusively in the domain of images, not data.

In contrast, the hybrid spaces and bodies imagined several decades later for James Cameron's *Avatar* (2009) aggressively translated and synthesized lens-based and computer-generated images into a seamless unity. In *Avatar*, the large blue feline-humanoid characters of the Navi were realized through a process of translation by which motion-capture and facial-capture data were converted into digitally generated animations. The spaces of the film were likewise captured with a combination of live action and virtual cinematography. Each element of Cameron's synthetic frame was defined equally by its relation to data—that is, 3D spatial coordinates within the scene—and the live action images captured there. The cinematic space of these scenes is a fully instrumented and computable volume. Every element, including the live action camera, "knows" where it is in relation to every other. Actors respond to physical objects while computer-generated figures obey the computed physics of a congruent virtual environment. These include elements such as gravity, light, reflectance, momentum, collision, and friction, as well as actions or movements that have been programmed to take place at specific moments. In short, *Avatar*'s combined conversions of images into data, and data into images, represent an apotheosis of the synthetic mode.

Avatar has been widely analyzed, along with the technologies that made its hybrid world possible. The film also marked a watershed moment not only in Hollywood but in the games industry, where a similar combination of motion capture and virtual cinematography was used to create the cut scenes in *Resident Evil 4* (2009). My primary interest here is not the role of visual effects technology in either the film or games industries. Nonetheless, it is worth taking seriously the process by which movies and games become conceptual metaphors for real-world technologies. The hybrid production environments created for commercial products such as *Avatar* and *Resident Evil* offer a model for reconceiving physical spaces off-screen.

Like the hybrid physical-virtual production sets of an effects-driven Hollywood film, many everyday spaces are increasingly instrumented and computable. The built environments of modern cities are replete with sensors, vastly outnumbering surveillance cameras. Although less obtrusive and less frequently noted for their potential intrusions on privacy, sensors that monitor temperature, lighting, energy, and network traffic generate streams of data from which it is possible to derive information about occupants and their activities within an instrumented space. The data gathered by environmental sensors may also be correlated with images and data from devices that connect automatically to data networks. In other words, urban environments are coming to resemble the type of fully computational hybrid spaces we see in *Avatar*, where data and images are fully integrated, constituting a synthetic regime of knowledge and—in multiple senses of the word—control.[3]

Beyond the world of commercial entertainment, the technologies used for various media art projects also contribute to the evolving relationship between images and data. In 2016, the Ars Electronica Futurelab created an art project, sponsored by computer chip manufacturer Intel, called *Drone 100*. Reportedly setting a world record for the most drones aloft at one time, *Drone 100* orchestrated the movements of LED-equipped quadcopters at a German airfield to create a series of volumetric light sculptures against the night sky. In addition to producing a dazzling aerial spectacle accompanied by a live orchestra, the project's designers proposed that it represented a unique means of transforming the empty spaces of nature into addressable volumes of spatial pixels—or, in Futurelab parlance, "spaxels." The result of more than a year of R&D preparation—aptly supported by Intel because of the project's processor-intensive demands—the project was technically complex enough to warrant documentation that devotes more time to describing the mechanisms for controlling the drones than showing the display itself. Once aloft, the matrix of drones succeeded in forming a series of colorful, synchronized 3D formations, depicting figural shapes, such as a teakettle, and various geometric patterns and designs.

On one hand, this might seem like an instance of artist-technologists being enlisted to rehabilitate the public image of drones in an era when their weaponized siblings continue to kill human beings in military actions around the globe. On the other hand, one could argue that Futurelab's artists are engaging in a noble tradition of repurposing military technology in the interest of spectacle. In the documentation video, a project engineer explains, "As soon as you call them drones, people immediately think

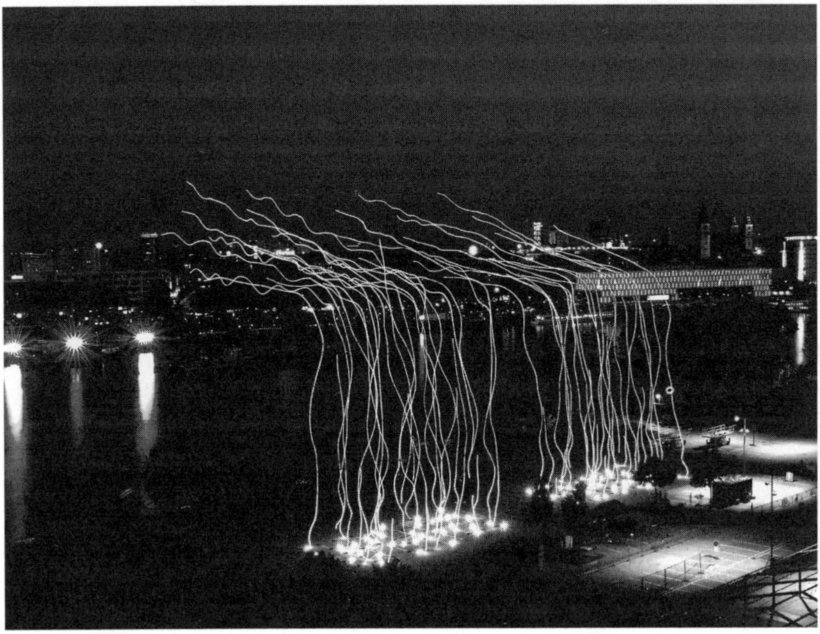

Figure 3.4
Intel sponsored Ars Electronica's Futurelab to choreograph large-scale 3D matrices of LED-equipped drones. *DRONE 100—Spaxels over Linz* (2016). Photo by Martin Hieslmair.

'dangerous' but it isn't really. It can be beautiful."[4] Another project participant waxes philosophical about the potential of large-scale drone matrices to become the future of 3D displays, in turn restoring curiosity and hope to humanity. But the drone's final formation really tells the story: in the video, the orchestra's final notes are replaced by an advertising jingle while the drones overhead strike a perfectly choreographed outline of the Intel logo.[5] Data space is also corporate space.

Futurelab's elaborately choreographed matrix of spaxels may be understood as an unusually literal interpretation of the idea of a point cloud manifested in physical space. More conventionally, point clouds are the visual representation of physical surfaces translated into an array of 3D coordinates for display or manipulation with software. Point clouds are both useful as an intermediate stage in 3D scanning or modeling and an aesthetic form in their own right. In 2009, designer James Frost and technology director Aaron Koblin famously created a "cameraless" music video to accompany the Radiohead song "House of Cards." Instead of cameras, performances were captured using LIDAR, a form of laser-based radar imaging developed for aerial cartography. Although common in modeling and topographical mapping software, in 2009 the point-cloud aesthetic was not yet a familiar effect in visual culture. Despite the effects-heavy landscape of music video, Frost and Koblin's lifelike animated point clouds succeeded in innovating a unique visual style. Describing his part in making the video, Koblin compared lens-based images with oil paint, while he likened LIDAR to sculpting with a putty knife. The process described by Koblin initially yields a grosser, less fine-grained image; to this he then introduced a variety of reflections, surface effects, and distortions of the data to create artificial glitches. Frost further proposed that the result was "a reflection of where we are as a society—everything is data."[6] "House of Cards" was released in conjunction with an open source version of the code used to make the video, and Koblin distributed a free Processing application, which invited users to remix the LIDAR data to create their own versions of the video.

Less than two years after "House of Cards," the Microsoft Kinect motion sensor was released in late 2010 as a supplement to its Xbox gaming system. As a consumer product, the Kinect was aimed at broadening Microsoft's still barely profitable niche in the console gaming market. The device was inexpensive and novel enough to sell eight million units in its first two months. The company followed up with a software developer's kit that encouraged users to hack the device's relatively simple mapping of spatial data into new forms of interface and image capture. One of the earliest and most innovative nongaming uses turned out to be the ability to generate point clouds based on distance data captured by the Kinect. For the first time, ordinary users, who had spent less than three hundred dollars for the device, could generate point-cloud models resembling the Radiohead video in a matter of minutes. The result was to render the point-cloud effect both technologically trivial and culturally familiar. How did a transformation of an essentially new mode of imaging happen so quickly? The answer lies in the indirect development of visual-digital literacy taking place across multiple domains of media culture at this time. These included experiments with spatial dynamics and paradoxes, such as in the *Portal* series of videogames (Valve 2007; 2011) and feature films such as *Avatar* (2009) and *Inception* (2010), among many others. Through continuing and varied exposure, hybrid and reconfigurable data-image spaces became increasingly established as an everyday part of the cultural vernacular.

Although it was colloquially known as a sensor, the Kinect unit, which was discontinued in 2016, functioned by capturing a combination of depth data and stereoscopic, lens-based pixel data. When both types of information are captured or combined, the result is termed "photogrammetry." Originally developed for topographical mapping, photogrammetry is now commonly used for high-end visual effects and in consumer systems for converting sequences of photographic images into 3D models. Although photogrammetry currently has limited utility for users who do not work with 3D animation, modeling, or game software, platforms such as Google's Project Tango, Microsoft's Hololens augmented-reality headset, and mobile devices equipped with multiple lenses and sensors for depth capture promise to make the synthesis of photographic and spatial information increasingly ubiquitous.[7]

Consumer electronics that shift previously specialized technologies into common usage help raise the computational literacy of participants in visual-digital culture. As synthetic imaging technologies proliferate, the result could veer toward an optimistic reconception of digital space or a troubling capitulation to the totalizing logic of immersion. Like motion capture, there is nothing about the internal logic of photogrammetry that destines its use for mimetic reproduction. While industrial applications continue to favor the seamless integration of data and images, the potentials for deliberate misuse, hacking, or alternative experimentation is equally afforded by the technology itself.

In 2008, Microsoft's Photosynth emerged precisely at the intersection of photography and geolocative data. Photosynth generates 3D models from photographs taken of objects from multiple angles. The resulting "synths" combine point-cloud data describing objects in space with photographic layers that are automatically registered to that model. The software then enables viewers to perform virtual camera moves to explore the resulting data models from multiple angles or to perform virtual dives through multiple layers of photographic imagery. Describing the software's origins, William Uricchio writes, "As we explore the new affordances of the algorithmic, and as our capacities to deploy them grow in tandem with the progression of Moore's Law we might also begin to reflect more critically about the differences in emerging modes of representation."[8] The stable

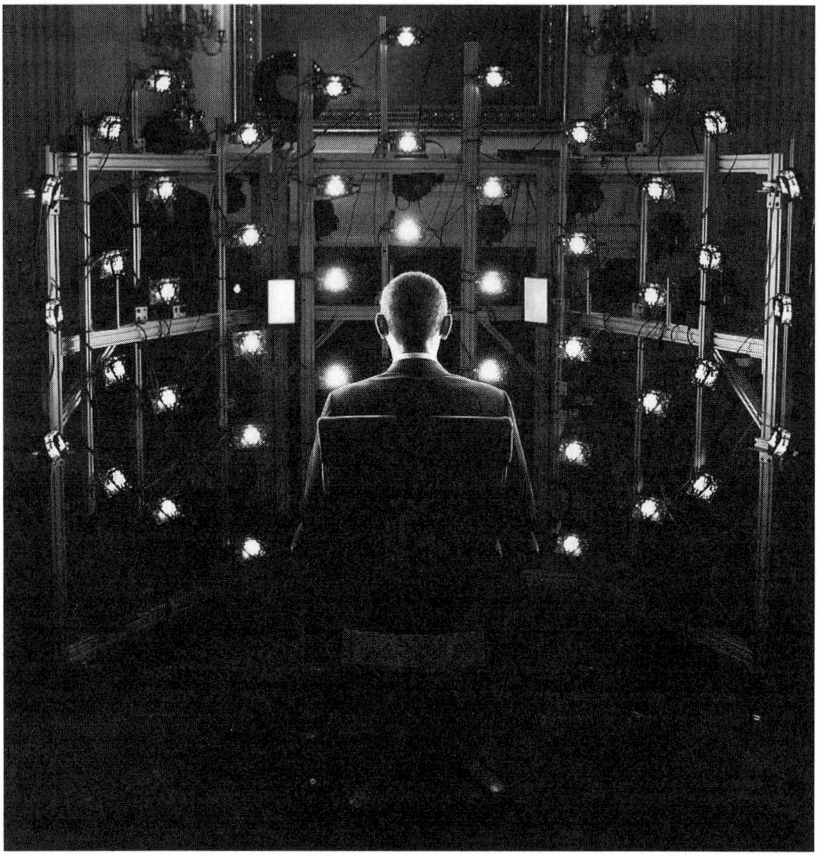

Figure 3.5
A multiperspectival hemispherical camera array used photogrammetry to capture the first 3D scan of a sitting U.S. president on June 9, 2014. Official White House Photo by Pete Souza.

relationship between viewer and viewed that is taken for granted in three-point perspective, exemplified for Uricchio by a Renaissance painting by Canaletto, is "fundamentally repositioned by the algorithmic regimes that now stand between subject and object."[9] Where photographic and cinematographic imaging—like the camera obscura before them—were implicated in the ideology of quattrocento representation, computational images may occupy multiple or indeterminate positions in space, decentering the eye in relation to its viewed environment. What is centered instead is the digital apparatus itself, to which the viewer may correctly be regarded as a kind of sentient appendage. For Uricchio, what intercedes is the algorithmic turn, which multiplies the possible number of viewpoints. In Photosynth the relation between image and viewer is provisionally determined by algorithms that generate a 3D point cloud on which to map a multiplicity of photos. Interestingly, later releases of Photosynth have made it more difficult to access the system's point-cloud view, suggesting that the point-cloud aesthetic, once crucial to visualizing the transformation of images into models, is no longer necessary.

Another revealing instance of the transition from human-centered to computational modeling is evident in the case of Google's SketchUp software. In 2004, Google acquired the digital mapping company Keyhole. Keyhole's software and image databases were incorporated into Google Earth, along with a gamelike "Flight Simulator," designed to retrain users' expectations of digital mapping software to be about visual exploration and discovery rather than mere location finding. Two years after the Keyhole acquisition, Google acquired SketchUp from @last Software. Promoted as "3D modeling for everyone," SketchUp offered a user-friendly environment for creating architectural forms that could be easily embedded in Google Earth. At the time, one of the limitations of Google Earth was the lack of basic topographical or architectural depth in the landscapes captured by Keyhole's satellite imaging system. Google sponsored several "Model Your Town" competitions using SketchUp in the hopes of crowdsourcing the monumental task of converting flat maps into 3D environments.[10] Although partially successful, especially in highly developed urban areas, human-centered modeling turned out to be too slow, inaccurate, and incomplete for Google's aspirations to "organize the world's information and make it universally accessible and useful."[11] In 2012, Google sold its SketchUp division to an architecture firm and expanded its focus on photogrammetry-based models, thus signaling a victory for computational over human modeling in the construction of large-scale 3D environments.

The digital literacy of the late 2000s that empowered Photosynth viewers to grasp the automated compositing of images, and Kinect users to create their own 3D point clouds, would not have been particularly useful for understanding previous generations of imaging technology. In commercial cinema, visual effects are considered most successful when they convey a desired meaning without drawing attention to the process by which they were created. This was not true for the "bullet-time" effect deployed in *The*

Matrix (1999). In this case, the effect of frozen movement erupting out of an action sequence was promoted as part of the film's marketing strategy. In light of the predominant use of digital effects in Hollywood, many viewers probably assumed that bullet time's simulation of camera movement within a 3D volume was a digitally generated effect. To highlight the novel process used,[12] Warner Brothers distributed an elaborately produced behind-the-scenes documentary in conjunction with the film's DVD release. Instead of digital effects, bullet time was achieved through a revival of the multiperspectival mode seen in Eadweard Muybridge's camera array, used for studying animal locomotion. Instead of creating a 3D model of the space depicted in a bullet-time sequence and performing a virtual camera move in postproduction, the frozen moment was captured in-camera by positioning an array of 35mm still cameras around the scene of action and triggering the camera shutters in precise synchronization.

In Dutch artist Michiel van Bakel's experimental short *Equestrian* (2003), the bullet-time effect was cleverly updated using live action video cameras from which van Bakel extracted, synchronized, and composited a combination of individual frames and motion sequences. *Equestrian* represents a conceptual investigation of the spatial and temporal transformations that are enabled by the multiperspectival mode. Instead of concealing the videographic apparatus by which its exquisite motion studies are carried out, van Bakel instead revels in them, evincing a nineteenth-century-style fascination with the cinematic apparatus. The video also cleverly invokes one of cinema's originary moments when Muybridge and Leland Stanford used serial photography to test whether all four of a horse's hooves are off the ground at the same time when running at a gallop. In *Equestrian*, when this moment arrives, the "camera" enters a radial bullet-time mode that pans around horse and rider in an ecstatic spiral. Like the rapid transformation of point clouds from high-tech innovation to amateur home gadget, once the conceptual door was opened on bullet time, its intervention in cinematic time and space was rapidly integrated into the cultural vernacular.

The Second Wireless Age

Before I dive into additional technologies of vision that have shaped relations between images and space in the twenty-first century, a digression into the early twentieth century is called for. Imagine the transition experienced by Americans at the end of the nineteenth century when wireless radio and telegraph transmission became part of the cultural vernacular. Telephone and telegraph wires, once a symbol of industrial progress, had become a blight on city skylines. Like air pollution and noise abatement, they were a sobering reminder of the environmental price paid for unfettered modernization. The seeming immateriality of wireless telegraphy reportedly stole the show from cinema at the 1900 Paris World's Fair. Just a few years after its introduction, cinema was readily legible as the clever recombination of familiar optical and mechanical technologies. The ethereal transmissions of wireless, on the other hand, seemed to fulfill Thomas Edison's vision of communicating not only across geographic distances but across spectral planes, providing connections to the afterlife, angels, demons, and all manner of spirits.[13]

Even if not always accompanied by the clearest scientific foundation, understanding the affordances of the electromagnetic (EM) spectrum—known as Herzian waves or "invisible light"—represented a major shift in the early twentieth century's technocultural imagination. Conceptually, it was a shorter step from radio to television broadcasting than from wired to wireless signal transmission. At stake was a contest not between data and images, but between physical and ethereal. Even the human body had to be conceptually reimagined as a conduit through which lower frequency waves of the EM spectrum easily passed. The growing ubiquity of commercial radio broadcasting in the decades that followed attested to the fact that we were all awash in electromagnetic signals wherever we went. Distinct from the damaging effects of ultraviolet, X-ray, and gamma radiation observed at the higher end of the spectrum, those at the lower end seemed comparatively benign. Radio and television waves brought news and entertainment into the domestic sphere, ostensibly knitting families closer together around an electronic hearth.

Whereas higher frequency X-rays and gamma rays caused cellular damage, lower ones brought a different kind of danger in the form of public persuasion. Radio suggested the potential for mass mobilization, manipulation, and possibly mind control, exemplified by Hitler's National Socialist Party, while television would later be characterized by its own FCC chair Newton Minow as a "vast wasteland" devoted to hoodwinking fools with low-brow entertainment, product advertising, and political demagoguery.[14]

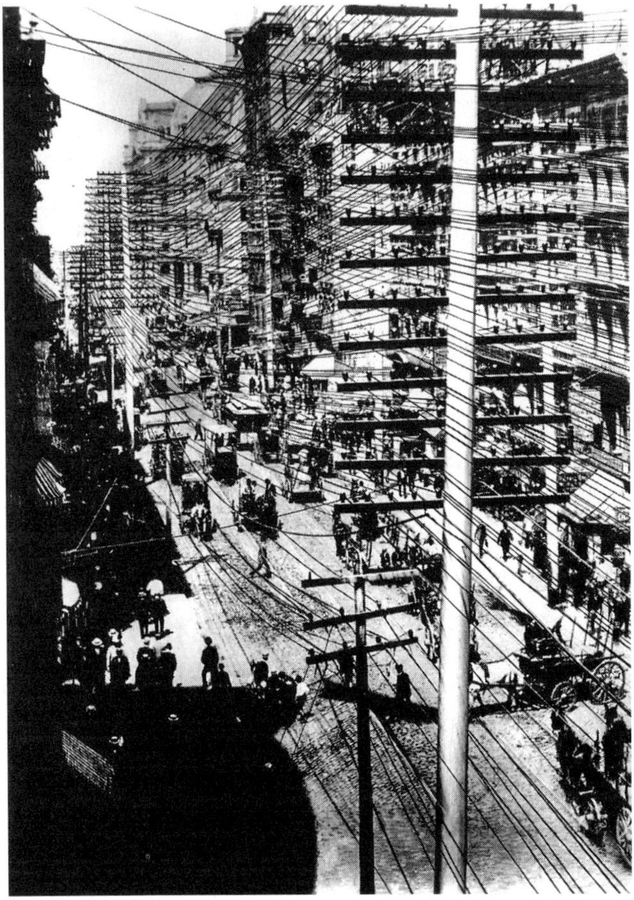

Figure 3.6
The congestion of telephone and telegraph wires in New York City (ca. 1903) highlights the contrasting infrastructures for wired and wireless communication.

The film industry barred no holds when airing its grievances against broadcast television. The postwar economic challenge TV posed may have threatened the film industry economically, but what really mattered, its large screen cautionary tales insisted, was TV's potential to turn viewers into the bumpkins, morons, and bloodthirsty corporate dupes seen in films such as *A Face in the Crowd* (1957), *Death Race 2000* (1975), *Network* (1976), *Being There* (1979), *Videodrome* (1983), *The Running Man* (1987), and many others.

Whatever ills might attend them, television and radio did not address viewers as individuals. Broadcasters could barely understand their audiences in terms of gross demographics, never mind who or where we were or what kind of attention we were paying to the screens and speakers around us. Except for a handful of demographic "types" who submitted to monitoring by the Nielsen Company, television viewers and radio listeners were anonymous and dislocated. It was up to individuals to manage the physical relationship between broadcast signals and the devices used to receive them: antennae could be repositioned or receiver dials fine-tuned to minimize signal disruption. Broadcast towers strategically positioned in urban centers, on nearby hilltops, or on downtown skyscrapers offered reminders of the physical infrastructures subtending invisible communication. Media broadcasting played by rules familiar from the experience of light and sound regarding geographic proximity and lines of sight.

The shift from wired to wireless communication that began at the end of the nineteenth century ironically reverted to the rewiring of communication networks in the latter part of the twentieth. In the 1980s, cable television reasserted the need for physical connection to a technical infrastructure to deliver home entertainment. Unlike broadcast media, connecting to this new network of copper cables brought monthly charges, but the promise of exponentially increased choices made it seem a small price to pay. So consumer-viewers were once again connected to a vast network from which they could receive images and sounds of marginally higher fidelity and more consistent quality. Individuals' actual viewing habits remained largely opaque to content providers, but the concept of narrowcasting at least acknowledged the potentials of targeting more specific slices of the oversize demographic categories imagined by Nielsen.

By the 1990s, most American households were wired into not one but three physical networks. It took a combination of phone, electrical, and television wires to provide the physical infrastructure for networked home computing. The geography of these physical networks was similar to that of broadcast media. Some places were too far away from a city center to be profitably reached by digital subscriber lines (DSL) or TV cables, a constraint that was economic, not technological. In the early twentieth century, it took an act of Congress to bring wires for telephones and electricity to rural areas—FDR's New Deal program for rural electrification in the 1930s sought to knit all but the most remote parts of the nation together via wires stretching back to nodes on a central grid. We quickly became dependent on this infrastructure for the basics of life, and it compliantly expanded to include the ability to talk on the phone and receive advertisements for consumer goods. Access to communication networks is sometimes described as a "right," and federal agencies are tasked with regulating it as such, on balance with the industry profits that depend on it.

Obviously, this coarse mapping of the comings and goings of wires and wirelessness in communications technologies is historically reductive, but my hope is that it will resonate on a metaphorical level. As data-intensive consumer technologies such as "virtual reality" once again tether humans to their computers with thick cables, the dreams of wireless image transmission, light field capture, and holographic display continue to lurk enticingly just over the horizon. The point is that the physicality of technical infrastructures is dynamic and recursive, not linear or progressive. Our perceptions of space continue to be shaped by the media through which we experience it and the physical effects it has on our bodies.

We are now in the midst of a second wireless age. We inhabit spaces that are mapped and penetrated by overlapping frequencies of the electromagnetic spectrum through increasingly ubiquitous Wi-Fi and cellular data signals. The generation that once confused the difference between cellular and cordless phones has largely passed, but the functional difference between Wi-Fi and cellular data is beginning to seem arbitrary and pedantic to generations who have grown up immersed in both. What's the difference, as long as we are willing to continue making monthly payments for both? We also pay with time spent enduring precisely tailored advertising and, most of all, with our consent to being tracked and quantified as a means to generate *more* precisely tailored advertising.

In the twenty-first century, we find ourselves once again inhabiting a world of invisible light. Spaces both public and private that are *not* awash in wireless data seem like an impoverished exception rather than the rule. Such places are negatively marked as "without service" rather than the other way around. The ubiquity of the cellular network is still an issue, judging by the exaggerated claims made by providers about what percentage of the nation they serve. In practice, we know that mobile phone signals come and go willy-nilly and we tolerate lousy connections and unintelligible conversations at a level that would have been unthinkable in the wired age. This, too, is part of the price we pay for inhabiting a wireless future just a little bit ahead of schedule.

Here's the difference. Our radios never phoned home to tell broadcasters which freeway we were driving on or what station we were listening to. TV sets never watched us in our homes. Television and radio were, in a word, stupid. In 1995, Nicholas Negroponte declared television sets to be "perhaps the dumbest appliance in our home."[15] The problem was not just TV sets' lack of microprocessors, as Negroponte argued—a void that has been long since filled. It was instead the entire medium's basis on one-way transmission and reception. Systems of broadcast media in general knew nothing about where, how, or by whom they were being used, and high-priced advertisements were bought and sold largely as an article of faith. We, in turn, treated these devices like the one-trick reception objects they were; if a signal was weak or an image obscured by static, a punitive slap to the side of the box just might fix it. If our identity was wrapped up in the broadcast content of television and radio, it was because of our affection for individual shows, stations, or characters, not some imagined cybernetic merging with the device itself. We may, on occasion, smash, stomp, burn, blend, drop, or microwave an outdated cell phone to post the results on YouTube, but we do not administer the same kind of corporal punishment to digital devices that once made perfect sense to unleash on TV sets.

Before the digital era, science-fiction writers might have imagined the transmission of evil spirits or voices of the dead via broadcast media, but they did not imagine human consciousness being uploaded to broadcast networks. Even *Max Headroom*'s star reporter Edison Carter had to be translated into a glitchy, low-polygon computer model before he could begin traversing the cable networks and hard drives of Network 23. Innumerable cyberpunk fantasies have since imagined both the utopian and the dystopian sides of being uploaded to the network, leaving all the inconveniences of physical bodies behind while risking psychosis and alienation from essential humanness.

Cyberpunk fiction of the 1980s imagined digital space as a lawless frontier hospitable only to anarchist nomads and skilled mobile privateers. Travel within those worlds was nearly instantaneous, taking advantage of the light speed at which electrical impulses move through computer processors. Ideally, such travel did not involve physical bodies at all, but required only a consciousness that was free to traverse digital networks to their limits. If humans—or at least sci-fi writers—of the 1980s imagined making their escape into an artificial environment, what exactly were they escaping *from*? The societies inhabited by William Gibson's antiheroes were only slightly more dystopian than those of Ronald Reagan's millenarian Cold War America. The world seemed closer to apocalypse in those days, but it's hard not to look around and feel that things now are so very much worse. The end, though possibly less imminent, is certainly more inevitable. Perhaps this is why the desire for an alternative to lived reality went from psychedelic fantasy to multibillion-dollar investment opportunity practically overnight.

Virtual Realities

A fundamental divide remains between lens-based images and computer-generated ones, both in technology and in the cultures that surround their production contexts. In the world of 3D games, images are not images but volumes, meaning they are encoded with depth information that affords players the experience of moving around a space and viewing surfaces from different angles. The grid of pixels that appears on-screen at any given time is merely a series of rendered planes computed from the code that defines the volume. By contrast, in the world of motion pictures, the images on screen—regardless of their origins—are neither more nor less than the two-dimensional pixel grids they appear to be. Practitioners of the art of cinematography, of course, might justifiably object to having the images they create characterized as "flat." Much of the artistry of the field is precisely devoted to eliciting the *illusion* of depth and the complexities of space through lighting, framing, contrast, and movement. Simply characterizing such images as "flat" by comparison to a 3D volume is misleading, even if empirically true.

This apparent conflict is exemplary of the transition we find ourselves in now, when lens-based and computer-generated imagery compete for dominance in industries devoted to film, TV, and digital games. The real difference, though, is not about surface and depth; it's about self-knowledge. In other words, the problem is not that cinematic and televisual images are flat; it's that they're dumb. Lens-based images are produced by capturing the light that falls on a planar surface inside a camera. In film emulsion, this is enabled by light-sensitive silver nitrate crystals; in video, it is typically some kind of CCD image sensor, which captures a grid of pixels expressing a combination of chroma and luminance. The cameras that capture these images may be able to reproduce the visual qualities of the reflective surfaces and the light sources in front of them, but they do not know what they are or where they came from. When viewed, these images don't know what to do if they are rotated in space or how to behave if another object bumps into them; they don't inherit qualities from adjacent images or pass on behaviors to others of their kind. These are paradigms of object-oriented programming and procedurally generated environments that are now sufficiently ubiquitous to stand as the computational counterpoint to the successive delivery of 2D frames as the basis of motion pictures.

The images that come from camera lenses can be manipulated by humans after the fact, to be sure—varied in size, color, opacity, or tonal value; they can be creatively multiplied, filtered, captioned, combined with other images, or coupled with sound; they can be made to move, morph, or tween—but for the most part, such images remain slaves of human intention. Increasingly, even consumer-grade digital cameras capture various forms of metadata along with reflected light: information such as what devices are in use; what exposure duration, lens aperture, and compression settings are active; the theoretical ISO sensitivity of the capture chip; what file format is generated; and the date and time of its capture. If equipped with GPS, the photos may be tagged with coordinates that locate the position and orientation of the camera on the surface of the earth. Future generations of these devices will routinely capture additional data describing not just the location of the camera, but the dimensional and physical characteristics of the objects photographed and more.

The idea that cameras should capture volumetric metadata has long been active in the film industry to facilitate the integration of live action footage with computer-generated images, effects, and characters. It is an unfortunate artifact of our present historical moment that we continue to ascribe a hierarchy to these two different forms of (primary) image data and (secondary) metadata. To speak of "image data" is no longer a non sequitur, but information such as latitude/longitude coordinates and volumetric data remain "meta," denoting a second-tier system of signification that is useful only in relation to external systems of meaning—the Cartesian coordinates describing locations on the earth's surface, for example. We are rapidly approaching a moment, however, when we would do well to dissolve the distinction between data and metadata. Through the integration of these forms of data, contemporary images are truly constituted; the fundamental relationship between image data and metadata should be recognized as one of interdetermination, not hierarchy.

In contrast, the computer-generated, object-oriented spaces created by 3D engines have never observed this distinction. Volumetric spaces may be displayed on 2D screens, but this does not represent the full extent of their "self-knowledge." The contents of image volumes are sometimes described with clumsy neologisms such as "voxels" or "spaxels," invented to indicate the conjunction of "pixels" with "volumes" or "spaces." Although they may be graphically complex, they can also be economical in terms of required bandwidth. Sometimes generated mathematically, rather than as points in a fixed matrix, they can be programmed to act, respond, or evolve in dynamic ways. Importantly, they can also learn from or adopt the actions, responses, and behaviors of others like them. The logical extension of these systems terminates in what we now call "artificial intelligence," but good arguments can be made that the likely forward trajectory of intelligent systems is not as an "other" to human intelligence but as an extension, hybridization, or transformation of it.[16]

Among the parallax modes described in this book's introduction, contemporary visual-digital culture is preoccupied by the translational and synthetic modes. This is not surprising. A long tradition in art history and media studies—to say nothing of the entertainment industries—privileges the Gesamtkunstwerk, or total artwork, capable of achieving a seamless integration of all other audio and visual media. This is at the heart of the translational and synthetic dynamics of data and images. At the time of this writing, nothing is so aggressively and unselfconsciously recycling the promise of the total artwork than the reburgeoning field of virtual reality.

What we have learned to call "virtual reality" in the mid-2010s has lost much of its original focus on the idea of "telepresence," that is, the perception of occupying a different space than where a person's physical body is located. This concept was important enough for artist-engineers Scott Fisher and Brenda Laurel to name their startup company Telepresence Research in 1991.[17] Among the most important VR researchers of the 1980s, Fisher also notably resisted using the term "virtual reality" in favor of the location-oriented phrase "virtual environment." Although Fisher's term offered the benefit of greater precision, it apparently held less marketing appeal than VR, which was attributed to the consummate entrepreneur of the field, Jaron Lanier. In a 1989 article titled "Virtual Environments," Fisher avoids the term VR entirely and only brushes against it in his final sentence as an implicit challenge to those who conceived it in a singular monolithic form. He writes, "The possibilities of virtual realities, it appears, are as limitless as the possibilities of reality. It provides a human interface that disappears—a doorway to other worlds."[18]

In retrospect, we might imagine how the first-generation hype cycle for VR of the eighties and nineties might have evolved differently if the transformation proposed by the technology had been the sensation of remote presence within an artificial environment rather than the virtualization of reality itself. Ultimately, it was the idea that technology—like the psychedelic drugs of 1960s counterculture[19]—could be used to transform reality that contributed to the public disillusionment with the real-world capabilities of first-generation VR.

In a report summarizing the work of his lab at NASA Ames Research Center in Mountain View, California, Fisher stated the goals of the VIEW (Virtual Environment Workstation) project in modest terms: "Complex operational tasks such as control of remotely operated robotic devices and vehicles that require a sufficient quantity and quality of sensory feedback to approximate actual presence at the task site."[20] Despite the tactical understatement of Fisher's project description, the system he outlined in 1985 included numerous features still not implemented in the current generation of commercial VR. In a diagram created by Fisher's lab to describe the aspirations of its "Virtual Interface Environment," the operator is not required to occupy a fixed position in space and is not constrained to a single form of user input. Full-body tracking allowed mobility within a predefined space, and interaction with the computer took place through a combination of voice, gesture, and tactile input, with dimensional sound, stereoscopic vision, and haptic feedback in response.

The expectation of being able to move one's body and interact manually with the environment was taken for granted in the VIEW system. Fisher, in fact, described the goal of the project as "matching visual display technology as closely as possible to human cognitive and sensory capabilities in order to better represent 'direct experience.'"[21] Whatever technological

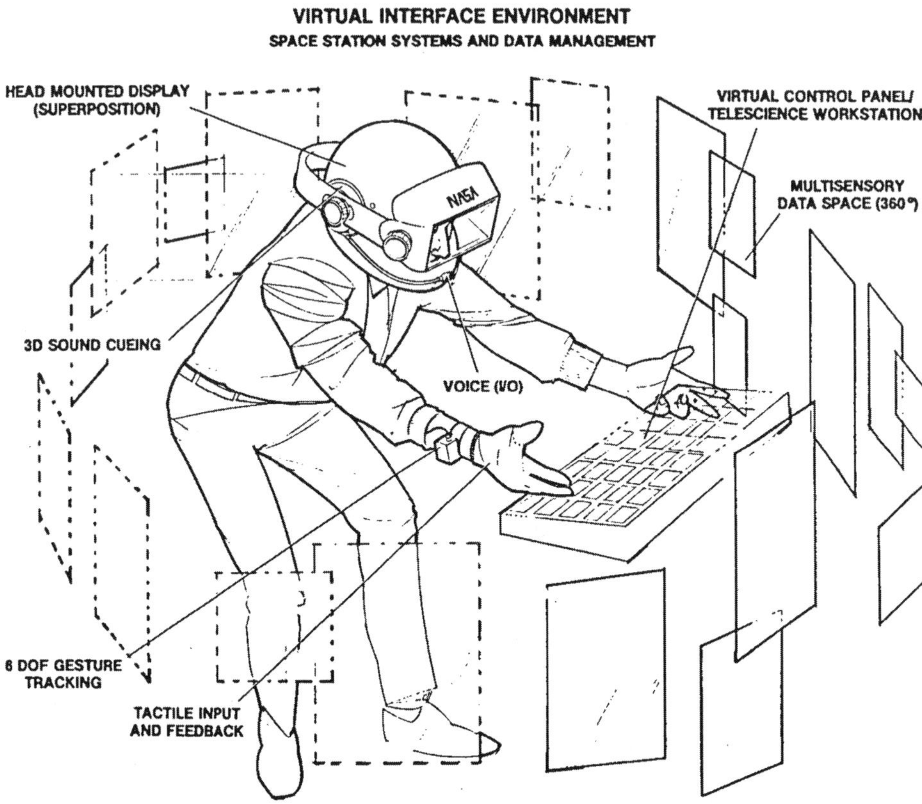

Figure 3.7
A 1985 diagram of Scott Fisher's VIEW system for NASA Ames Research Center maximized affordances for user interface, feedback, and mobility.

limitations might have beset the first generation of virtual environments, Fisher's vision did not compromise on what the experience of telepresence should look and feel like. His report continues, "With full body tracking capability, it would also be possible for users to be represented in this space by life-size virtual representations of themselves in whatever form they choose—a kind of electronic persona."[22] In 1985, the VIEW system thus anticipated multiuser applications and interactions with customizable 3D avatars, which are only beginning to enter the conversation about VR three decades later.

VR 2.0

It is remarkable how repetitive the tropes of virtual reality are when depicted in commercial cinema of the past three decades. And while the technologies driving VR have evolved, the promise of their actualization and the ways they interface with human bodies have remained relatively static within the cinematic imaginary, especially the possibility of experiencing illicit, dangerous, or forbidden actions through a first-person camera point of view. Another way of looking at this is that VR provides an excuse for Hollywood cinema to indulge in a renewed frenzy of the visible, while distancing itself from the technology that is diegetically responsible for presenting such content to audiences.

A survey of movies and TV since the early 1980s reveals the overinscription of standard tropes of VR—complex technological apparatuses that deliver "safe" (but never completely safe!) experiences that are denied in everyday life—particularly extremes of violence, sexual pleasure, and other kinds of exoticism. The apotheosis of these depictions in American entertainment came in 1995, with the release of more than a half-dozen feature films and TV shows within a few months. Among these, the films *Strange Days* and *Virtuosity*, and the Fox TV series *VR5*, all constructed a vision of virtual reality that was indistinguishable from real life—that is, complete sensory and emotional immersion in worlds that are entirely generated by a computer.

In 1995, if TV and movies were to be believed, consumer-grade VR was poised to deliver virtual experiences that were indistinguishable from the real world. Ellen Strain termed this phenomenon of the cinematic imaginary "virtual virtual reality," noting that Hollywood fantasies of VR led to impossibly high expectations in comparison with existing technologies of the 1990s.[23] By the time Nintendo released the Virtual Boy game system in 1995, consumers, who paid nearly two hundred dollars for the device, experienced not complete sensory immersion but a monochromatic display with red LED images 224 pixels wide. Nintendo went on to release a limited number of cartridges based on existing Game Boy titles such as *Mario Tennis, Bowling, Golf, Baseball, Pinball, Boxing,* and *Tetris*. Unfortunately, the device never lived up to Nintendo's promise of "totally immersing players into their own private universe," and the Virtual Boy was discontinued the following year.[24] The previous year, Sega had discontinued development of its own head-mounted VR system, issuing a tongue-in-cheek public explanation that the virtual reality experience had been so realistic that test subjects were injuring themselves by attempting to walk into virtual spaces while wearing the visor.

As a skirmish in the war between data and images, we can consider this an instance of the movie industry launching a highly effective attack against the gaming industry, successfully raising consumer expectations to the level of big-budget Hollywood feature films. The demise of VR in the decade that followed is well documented, as R&D funding for VR labs at Atari and NASA Ames were eclipsed by the frenzy of speculative investment in the internet, leading to the dotcom bubble and collapse just five years later. To overstate the case only slightly, "virtual virtual reality" on TV and in movies *killed* real virtual reality as a medium for commercial entertainment in the mid-1990s.

Regardless of whether the current generation of head-mounted displays succeeds as a delivery mechanism for home entertainment—and perhaps one day a reconceived sense of telepresence—the manufacturers of these devices will have achieved the goal sought by numerous villains and sociopaths of Hollywood VR narratives: to make the transition from an immaterial existence in "cyberspace" to the physical world. As owner of Oculus VR, for example, Facebook is no longer limited to tracking social media users' actions online but has direct access to user data collected through networked hardware devices installed in the homes and integrated into the leisure time of millions of consumers.[25]

Jonathan Crary's argument that it is nearly impossible to imagine a history of nineteenth-century technologies of vision that is not in service to the history of cinema resonates when looking back on the history of VR. We don't know what new "cinema" might be looming at the end of the current century or decade, waiting to impose a narrative that swallows all deviant alternatives. Admittedly, the symmetry of VR's cinematic apotheosis in 1995—cinema's centennial, after all!—makes it seem a promising heir. Certainly VR's many bright-eyed evangelists of the 2010s would love to occupy such a role, but the historiographical logic of a lone technological platform dominating an entire century's entertainment no longer holds the allure it once did. Narratives of convergence notwithstanding, signs point to various entertainment technologies and genres affording mediated experiences that are multiple and contradictory rather than singular and unifying.

The cluster of media technologies and delivery apparatuses associated with "VR" in the mid-2010s includes projects and platforms that are quite diverse in terms of technical affordances, content genres, and intended user/viewer experiences. Even in the early years of this second wave of commercial development, the singular term "virtual reality" is clearly inadequate to account for such a range of practices, suggesting that its primary utility lies—as it always has—in the domain of marketing.[26] Content created for these platforms comprise a full spectrum of forms, including spherical live action video, and computer-generated environments that may be entirely prerendered, procedurally interactive, or a combination of both. Various forms of interactivity are also deployed, ranging from head, hand, eye, or body tracking to custom controllers, gestural controls, raycasting, and biofeedback. The rapid evolution of technological development and content creation in this space makes it a bad time to anchor too much of my analysis to specific platforms or projects. Nonetheless, the model established in this book's opening chapter, taking account of the parallax relationship between data and images, continues to serve the analysis of these forms so long as mimesis and computability remain in a state of tension.

A return to early cinema theory's description of the relationship between camera and viewer illuminates some of the ways "VR" differs from conventional media production. The notion of the profilmic, or that which appears in front of the camera lens, is already troubled by the spherical display capabilities of the head-mounted display (HMD). A viewer who allows suspension of awareness of the wires and bulky apparatus affixed to her head may momentarily experience the dissolution of the filmic apparatus itself. This is an issue of some curiosity when viewing a visual field captured with a 360-degree camera array. The question of the camera's point of view is answered simply—it is congruent with the centered position of the viewing subject. But in a computer-generated environment, the concept of an afilmic reality existing "behind the camera" makes no sense. An immobility even more radical than that of early sound cinema, when cameras were often confined to soundproof enclosures, constrains the experience of many consumer VR systems. Viewers are not psychologically sutured into profilmic events as they were according to the principles of cinematic montage, but are confined by virtual props or boundaries. This explains the effectiveness of narratives set in confined spaces that are narratively justified, such as occupying a solitary confinement cell (*6×9*, 2016), riding an elevator to the top of a massive ice wall (*Ascend the Wall* 2014), or being trapped in a car where a bomb needs to be defused (*I Expect You to Die*, 2016). These experiences may be as physically disembodying as they are perceptually immersive, but the former is generally suppressed in the interests of celebrating the latter.

Thinking clearly about the platforms and technologies that are currently gathered under the "VR" marketing umbrella requires noting significant differences between these various forms. Live action video viewed from a single position with a fixed time base represents a very different experience than a procedurally generated 3D game environment with position tracking and an indefinite time base. If not for the shared requirement of mounting displays on users' heads, it would make little sense to equivocate among such divergent media forms and genres. Along with this slippage, the cultural discourse surrounding virtual reality repeatedly attempts to claim a selective history for the medium. Given the technology's previous failure to meet market projections in the 1990s, it is not surprising that this period would be downplayed or forgotten, along with other technologies of immersion that achieved limited success despite significant investments, such as stereoscopic 3D (S3D) and three-strip Cinemascope. In a selective rereading of past moments of technological emergence, VR's illusion of presence is compared with painful frequency to the image of viewers running screaming from the theater upon seeing the Lumière brothers' *Arrival of a Train at La Ciotat* (1895), long after cinema history abandoned this origin myth as an apocryphal—and frankly rather silly—fantasy.

The genealogy of VR is correctly linked to Ivan Sutherland's invention of a head-mounted display known as the "Ultimate Display" in 1968, but that engages only one aspect of the medium's already fetishized display apparatus. Other experiments with interactive and immersive media in the 1960s laid an equally important conceptual foundation, such as Thomas Furness's Super Cockpit flight simulator, created for the U.S. Air Force, or Morton Heilig's Sensorama S3D cinema viewer, which featured motion and aroma effects. We should also be suspicious of any history of VR that focuses solely on HMD delivery, ignoring rear projection-based displays such as the Cave automatic virtual environment (CAVE), developed by Thomas DeFanti, Daniel Sandin, and Carolina Cruz-Neira in the early 1990s. With their exponentially greater spatial and technical requirements, including multiple projectors, processors, and rear projection screens, CAVEs may be less readily digestible by a consumer market besotted with the idea of in-home VR, but compelling research continues in virtual projection environments, such as Hiroo Iwata's Large Space facility at Tsukuba University. At 25 meters wide, 15 meters deep, and 7.8 meters high, and requiring twelve stereoscopic 3D projectors—to say nothing of its counter-weighted, traveling pulley apparatus, which enables visitors to "fly" around the space—it is currently the largest fully instrumented virtual environment in the world, modeling a very different vision of embodied—and natively multiuser—virtual environments.

But it's really not my job to correct this historical record—nor to decry the collusion of ignorance and instrumentality required to rewrite VR history as starting with Palmer Luckey's Kickstarter campaign for the Oculus Rift. Still, we should not underestimate the importance of the cultural and historical discourse by which emerging media are framed. My real concern is to articulate a relationship between explicitly mediated technologies of vision and their impact on our ways of experiencing, knowing, and acting on the world. The instrumented synthetic environments of virtual and augmented reality offer revealing crucibles for thinking about the increasingly instrumented world of everyday life. If we think about issues of perceptual hybridity and instrumentation only when writing about or wearing head-mounted displays, then we fail to ask broader and more important questions about contemporary technoculture.

Let me say this another way: just as the technologies of rail travel and cinema transformed the visual culture of industrialization in the nineteenth century, immersive media technologies are reshaping the experience of urban environments in the twenty-first. At stake in this investigation is understanding how the contested relationship between data and images is shaping our perceptions and agency within the culture of neoliberalism. The explicitly instrumented confines of a motion-tracking volume represent a microcosm of the instrumented urban spaces of a city, populated by cell phone towers, Wi-Fi signals, license plate readers, satellite transmissions, near field communications, Bluetooth, RFID, and various forms of environmental sensor, area, and mesh networks. All of these technologies contribute to the enframing of human behaviors as readily trackable and computable quantities. The enlistment of everyday actions—shopping, searching, texting, dating, traveling, sharing—within the operational logic of these systems deflects awareness from how these technologies, in aggregate, constitute a radical threat to personal liberty.

All of this leads to a sobering proposition. The more we believe our physical world to be interchangeable with the digital one, and the more physical space begins to resemble instrumented volumes, the less resistant we will become to the logics of neoliberalism in converting everyday activities into marketable commodities. Likewise, the more readily we accept digital traces as surrogates for human actions and desires, the less conscious we will become of concrete human struggles for justice and equality, class conflict, and challenges to authority. Data space, in the end, is controllable space.

Virtual Bodies

The renewed discourse of virtual reality in the 2010s remains anchored to the phenomenological and perceptual resemblance between the "virtual" and "real" worlds. Today's computational systems can and do allow for experiences that approximate certain aspects of perceptual realism, but claims that "VR" therefore inherently functions as an "empathy machine" ring naïve and anachronistic. In December 2014, producer Chris Milk and director Spike Jonze captured a spherical documentary video of the Millions March that took place in New York City. A reported sixty thousand protestors took part in the march, focusing attention on racial profiling and violence by police toward African Americans. Handheld video footage captured while moving among the marchers resulted in a series of continuous-take sequences that allowed viewers to experience a powerful semblance of the sights and sounds of the march.

In a *TechCrunch* article titled "The Empathy Machine," Milk is quoted saying, "Journalism is about bringing people to an event or something that they couldn't attend. ... Here the viewer feels transported to that place. There's no translation. They're witnessing it first-hand themselves." Indeed, the 360-degree video allows viewers to observe the action in any direction; it also features a field reporter from Vice News who solicits interviews with march participants, culminating in an impassioned monologue by a young African American woman, who summarizes the motivations and urgency of the event. In conclusion Milk notes, "There's something about this format that touches a more emotional place in the mind and the soul."[27] I would argue that the frequently paired presumptions that journalism is "about" empathy and that VR is "about" immersion do a disservice to both. Immersion and empathy are factors that may be mobilized by *any* medium, but they are far from the best or only way to think about what is possible when working in formats with complex and varied technical affordances, such as stereoscopic 3D, navigable virtual environments, and spherical video.

The previous generation of artistic experiments with VR in the 1990s modeled some compelling alternatives to a focus on empathy. These included the somatic interfaces and generative abstractions of artist Char Davies, such as her *Osmose* (1995) and *Ephèmeré* (1998). Davies's work was predicated on the refusal of photorealism and conventionalized interfaces as primary means of achieving virtual experience. Instead, Davies's work promoted emotional and personal reflection achieved through a deliberate distancing of the data/images parallax, immersing users in entirely non-lens-based visual environments.[28] In stark contrast to the disembodied virtuality of William Gibson's vision of cyberspace expressed in "Burning Chrome" (1982) and *Neuromancer* (1984), Davies insisted on a deeply embodied mode of engagement with virtual spaces. Her wearable harness included sensors for breathing, balance, and biofeedback, which served as user input for audiovisual stimuli. The digitally generated environments through which her users were invited to move offered abstractions of the natural world, fractal images floating in a weightless void, suggestive of outer space or an undersea world. Whereas Gibson's conception of uploading human consciousness to a network represented the ultimate in pure, disembodied cognitive experience, Davies was interested in embedding the body and all its sensations in an unmistakably artificial, computational environment. Variations in breathing and physical movement directly affected the user's position in the perceived virtual space, which was thereby rendered at once more tangible and more ethereal.

Davies's work remains exemplary for its explorations of visual abstraction and attention to the central role of bodily sensations for producing an immersive experience. Contemporary VR producer Nonny de la Peña, working in an entirely different mode she dubs "immersive journalism," shares with Davies an interest in embodied interaction. Each of de la Peña's works to date invites participants to serve as witnesses to a historical—often violent or traumatic—event. These experiences range from witnessing an exploding bomb (*Project Syria*) to viewing a brutal beating by the border patrol (*Use of Force*). Like Milk, de la Peña describes her work in terms of its capacity to produce emotional or empathetic responses to real-world events. Interestingly, rather than emphasizing the visual verisimilitude of live action video or high-end computer graphics, de la Peña's work bases its "truth claim" instead on documentary audio, which is accompanied by comparatively low-res 3D models and animated figures. Rather than serving as a distraction, the low-fidelity visuals create a productive tension among what we see, what we hear, and what we think we know as a result.

De la Peña frequently cites the desire among viewers to participate more directly in the virtual events unfolding around them. She notes attempts ranging from cradling the head of a seizure victim to whipping out a real-world cell phone to call for help in *Hunger in Los Angeles*. This may be understood in relation to Hal Foster's "traumatic realism," in which an artwork simultaneously elevates and denies the lived experience of the original trauma.[29] Written two decades ago, in the wake of VR's first-generation boom-and-bust, Foster's *The Return of the Real* poses questions about artistic and theoretical responses to a culture marked by trauma that seem no less relevant today. "Why this fascination with trauma, this envy of abjection today?" Foster asks, suggesting that the dismal state of the world, marked by poverty, disease, and broken public trust, had resulted in an artistic focus on trauma and abjection as points of resistance to the fantasy of capitalist consumerism.[30] Foster continues, "For many in contemporary culture, truth resides in the traumatic or abject subject, in the diseased or damaged body. To be sure, this body is the evidentiary basis of important witnessings to truth, of necessary testimonials against power."[31] At a moment characterized by electoral disempowerment and waning connection between media and truth, perhaps the immediacy and intensity of de la Peña's virtual traumas offer momentary reconnection to something recognizable as "the real."

To be clear, all of de la Peña's immersive journalism projects thus far are entirely prerendered and replayed on a fixed timeline; they are not procedurally responsive to a user's actions. When fully installed with a position-tracking apparatus, viewers are empowered to walk around inside a simulated environment and to focus on specific aspects of the action, but this is the limit of one's capacity to interact with events as they unfold. Viewers cannot alter the course of an immersive journalism event any more than they could a live TV news report. Thus, the experiences created by de la Peña and others uniquely elevate the experience of witnessing over that of agency by delivering a cathartic sense of having "been there."

In *Project Syria* (2014), for example, viewers find themselves on a street in Aleppo where a young girl sings a song before a bomb explodes. De la Peña describes the project's goal as to "make you feel like you're witness to an actual event. You're not separated by a television or a screen. You actually feel like you're there."[32] The effacement of the medium's display apparatus and focus on viewers' emotional response aligns de la Peña's conception of immersive journalism with a tradition of social issue documentary, in which photographic or cinematographic representation aims to catalyze changes in social policy. What else is at stake in this type of witnessing? Respect for the dead and victims of violence, certainly. In de la Peña's case, it is also about the desire to incite personal action, as is made clear by the PSA-style calls to action that punctuate many of her projects. This desire may also be understood in the context of de la Peña's history as a print journalist for *Newsweek* and as the director of the feature-length documentary film *Unconstitutional: The War on Our Civil Liberties* (2004), about the Bush administration's erosion of civil rights under the PATRIOT Act.

Prior to creating her first work of immersive journalism, de la Peña collaborated with Peggy Weil to create *Gone Gitmo* (2009), an interactive simulation of the U.S. government's Guantanamo Bay prison in Cuba, created as a sim in the multiuser virtual environment Second Life. Developed with support from the MacArthur Foundation and the Bay Area Video Coalition, *Gone Gitmo* allowed Second Life users to navigate a 3D model of Guantanamo, a space that was notoriously inaccessible to journalists. Visitors to the sim could explore the grounds of the prison, where embedded video interviews excerpted from *Unconstitutional* testified to the dehumanizing experience of imprisonment in the camp. The space was also scripted to create a noninteractive simulation of being immobilized, hooded, and transported to a jail cell, where the user's avatar was placed in a stress position, an early experiment with the emotional identification that could be activated between user and avatar. *Gone Gitmo* was thus a supplemental data-image space populated by 3D models, computer-generated avatars, documentary audio/video, and a uniquely embodied experience that momentarily deprived users of the agency one ordinarily expects from a virtual environment. Each of these elements has persisted in various forms in de la Peña's subsequent work.

The transition from *Gone Gitmo* to a fully articulated vision of immersive journalism took place in the Mixed Reality (MxR) lab, directed by Mark Bolas, at USC's Institute for Creative Technologies (ICT), where de la Peña was enrolled as a doctoral student in the School of Cinematic Arts. ICT was founded in the wake of the terror attacks on the World Trade Center and the Pentagon in 2001 as a research and development space at the intersection of entertainment, engineering, and the military. The explicit charge for the facility was to combine the technologies of Silicon Valley with the visual vocabulary of Hollywood to assist in the Bush administration's war on terror. Bolas, who had been a researcher in Scott Fisher's NASA Ames lab, founded MxR on the same open source ethos modeled at Ames a generation earlier.[33] Virtually all software developed in the lab was freely distributed to encourage development in all areas of immersive and stereoscopic research, and the lab was known for welcoming short- and long-term projects by students and researchers regardless of institutional affiliation.

In this context de la Peña created her first "VR" project, working with a team of MxR lab technicians, including Thai Phan and Palmer Luckey. The result was a prototype head-mounted display, with a custom apparatus for position tracking that allowed viewers to walk around a predefined 3D space. The project *Hunger in Los Angeles* premiered at the Sundance Film Festival's New Frontier exhibit in January 2012. Development of the prototype HMD—minus the position tracking—was continued by Luckey with funding from a Kickstarter campaign later in 2012. This led to the creation of the Oculus company, which was acquired by Facebook for $1.6 billion in March 2014.

Although primary funding for MxR came from military contracts through ICT, Bolas created a fertile space for experimentation across a spectrum that included military, consumer, and artistic applications. Among the most notable of these was the FOV2GO, a low-cost foam-core stereoscopic VR viewer designed by Bolas to work with software written by Perry Hoberman. The FOV2GO was distributed free at a Google TechRaking event in April 2012, then later at the SIGGRAPH conference in Los Angeles in conjunction with a simulation of NASA's Curiosity Rover landing on Mars. Promoted as "Virtual reality in an envelope," FOV2GO was accompanied by open source software for generating stereoscopic imagery on an iPhone, along with templates and instructions for assembling a home DIY viewer. A similar design obviously modeled on the FOV2GO was later marketed as Google Cardboard and famously distributed as NYT VR to one million subscribers of the *New York Times* in November 2015.

Drawing on the parallax models outlined in this book's introduction, a revealing juxtaposition may be found in two projects featured at the Sundance Film Festival's New Frontier showcase in 2015 and 2016: Vincent Morriset's *Way to Go* (2015) and Nonny de la Peña, Brad Lichtenstein, and Jeff Fitzsimmons's *Across the Line* (2016). These two projects offer a stark contrast in tone and content. Whereas *Across the Line* is a somber work of politicized journalism confronting head-on the issue of health clinic protests by antiabortion activists, *Way to Go* is as light as a feather, inviting users to go on a reflective walk in the forest. What makes these two projects exemplary for my purposes is how they deploy differing strategies for handling the disjunction between data and images in "VR."

In *Way to Go*, the lines between live action, digital effects, and animation are deliberately blurred, but not through the creation of synthetic illusions. At the beginning of the project, viewers are introduced to a simply animated humanoid figure with a cube-shaped head that is inserted into an otherwise live action, spherical video landscape. The white cube-head figure invites us to follow it down a path that runs through a forest alongside a river, and whichever direction we look, it is there, walking, running, or flying to match pace with the progress of the video. The timeline is unidirectional, allowing viewers to walk, run, jump, fly, or stop, but not to reverse direction on the path. The path through the forest is designated by what looks like a white chalk line sprinkled on the dirt to indicate where we should walk. When the animated figure jumps and then lands back on the path, the "chalk" gives itself away as a digital overlay, subtly registering impact with a glowing cloud that sends an electric pulse along the path ahead. The relative crudeness of the line-drawn animation contrasts starkly with the videographic detail of the surrounding landscape, but even the live action imagery turns out to have a surreal side.

A familiar trope of spherical video capture is the presence of a camera operator, usually located in the center of the lower hemisphere of the video. In *Way to Go*, the operator appears as a figure dressed all in black, with an oversized black cube-shaped head resembling that of the animated figure. As we travel through the forest, we come across a few more of these figures, first an animated cube-head that is black instead of white, then a nearly identical live action figure dressed in black, who lurks behind trees,

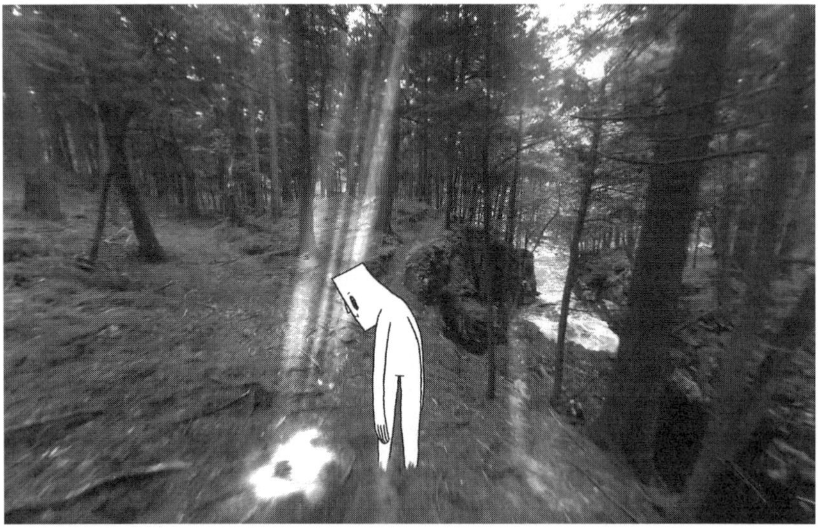

Figure 3.8
Conventions of live action video, 2D animation, and computer-generated environments create hybrid data-image spaces in *Way to Go* (2014). Image courtesy of Vincent Morisset, http://a-way-to-go.com, National Film Board of Canada (2015).

traveling alongside us for a while before being joined by two other black cube-heads. Sometime later, all of them disappear back into the forest. After a while, users may stop trying to distinguish between live action and animation. In fact, the live action figures are equipped with line-drawn faces and eyes that blink, even when the video frame is frozen, providing just enough movement to suggest a timeless space rather than a broken diegesis. Although the cube-head figures never interact with us directly, their dual presence as animation and live action creates an uncanny feeling of presence in a space that is neither entirely physical, nor animated, nor digitally generated.

A few minutes into the walk, the landscape makes a transition from the lens-based forest to a digitally generated one. The animated figure remains the same, as does the chalk line on the ground, but looking down, we notice that the camera operator has disappeared, a sure sign that we have entered digital space. Farther down the path, the landscape grows increasingly dreamlike; the sky glows in multiple colors, and trees give way to a field of grass. Still the ability to move remains constrained to the marked path—our movement is, in videogame parlance, "on-rails"—an effect that was previously attributable to the constraints of live action video. In this sense, *Way to Go* trains viewers how to behave in a world that is a hybrid of data and images, initially porting affordances from animation and procedural media into a space that otherwise appears to be live action; then later borrowing the constraints of lens-based media to shape viewers' behavior within an entirely digitally generated space. Eventually, the animated figure reaches a clearing and a provisional end title appears, followed by an invitation to either continue exploring the digitally generated world, which no longer has any spatial or temporal constraints, or to return to our real-life adventure, in which we may begin to differently perceive freedoms and constraints—both digital and physical—that we were not aware of before.

An opposite effect results from the strict bifurcation between the lens-based and computer-generated segments composing *Across the Line*. Whereas *Way to Go* melds data and images, *Across the Line* separates them. The project opens with two live action segments. First is an improvised reenactment that takes place in a health clinic, where a young woman talks to her doctor about an unwanted pregnancy and the difficulty of accessing the clinic because of protestors. We then move to a flashback scene in which the woman, who is playing herself based on real-world experiences, arrives at the clinic by car and has to pass by a group of antiabortion protestors who try to talk her out of entering the clinic. Interestingly, this scene is staged as a hybrid of documentary and fiction, with actors in the car confronting real protestors outside a Planned Parenthood clinic. Although staged, the interaction between the women in the car and the protestors captured by a 360-degree camera rig positioned in the back seat of the car are unscripted. Following this segment, the viewpoint shifts from third-person to first-person perspective, and depending on the installation, viewers gain the ability to look or walk around while a line of computer-animated figures unleash a verbal assault in the direction of the viewer. The voices in this sequence are documentary audio selected from real-world abortion protests around the country, intended to viscerally simulate the kind of hostility and derision to which women are routinely subjected when attempting to enter reproductive health clinics.

While the live action sequences establish a narrative context, the experiential center of the project lies in this final hybrid experience of documentary audio and computer-generated animation. Because viewers are

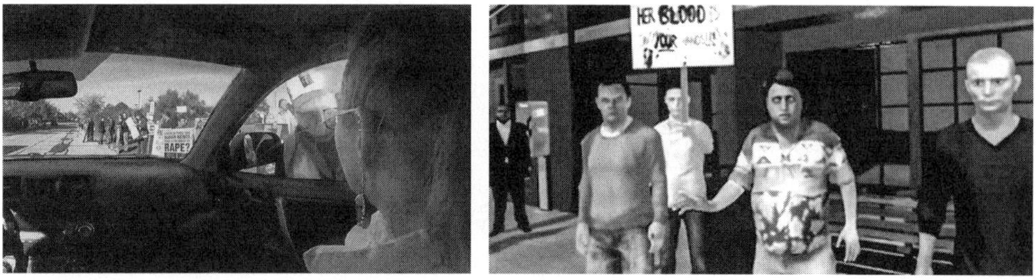

Figure 3.9
Videographic images and computer animation construct adjacent but unblended virtual experiences in Nonny de la Peña, Brad Lichtenstein, and Jeff Fitzsimmons's *Across the Line* (2016). Image courtesy of Nonny de la Peña.

no longer shielded from the action on-screen by the actor around whom the narrative is framed, the experience for many viewers is an emotional response, coupled with intellectual recognition of the intensity of these everyday experiences for women in the real world. For this strategy to succeed, the veracity of the audio recordings of antichoice protestors, which functions in support of comparatively low-fidelity digital reenactments, is all important. In this regard, immersive journalism belongs to a well-established tradition within documentary media that accepts once taboo strategies of reenactment and animation as legitimate forms of expression. De la Peña's work is a rarity, however, in giving priority to audio rather than video in a medium that otherwise uniquely privileges the visual register.

Although she continues to focus on timely issues and events, de la Peña remains devoted to a process that aspires to forensic accuracy. In the case of the Trayvon Martin project, *One Dark Night* (2015), for example, the 3D environment where the murder takes place was modeled on real-world architectural plans; others, such as *Project Syria* and *Hunger in Los Angeles,* were based on photographic documents of their actual urban environments; and in *Use of Force,* the primary real-world witness of the events had her face and body 3D scanned and motion captured for the purposes of a virtual reenactment. In this sense, de la Peña's work occupies a liminal space that neither simply fetishizes verisimilitude and indexicality nor totally eschews their value. These multiple ambiguities are precisely how immersive journalism makes a notable contribution to the evolving ethics and aesthetics of VR witnessing. As decades of documentary theory have demonstrated, the most interesting representations of reality are those that are irreducible to empirical verifiability or viewer empathy.

Sam Gregory, program director of the activist media organization Witness, argues that the ability to elicit viewer empathy—frequently touted by VR creators and promoters—is not the most important factor when producing media for social change. Rather than focus on the potential for producing *empathy toward victims* of injustice, Gregory advocates strategies that produce *empathy with activists* on the front lines of social struggle. The problem, according to Gregory, is that empathy does not elicit action as effectively as feelings of compassion and solidarity. If the goal is to find "better ways to engage people and to translate that engagement into meaningful actions," Gregory argues, then the real potential for "VR" lies not in creating a stronger sense of presence for viewers but a stronger sense of copresence among activists—a feeling that their work is recognized and supported by a broader public.[34] Rather than walk *in* another person's shoes, Gregory argues, it is more effective to position subjects in "VR" as walking *next to* a person who is engaged in direct action. In an important reversal of the logic of "VR" as a tool for social impact, Gregory emphasizes the potential influence of the technology on the front-line activist rather than on the viewer at home.

In either event, the purported sense of empathy experienced by "VR" viewers is largely ineffective for informing them about historical contexts and structural inequality, which are necessary to pose an effective critique of power. Gregory sees potential in what he terms "co-presence for good," defining it as "using the sense of being together with other people in a remote environment to drive concrete, productive actions, engagement and understanding across barriers of geography, exclusion and time zones."[35] The often fetishized agency bestowed on users of interactive media does nothing to support the agency of people—often those depicted in a documentary context—to more effectively engage in real-world struggles. Among practitioners of immersive documentary, then, principles of user-centric or player-centric design, imported from interactive media and games, may not be the most effective ways to think about user-experience design in "VR." Instead, given the powerful potentials of immersive media to engage issues of social consequence, it is important for creators to develop sophisticated models for tracking and understanding the relationship between perceptual experiences and concrete action in the world.

The contemporary resurgence of critical attention to virtual reality has much to learn from previous generations of theory devoted to issues of representation in fields such as documentary and ethnographic filmmaking, visual anthropology, and journalism. I would further argue that immersive media is uniquely positioned for experimentation with a negotiated relationship between the representational affordances of lens-based and computational media. While much contemporary "VR" production is dominated by the translational or synthetic modes—synthesis of live action imagery into navigable screen spaces; translation of motion-capture data into lifelike animations, and so on—there is great potential in exploring points of strategic discontinuity and friction.

One remarkable example of such discontinuity is found in Arnaud Colinart, Amaury La Burthe, Peter Middleton, and James Spinney's *Notes on Blindness: Into Darkness* (2016), which offers an illuminating instance of the negotiated mode. The project comprises a series of four short VR experiences based on two films—both sharing the *Notes on Blindness* title—about theologian John M. Hull's experience of losing his sight. Both the films and VR experiences are based on a collection of audiocassette tape recordings made by Hull in the 1980s as he reflected on the ways his life was changing. In the films, Hull's life and family are primarily depicted through dramatized reenactments and occasional interviews, accompanied by Hull's original voiceover recordings. In the "VR" iteration, the user experience is designed to approximate a visceral rendering of Hull's personal sensory experience. Selected threads within Hull's voluminous recordings are accompanied by a densely layered, positional soundscape that offers an audio interpretation of the scenarios described (a day at the park, a rain storm) and an ethereal, highly stylized visual experience.

At the beginning of *Into Darkness,* the user peers into a dark landscape in which only a digitally generated flow of white particles resembling a river is visible. As sighted viewers' eyes adjust to the darkness, shapes start to form as if conjured by desire or memory, mixed with the words of Hull's gentle, reflective narration. "Rain brings out the contours of what's around you," he says. "It introduces a continuous blanket of differentiated and spatialized sound, uninterrupted, which fills the whole of the audible environment." With this observation, Hull articulates a way of thinking about his world that may be compared with the concept of instrumented volumes in digital space. Objects that are "invisible" to him become acoustically perceivable

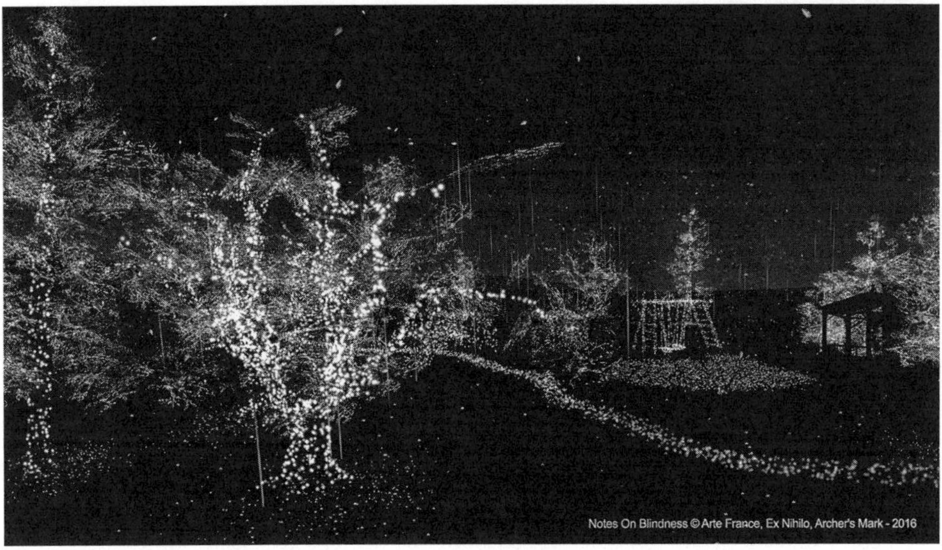

Figure 3.10
The use of minimal visuals in *Notes on Blindness: Into Darkness* (2016) shifts viewers' sensory experience to a dimensional soundscape. Image courtesy of Arnaud Colinart, Ex Nihilo—Archer's Mark—Art France.

when struck by rain drops, just as bodies in space might be recognized by infrared sensors or a LIDAR scan. Whereas digital instrumentation registers interruptions in the electromagnetic field, Hull's audible environment is a volume that is perceptible only when saturated with falling raindrops.

In the realm of cinema, the nearest thing to the combined audiovisual experience of *Into Darkness* is Derek Jarman's final feature film, *Blue* (1993). In *Blue,* Jarman narrates a series of memories and reflections, interlaced with audio reenactments related to his struggle against AIDS-related afflictions, including blindness. Completed just a few months before the filmmaker's death, *Blue* remains an extraordinarily moving spectator experience—because of not only the richness of the audio landscape, but also the increasingly rare visual experience of film projection. Viewers who are able to watch *Blue* on film—as opposed to projection from a digital source—grow uniquely attuned to the granularity of the film emulsion that is ordinarily obscured by conventions of cinematic representation: characters, objects, locations, actions, *story*. In *Blue,* all these things are conjured in the minds of viewers in dialogue with the irregularities of the film frames and light passing through the gate and lens of the projector.

The world of *Into Darkness* is black, not blue. From the darkness, numerous traces of visual experience emerge, especially features of the landscape that have sound associated with them: trees, a stream, a wind chime, a swing set. Some of the figures are entirely digitally generated, while the majority appear to have originated as live action video or motion-capture data. These figures were then isolated from their surroundings and spatially composited into a virtual environment, created using the Unity game engine. These enigmatic figures appear as vague moving shapes that appear to be lighted from within by flickers of bluish light. Appropriately, these unmistakably live action figures—children playing, ducks swimming, boats passing, a person reading a newspaper on a park bench—resist being fully resolved in the eye of the viewer. Ultimately these figures—and even their color palette—resemble nothing so much as the LIDAR-based point-cloud data seen in Radiohead's "House of Cards" music video. This creates an abstract but recognizable variation on a 360-degree environment that could have been captured or composited with entirely lens-based images. At one point, viewers are reminded of the environment's constructed nature by a clap of thunder followed by a shockwave of light that inverts the usual priority of visual experience. The thunder comes first, then a wave of intense white light surges toward the viewer, more like the visualization of a soundwave than a lightning flash experienced by a sighted person in the real world.

In another segment titled "The Wind in the Trees," Hull's voice intones, "In the blind person's appreciation of weather, wind takes the place of sun." In this segment, a gamelike mechanic is introduced that invites viewers to project gusts of wind into the landscape. With a simple touch of the controller, blue-white arrowhead-shaped geometric figures flock and swarm in the direction of the user's gaze, causing the blue crystals of tree leaves to flicker and glow as if absorbing energy from the wind or reflecting the light of the arrowheads. Although hardly the stuff of first-person shooter games, this mechanic is distinctly that of a world that is procedurally aware and receptive to user input in a way that far exceeds the affordances of typical lens-based environments. Together, the combination of Hull's understated but emotionally wrenching narration, an extraordinarily rich sound environment, and a precisely motivated visual minimalism makes *Into Darkness* a richly evocative instance of the negotiated mode. Rather than an obstacle to be overcome, the functional divide between image and data offered by *Into Darkness* becomes a creative variable enabling a unique conjunction of visual and narrative experience.

Movies and Maps

As televised sports, visual effects, and virtual reality offer crucibles to explore various negotiations of the relationship between data and images, another vector of investigation is panoramic imaging systems that combine physical with virtual immersion. Many artists, including Jeffrey Shaw and Luc Courchesne, have investigated this intersection, but none so tenaciously as American media artist Michael Naimark. At first glance, Naimark's enticing celebrations of large-scale immersive imaging—cylindrical, panoramic, navigable, comprehensive—suggest a vexing contradiction to my critique of the desire for totalization. Yet, when viewed in a historical context that accounts for both content and form, this work represents a crucial moment in the ongoing dialogue between art and industry; politics and entertainment; new and old. Naimark has worked with and without the direct support of industry and institutions. In addition to his longtime residency at Paul Allen's Interval Research lab in the 1990s, Naimark helped shape research efforts at Atari, Apple, and Lucasfilm, and in 2015, he was installed as the first resident artist at Google VR. A veteran of the Architecture Machine Group (predecessor to the Media Lab) at MIT, Naimark has also taught at NYU's Interactive Telecommunications Program and USC's Interactive Media Division, among others, and is known as a tireless advocate for lens-based imaging in a world increasingly dominated by the logic and technologies of CGI.

While a graduate researcher at MIT, Naimark was part of the team, led by Andrew Lippman, that created the *Aspen Movie Map* (1978). Using newly available laserdisc technology, and with funding from DARPA, the *Aspen Movie Map* presented a navigable photographic record of Aspen, Colorado, captured from a panoramic four-camera array mounted on top of a vehicle and triggered at precisely measured intervals. Using a touchscreen display to index a database of thousands of images, the project allowed users to navigate every street in the town. The key word in this description, as in much of Naimark's subsequent work, is "every." Naimark himself has written and lectured widely on the technical and conceptual similarities between the *Aspen Movie Map* and Google's Street View—launched nearly four decades later—which expands the desire for navigable photographic documentation to every street in every country of the world. The *Aspen Movie Map* was additionally prescient in its integration of historical images, 3D architectural models, and minidocumentaries (by Ricky Leacock, exploring the interiors of selected buildings in the city), all foreshadowing features that would be implemented by Google decades later.

Although Naimark was only one among a large and distinguished team responsible for the project, he remained uniquely devoted to the concept of "place representation" by means of photographic mapping. In the decades that followed, Naimark created *Paris VideoPlan* (1986), a navigable walking map of selected routes through the Madeleine district of Paris, as well as *El Camino,* part of the Apple Multimedia Lab's Visual Almanac, which presented a split-screen juxtaposition of images captured in 1975 by the California State Department of Transportation and images of the same mile-long stretch of Silicon Valley's El Camino Real rephotographed in 1987. He also returned to the concept of photographic mapping with *See Banff!* (1993–94), documenting more than one hundred paths through the wilderness around Canada's Banff Centre, using a jogging stroller outfitted with a stereoscopic 16mm single-frame camera. This, too, may be thought of as a predecessor to a Google project, Trekker, which launched some twenty years later.

Interestingly, Naimark and his collaborator Gilles Tassé presented the *See Banff!* image sequences to viewers by means of a replica of an Edison kinetoscope, activating a historiographical dimension that goes beyond technophilia and places Naimark among a select group that Erkki Huhtamo has dubbed "artist archaeologists."[36] But the project that most closely adheres to the original vision of the *Aspen Movie Map* is Naimark's *Karlsruhe Moviemap* (1991). Commissioned by the media arts organization ZKM in Karlsruhe, Germany, *Karlsruhe Moviemap* allows users to navigate every passenger train line in the city—more than 100 kilometers' worth—using an interface based on the control panel of a Karlsruhe city tram.[37]

Within the critical frame of this book, I must question the role of "movie maps" in illuminating the relationship between data and images. Unlike fundamentally synthetic technologies, such as motion capture and photogrammetry, movie maps function in a domain better characterized as supplemental. Spatial data—whether literally anchored to GPS-based latitude/longitude coordinates, or cartographically defined locations—is a subsidiary system for indexing and sequencing a database of conventional photographic documents. The primary visual experience of these images is not fundamentally transformed by its delivery through a computational system. In fact, the visual experience of Naimark's *Karlsruhe* project, with its physical props resembling a tram driver's station, resembles nothing so much as the early twentieth-century train-ride simulations popularized by Hale's Tours.

In both the *Aspen* and *Karlsruhe* projects, the central viewing space is augmented by a screen presenting an overhead view of the user's virtual location within the "playable" space of the map. This convention, which we now associate with videogames, served a practical purpose, steering users away from the boundaries of the project and displaying an otherwise unacknowledged aspect of the technological apparatus underpinning it. Writing about Naimark's mapping projects, Huhtamo notes, "Works like these combine two different perceptual approaches, overview and immersion. The former gives the user a 'bird's eye view,' the latter a 'labyrinth perspective,' which presents a restricted visual field, hiding most of the potential scenes 'behind the corner.'"[38] Naimark's inclusion of first-person and overhead views complicates assumptions about sensory immersion as the primary goal of the work, suggesting the value of multiple viewpoints and a relationship between data and images that ultimately merges the synthetic and supplemental modes.

Another project central to this discussion is Naimark's *Golden Gate Flyover,* which was commissioned by the San Francisco Exploratorium in 1987 and remained on display for more than two decades. The project enabled viewers to explore every segment in a ten-square-mile region surrounding the area's most famous landmark, the Golden Gate Bridge. The project's extended public installation attests to a continuing fascination with simulated flyover experiences, even as technological innovations such as satellite imaging and consumer-grade remote aerial photography have converted many of the project's original features into everyday experiences. Indeed, Naimark's project, which employs a trackball interface familiar from arcade-based videogames of the 1980s, predated the publicly available satellite imaging of Google Earth by nearly two decades. Part of the allure of the project is Naimark's image-capture method, which was customized for the experience of a comparatively low-altitude flyover. This method of imaging the earth's surface has a very different feeling than satellite images, which allow for no perception of parallax in the landscape. *Golden Gate Flyover* used an early version of GPS-based geolocation to array the images, captured using a gyroscopically stabilized helicopter camera, again more than a decade before these technologies entered the consumer marketplace. The real key to the experience lay precisely in *not* attempting to document or simulate a real-world experience. "The goal," according to Naimark, "was not to re-create a helicopter ride as much as to create a hyper-real experience, something impossible to experience in the physical world."[39] As a great deal of today's immersive development emphasizes principles of realistic simulation, it is worth considering models that instead explore potentials that are uniquely afforded by nonphysical spaces.

In the *Golden Gate* project, and throughout his oeuvre, Naimark has pushed the limitations of data-processing speed and storage defined by the

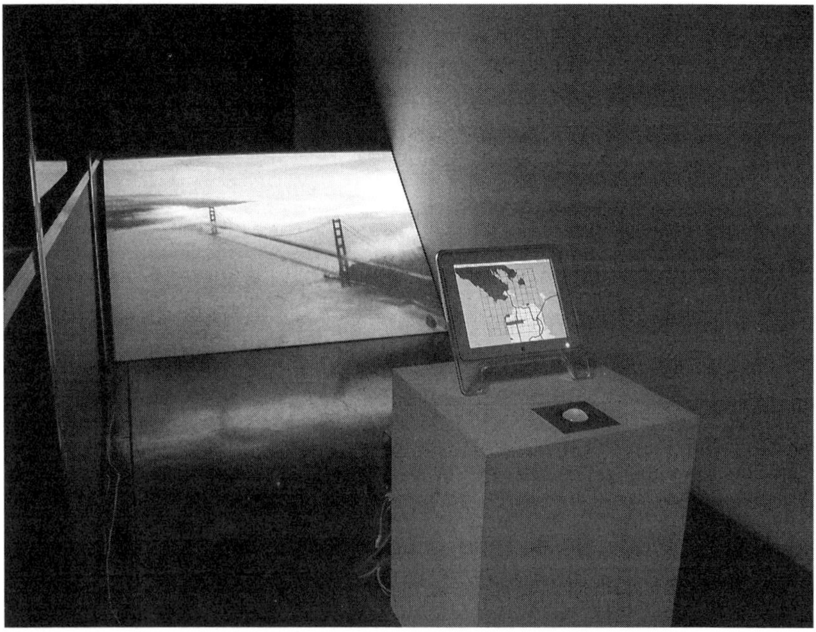

Figure 3.11
A videogame arcade-style trackball interface combined with an overhead map and first-person camera views create a hyperreal flyover of the San Francisco Bay in Michael Naimark's *Golden Gate Flyover* (1987). Image courtesy of Michael Naimark.

technological moment he is working in. But this explains only part of the longevity and prescience of his work. The fascination of *Golden Gate Flyover,* like the accelerated speeds with which one may traverse the train lines in *Karlsruhe Movie Map,* lies in the ability to simulate a heightened sense of mastery over space and time. This in turn creates a *resonance* with everyday experience, not its *reproduction.* User-viewers are invited to occupy a remote, sensorial space, but one where basic rules of perception and experience are altered, where space and time do not so much present technical challenges as provide creative variables. This agenda also offers a promising alternative to that of many contemporary "VR" experiences predicated on relocating viewers in artificial spaces with no necessary connection to their surrounding world.

Promises of totality, infinitude, and ubiquity may be inscribed in the deep structures of digital technology, but they need not be its primary purpose. The desire for total information systems has taken many forms, whether it involves creating a global map, a complete database, an encompassing archive, a global social network, a pervasive game world, a comprehensive

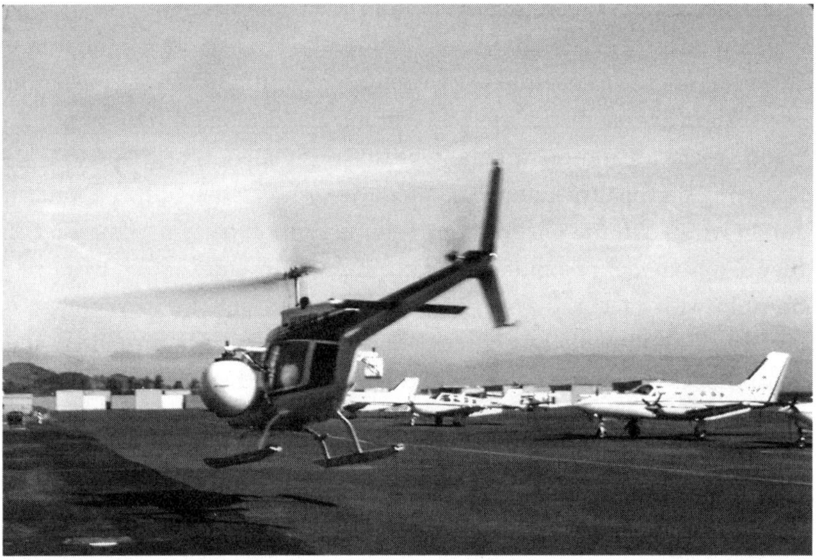

Figure 3.12
A helicopter with gyroscopically stabilized camera rig captured images and satellite data, covering a ten-by-ten-mile grid, for *Golden Gate Flyover* (1987). Image courtesy of Michael Naimark.

shopping venue, or an unlimited media-sharing service. Nonetheless, digital media (as I have argued elsewhere with regard to digital *history*)[40] is as well suited to creating recombinant chaos as it is to imposing totalizing order. I'll say it again: we should be suspicious of any argument that claims for digital media a natural or inevitable tendency to minimize chaos and constrain disorder. We would also do well to challenge broad or transhistorical attributions of ideological value associated with specific media forms. It is axiomatic to this book that technology is always inscribed with cultural values, just as culture is shaped by the technologies produced within it. Decoding ideological implications is among our central tasks, but such decodings are most convincing when historically situated and specific.

In *The Democratic Surround: Multimedia and American Liberalism from World War II to the Psychedelic Sixties* (2013), Fred Turner assembles an erudite and broad-ranging historical account of the evolution of multiscreen technology during the decades following World War II. He also analyzes the tension between eccentric multiplicity and totalizing order, paying particular attention to the political valences associated with each in their historical moments. Turner's book offers a succinct account of the deliberate shift among media producers away from the technologies of mass media, which were associated with fascism and totalitarianism during the thirties and forties, and toward the use of multiscreen, multichannel media displays. Turner explains this shift as a deliberate ideological response to the grand spectacles and one-to-many broadcasting models of the Nazi Party. Reflecting on the disparate media producers who eschewed this approach, Turner writes, "In the one-to-many communication pattern of mass media they saw a model of political dictatorship. ... To enter into such a relationship with media, many worried, was to rehearse the psychology of fascism."[41] Multimedia was posed as the antidote to such centralized, univocal modes of political speech, and while it may be tempting to form a linkage between the multimedia of the 1940s and the apparent freedoms of today's digital networks, Turner asserts that they are simply regulated by a different institutional logic, "in terms that have been set for us by distant experts: programmers, media executives, government regulators."[42] Turner also notes the near total lack of diversity among the authors of this movement, composed almost exclusively of white men, who unselfconsciously articulated a utopian vision of radical equality and democratic participation.

The antifascist ethos of the Bauhaus was also rigorously opposed to mass unifying spectacles and broadcast media generally. László Moholy-Nagy, Herbert Bayer, and others advocated the strategic use of multiple screens, fragmented images, and the possibility of individual choices for viewers as antidotes to the totalizing impulse. Viewers who were allowed to choose where to stand in relation to the screens and to circulate among an array of artworks in a sequence of their own choosing were thought to be participating in a democratic inoculation against the uniformity of fascism. According to Turner, however, the first Bauhaus exhibition at MoMA in 1937 was regarded by many visitors as chaotic and disorganized, suggesting that, despite their immersion in a democratic society, Americans were not up to the task demanded by the Bauhaus ideal.

In the immediate postwar years, the ideology of choice and multiplicity that flourished in art and technology came into revealing conflict with the desire to transform the logic of multiple screens into the logic of multiple *contiguous* screens. While Hollywood was developing technologies to synchronize film projectors into ultrawide screen-projection environments, such as Cinemascope and Cinerama, artists began to experiment with large-screen immersive spectacles that also retained some avowedly "democratic" characteristics. Charles and Ray Eames's multiscreen projection *Glimpses of America* (1959), for the American Exhibition in Moscow, encapsulated many of these tensions, presenting a combination of still and moving images on seven noncontiguous screens suspended on the interior walls of a dome designed by Buckminster Fuller. In the Eames's display, the images were choreographed in tight, formal patterns that sometimes approximated a continuous image or, through patterns and resonances, created a perceptually unified whole. Given the context of Cold War nationalism (the same exhibition space would famously serve as the backdrop for the Nixon/Khrushchev "kitchen debate"), the Eames's exhibition design cannot help but read as a deliberate refraction of cultural ideology.[43]

Viewed in terms relevant to this project, the 1959 Moscow Fair enacted an evocative separation of the domains of data and images at a moment when the ability of computers to process visual information was still severely limited. The exhibition featured an IBM RAMAC computer that was displayed in the entryway to the U.S. pavilion. Before entering the pavilion, Soviet citizens were invited to ask the computer questions about America; the computer's responses were as much about promoting a nationalist narrative as displaying the technological virtuosity of IBM, and as it turned out, it was also about aggregating the questions asked by Soviet citizens to better understand their attitudes toward the United States. While this data gathering and exchange was confined to the entryway, the interior of the dome was devoted to an intensely visual display, centered on the Eames's multichannel projections visualizing America's geography, industry, and people. Although it is no longer naïvely conceived as an antidote to fascism, today's multiplication of screens in the form of mobile phone and tablet devices invokes an additional Cold War–era freedom that was implicitly articulated in the exhibition of 1959: the freedom to consume.

Many of these Cold War tensions remained unresolved at the time of the Montreal Expo of 1967, where large-scale projection was among the highlights of the artistic exhibitions. Expo '67 also marked the first public performance of interactive cinema, *The Kinoautomat,* by Raduz Cincera for the Czech pavilion. Cincera's experiment presented audiences with a collective mode of "democratic" viewing that echoed the choice and multiplicity offered by the Eames's multiscreen displays. Taken as a metaphor for tensions within the ruling Czech Communist Party of the late 1960s, Cincera's *Kinoautomat* resonated with party secretary Alexander Dubček's "Prague Spring" democratic reforms, which precipitated a Soviet invasion in 1968 and the return to an authoritarian mode of centralized government less than a year after the closing of Expo '67. The utopian aspirations of the *Kinoautomat* were likewise crushed by the monolith of linear narrative feature films as the dominant mode of theatrical entertainment for decades to come.

In spite of a national ideology that hinged on personal freedom and choice, American cinema viewers were subjected to orchestrated efforts to stitch multiple screens together into a cohesive whole, reaching an apex in systems such as Disney's eleven-projector cylindrical apparatus Circarama (1955). According to Turner, the nineteen-minute *USA in Circarama* was both immersive and visually dynamic:

> Shot from the windows of automobiles and from the wings of a B-52 bomber, the film raced and swooped across the American landscape. Wheat fields in Montana melted into Yellowstone Park; Pittsburgh steel mills led to the Santa Fe Railroad. The film culminated in an airborne swing through the Grand Canyon and a sunset over the Golden Gate Bridge.[44]

Like Disneyland's later cylindrical projection *America Sings* (1974), Circarama was realized entirely through the mechanical synchronization of film projectors. Circarama essentially brought the immersive spectacle of the panorama to life through motion picture footage—especially magisterial, aerial flyovers that provided a sense of visual omniscience. Reports of the viewing experience note standing crowds of viewers leaning and swaying in unison to anticipate the centrifugal force of the vehicles, even though their own viewing platform remained entirely stationary. In the end, we might conclude that the Bauhaus ideals of multiplicity and freedom of choice were swallowed whole and then regurgitated by American media industries, which preferred for viewers to confine their expressions of individuality to brand differentiation in the consumer marketplace. In the decades that followed, the desire for all-encompassing visual spectacles resurfaced in the form of mapping systems that aspire not just to symbolic temporary experiences of immersion, but to creation of a global visual-digital archive for which the map would ultimately exceed the territory.

Synthetic Cartographies

Massively scaled corporate information systems are often presented as self-validating precisely because of their speed, scale, and aspirations to totality. Synthetic cartography[45] systems such as Google Earth or Street View require no narrative, historiographical, or critical justification; they offer themselves freely to the world like a public utility or natural resource. Within these systems, innumerable potential narratives and recombinatory meanings emerge. These are incidental to the functioning of a total information system, but they offer a revealing crucible for the intersection of data and images. Digital maps, for example, function as interfaces as much as they are geographic representations; satellite images and photographs of landscapes are tiles waiting to be mapped onto polygons, models, and point clouds in virtual environments. This synthesis represents a long-awaited step toward a photorealistic, computationally enabled geospatial web.

Since launching Street View in 2007, Google has worked to make its repository of geolocated images as globally comprehensive as possible. In fact, Google's mapping project extends well beyond paved "streets" to include hiking and mountain biking trails, captured using the Trekker system designed by Luc Vincent. Trekker is a body-mounted version of the

Street View capture system, configured to be carried by individuals into parts of the landscape that are inaccessible to vehicles. Trekker also offers a loaner program that encourages members of the public to take GPS-enabled spherical camera rigs with them on hikes off the beaten path, thereby crowdsourcing the system's implied conjunction of images and data. With such efforts, Google extends its visual reach beyond the edges of the built environment into nature itself, a veritable frontier of visual and locational data that uniquely depends on the mobility of human bodies traversing the wilderness.

Although less known than its read-only visual mapping platform, Google's Street View App empowers everyday users to capture and embed spherical images within the Street View online universe. The Street View App generates spheres that are automatically stitched together from images captured with mobile and tablet devices and incorporated into Street View according to GPS coordinates. Although it is not yet possible to use Street View to navigate from one spherical image to an adjacent one, it's easy to imagine such traversal being possible—especially in heavily documented locations—enabling a different kind of wandering than the mostly rectilinear paths mapped by Google's fleet of Street View cars currently permits.

The universality of Google's Street View, is bracketed on one side by spaces that *have not* been fully mapped by the available technological apparatus, and on the other side by spaces that *may not* be mapped. Taken in aggregate, Google's Street View, Earth, and Maps projects constitute a massively scaled attempt to synthesize a photographic vision of the earth's lived spaces with topographic and architectural data models. It is precisely the scope and audacity of Google's aspirations for these combined information-image systems that make them useful as a case study for examining their rare but revealing instances of failure and fissure.

To offer just one example, early in its mapping efforts in March 2008, Google was confronted with a Pentagon request to remove Street View images of the military base at Fort Sam Houston in Texas. Perhaps recalling the Defense Department's own financing of the technology behind the *Aspen Movie Map* as a potential strategic asset, Air Force General Gene Renuart of the U.S. Northern Command was quoted saying, "It actually shows where all the guards are. It shows how the barriers go up and down. It shows how to get in and out of buildings. ... I think that poses a real security risk for our military installations."[46] Google responded that photographing the military base had been in violation of its own policy to restrict Street View images to public roads and promptly withdrew public access to the images. This relatively trivial instance of conflict between the more commonly aligned interests of the military and technological complexes nonetheless highlights the anxiety that occurs when traditionally hierarchical technologies of vision—the military would rather see than be seen—become uncomfortably bidirectional.

A differently revealing instance of the disjuncture of data and images is evident in a Twitter thread that circulated widely on social media in early 2013. The thread was based on a Twitter user's suspicion that a Street View car, which was mapping Botswana—the first country in Africa to be captured by Street View—had run over a donkey.[47] This imputed event resonated uncomfortably with the long history of Western colonialism in Africa, especially in relation to the complicit role of photography in constructing and perpetuating that history. Responses to the tweet readily assigned blame to the Street View car, which quickly became a symbol of colonialist narratives of exploitation and violence.

In fact, the Street View image that circulated in connection with this discussion simply represented a failure of the synthetic mode observable in Street View's system for merging data and image. The original tweet, by "The Real Sheldon C," included an image of an apparently fallen donkey surrounded by clouds of dust, presented as visible evidence that a donkey had been flattened on a road in Botswana—as if the Street View car were a steamroller and the donkey were made of clay. A Google Maps project manager responded with a slightly flippant blog post, wittily titled "Never Ass-ume," accompanied by a subsequent image of the donkey standing by the side of the road as evidence that the creature had survived its encounter with the Street View car.[48]

This incident marks an unusually stark example of the persistent desire to trust the mimetic capacity of images, even in an age when logic tells us that a system such as Google's Street View is at best a computational hybrid, resulting from algorithmic reconstructions covering over gaps between optically captured images. Interestingly, Google has allowed imagery of the donkey to remain publicly accessible, presumably reflecting the company's confidence that the visible evidence it presents is ultimately exculpatory. Viewed from the proper angle, it is even possible to see the purportedly flattened donkey in the same Street View frame as a perfectly healthy-looking

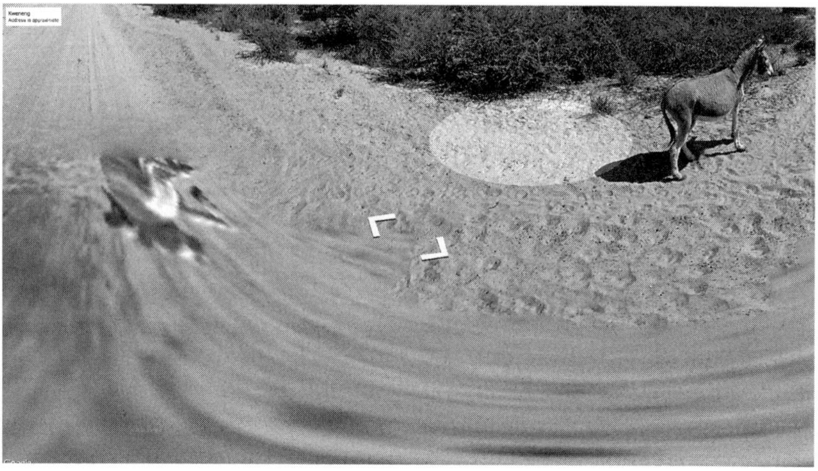

Figure 3.13
Google's attempts to seamlessly merge photographic documentation with algorithmically interpolated image textures can result in self-contradicting images and crises of signification. Street View coordinates: -23.527824, 24.72265 Kweneng, Botswana.

donkey standing at the side of the road. The flattened part of the image is clearly the result of the Street View algorithm's filling-in of missing imagery in the lower hemisphere of the spherical image.

In most cases, this type of algorithmic image generation is undetectable, as it is drawn from undifferentiated imagery of the ground over which the car is traveling. The proximity of the donkey to the car as it passed allowed donkey-like image textures to be integrated into the reconstructed imagery of the dirt road. At the time of the incident, Adobe's popular image editing software Photoshop did not yet include its "content-aware fill" tool, which allows sections of photographs to be removed and the empty space automatically filled in with image textures derived from adjacent areas of the image.[49] It is not possible to definitively track public awareness of the capacity for software to perform operations such as "content-aware fill," or for Street View to conceal gaps in its spherical image capture, but incidents such as these—and the cultural narratives that accompany them—allow us to speculate about the development of cultural literacy related to mimetic and computational imaging.[50]

Since its origins in the nineteenth century, photography has played a schizophrenic role in capturing and conveying information. While early photography was deployed in the interests of science, photography itself has also been associated with the occult. Spirit photographers purported to be able to capture images of the dead, and nineteenth-century supernaturalists looked to photography to visualize emotional traumas, spiritual auras, and other phenomena of the nonvisible world. Once photographic technologies and processes were more widely understood, these claims lost credibility, but it is interesting to note a related phenomenon within internet cultures devoted to identifying image anomalies within systems such as Street View and Google Earth. The automated stitching of images captured from a moving Street View car, for example, sometimes results in image composites that, like the donkey in Botswana, suggest alternate narratives. Ghostly images of truncated human bodies on city streets, lens flares and cloud formations that suggest alien abduction, and so forth recycle century-old narratives of photography as a conduit to the supernatural.[51]

When computational imaging systems function seamlessly, they contribute little to cultural awareness about their operation. A project that roughly coincided with the Street View donkey incident is artist Clement Valla's image archive *Postcards from Google Earth* (2013). Valla, who insightfully describes Google Earth as "a database disguised as a photographic representation,"[52] has amassed a collection of images that highlights the uneven synthesis of data and images. According to Valla, the images captured in his archive are almost immediately suppressed by Google's quality control, making his collection of image anomalies all the more remarkable. Valla's postcards come from the edges not just of the physical cartographic world, but of machine and human perception, where photography and algorithm meet head-on in a fiery crash.

Whereas the functioning of Street View's composite imaging may be understood in relation to software tools such as "content-aware fill," the anomalies documented by Valla are more complex and visually striking. In generating its photographically textured topographical maps, Google Earth engages in a massively scaled exercise in photogrammetry, which Google has dubbed "universal texture."[53] The process involves extracting topographical data from multiple flyovers of landscapes, then "draping" or "wrapping" the photographic textures over the resulting 3D models. If the 3D models line up with the visual features of the landscape, the result is an invisibly synthesized data-image. In Valla's *Postcards*, however, certain features of landscapes prove more difficult to translate into a data model, especially those involving significant variations in surface depth, such as ravines, waterfalls, bridges, and freeway interchanges. Valla describes these images not as glitches or errors in the system, but instead as the logical outcome of the process by which they are created. In all its iterations, Valla's project constitutes an unusually elaborate joke at the expense of the totalizing aspirations of Google Earth.

At the same time, *Postcards from Google Earth* celebrates the flawed aesthetics of photogrammetry. Algorithmic anomalies cause roadways to dip down into gorges or stretch and contort like a tangle of ribbons laid out on the landscape; texture maps of buildings with imperfect models beneath them melt and ooze into viscous lumps. Despite these anomalies, each "postcard" retains the basic visual attributes of a Google Earth image, which is contiguous with all other images in the system. Theoretically, there are no edges or negative spaces, nothing separating each frame from the rest of the landscape. The *Postcard* images provide a revealing glimpse of the way the system works and, more important, what happens when it doesn't. Valla continues, "These jarring moments expose how Google *Earth* works, focusing our attention on the software. They are seams which reveal a new model of seeing and of representing our world."[54] Valla's strikingly beautiful anomalies offer an artistic illustration of what can be learned from seams, imperfections, and failures in an otherwise opaque automated system.[55]

While Valla calls attention to the imperfections within a massive and seemingly totalizing system by showing how the gaps are covered by machine logic, the work of Japanese media artist Masaki Fujihata is fueled by an entirely different ethos dedicated to showing—and even reveling in—those gaps. With a body of work that predates Google's Earth and Street View platforms, as well as common technologies of locative media, Fujihata has long experimented with alternative ways of embedding images and video in geolocated data spaces. Beginning in 1991, Fujihata produced a series of location studies under the title *Field-Works*. The resulting digital landscapes are dominated by a void of blackness in which image planes are suspended at regular intervals. A user navigating the space can click on an image plane to play a video sequence, often an interview with local inhabitants. White GPS tracking lines loop through the space, connecting the images and illustrating their relative positions in space, while also reminding us of the path taken by Fujihata when traversing and documenting the area. Like the artist, users control a virtual camera to move around the space

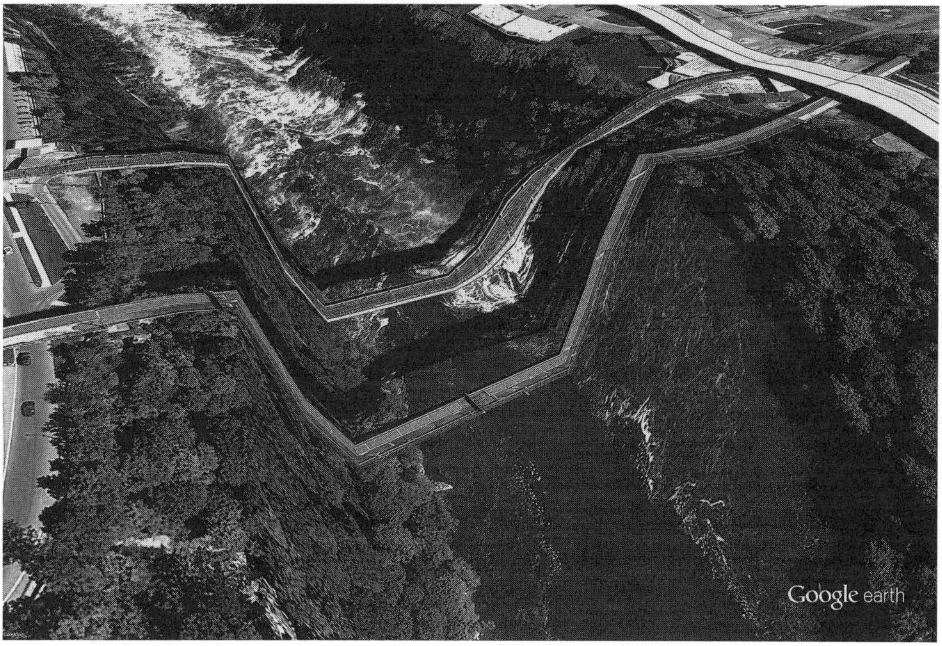

Figure 3.14
Image anomalies captured by Clement Valla's *Postcards from Google Earth* (2013) reveal the limits of Google's universal texture algorithm. Image courtesy of Clement Valla.

in three dimensions, viewing the videos from any angle or following the GPS lines to other parts of the landscape.

A variation on this visual strategy occurs in Fujihata's *Simultaneous Echoes* (2009), where image and video frames are placed not only in voids of blackness but in panoramic landscapes or cylindrical projections. Like the earlier projects in this series, *Simultaneous Echoes* acknowledges the limits of photographic and videographic representation through the juxtaposition of continuous and discontinuous imaging. Fujihata's use of frames within frames also suggests the arbitrariness of any given photographic view and affords viewers the option of zooming in on individual frames or pulling back to reveal a total environment. In all cases, the primary tension in the work is between things that are seeable and those that are not. The myth of total documentation and infinite navigability is thereby thrown into relief; the project is a reminder of the contingent and arbitrary nature of

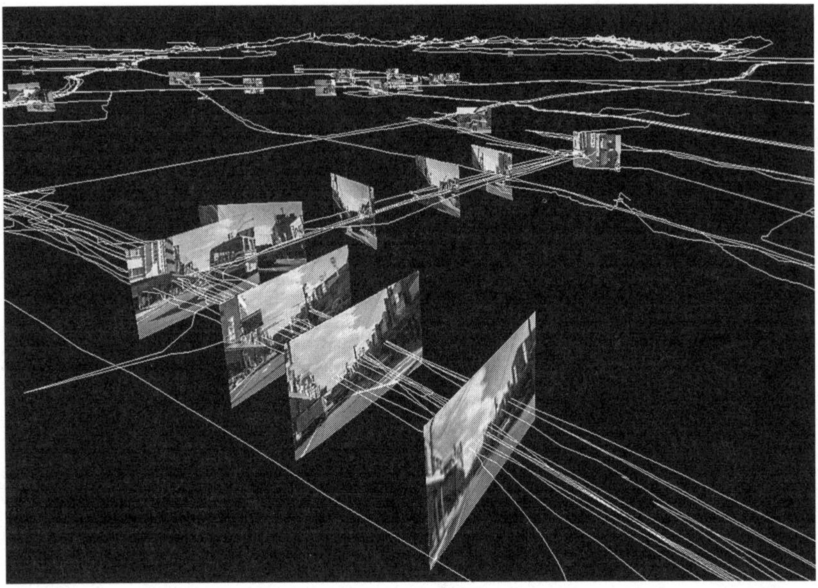

Figure 3.15
Masaki Fujihata's *Field-Works@Tsumari (Experiencing 1-inch Monk)* (2000) highlights the negative spaces between geolocated image planes. Photo credit: Masaki Fujihata, Takeshi Kawashima (technical support).

all documentation, even within systems designed to mobilize the power of both data and images.

Fujihata focuses on the relationship between the tangible and intangible—or visible and invisible—aspects of data used in computer graphics. Describing the evolution of the project as an extension of his early experiments with computer-based sculptures in the late 1980s, Fujihata notes, "I had felt frustration with the computer images, because the image was generated with 3D data but we cannot touch that 3D object. I had a strong desire to materialize the object which is from computer data, for touching the surface."[56] Although the *Field-Works* series does not allow users to physically touch the surface of either data or images—as a gallery installation, users navigate projected images with standard computer controls—Fujihata's strategy of representation is uniquely devoted to demonstrating the limitations of photographic and videographic documentation. At stake in these projects is a fragmentation of both space and time, which stands in stark opposition to geolocative systems architected to conceal gaps between images, and the role of image-data synthesis in creating an illusion of seamlessness. Where systems like Google Earth and Street View propose a ubiquitous totality for their visions of the world, Fujihata's work reminds us that seeing is really never more than glimpsing.

Both Valla and Fujihata work on the edges separating image from data, exploiting creative potentials of the disjunction between the two. Using technologies of laser and structured light scanning, the London-based creative studio ScanLAB Projects, led by Matthew Shaw and William Trossell, has produced a body of work that hovers at the periphery of data space, exploiting and even exaggerating the limits of volumetric data to represent physical spaces and bodies. Most commonly, LIDAR and other technologies for capturing volumetric data focus on faithful reproduction of the physical world, a capability that is useful in fields as diverse as cartography, architectural preservation, visual effects, and autonomous vehicles. But when misused or misappropriated, these technologies can produce images of remarkable beauty and idiosyncrasy. Instead of avoiding the anomalies and artifacts that result from scanning complex lived environments, ScanLAB cultivates and accentuates them. While capturing volume data from a vehicle passing through the streets of London, for example, ScanLAB produced a series of rainbow-hued abstractions that resulted from the scanning system incorrectly distinguishing between the relative motion and stasis of vehicles and buildings.

In one image, a double-decker bus is misrecognized as part of the city's architecture, causing the scan data to create the appearance of a motion blur that stretches the full length of a city block. This poetic aberration continues ScanLAB's longtime interest in work that acknowledges—even celebrates—uncapturable or unrenderable spaces. This is where the representational capacities of data and image come into most exquisite conflict. In 2013, ScanLAB devoted an entire show to such artifacts. *Noise: Error in the Void* features a series of images derived from a scanning project in Berlin. Outlying data resulting from reflections, clouds, or human figures is ordinarily removed before the rest of the data is incorporated into a 3D model. But in *Noise*, such "unclean" data is the point of the show. A scan of Berlin's Oberbaum Bridge, for example, radiates a psychedelic aura of reflections, echoes, and overmodulations emanating from the bridge structure. ScanLAB describes the process of capturing these images in poetic terms:

> The scan sees more than is possible for it to see. The noise is draped in the colours of the sky. The clouds are scanned, even though out of range. Everything is flat; broken only by runway markings. Traces of dog walkers spike up into the cloud. The ground falls away to the foreground in ripples. The horizon line is muddy with the tones of the ground and the texture of the sky. The center is thick with points, too dense to see through. Underground only the strongest noise remains.[57]

ScanLAB is uniquely interested in visually exploring the ways in which data systems are—and are not—able to see or sense the world. Writing about ScanLAB's involvement with a self-driving car project in the *New York Times*, architecture writer Geoff Manaugh illuminates ScanLAB's work as marking the transition from human to posthuman ways of seeing.

> ScanLAB's project suggests that humans are not the only things now sensing and experiencing the modern landscape—that something else is here, with an altogether different, and fundamentally inhuman, perspective on the built environment … As we peer into the algorithmic dreams of these vehicles, we are perhaps also being given the first glimpse of what's to come when they awake.

Although I would disagree with Manaugh's acceptance of dreams and other psychological states as the default metaphor for artificial intelligence,[58] the point that humans in urban environments inhabit a shared visual field with a broad array of scanners, sensors, and algorithms is well taken. As discussed in the first chapter of this book, machine vision and human vision have achieved a precarious balance that is currently playing out across various technologies of vision. The relationship of these two regimes is as irreducible to metaphors of human cognitive processes as to algorithmic ones.

In 2016, ScanLAB undertook an ambitious project commissioned by the Los Angeles County Museum of Art's Art + Technology program to create a series of more than 150 scans in Yosemite National Park.[59] The assignment was, in part, an exercise in perversity, unleashing the logic of data on one of the world's most commonly photographed natural spaces. The result was a protracted and genuinely spectacular negotiation of the boundaries between data and image. Although laser scanning is primarily used for capturing volumetric data in the form of point clouds, the scanners also capture color information that can be used to texture-map the resulting 3D models so that they resemble photographic surfaces. In their creative work,

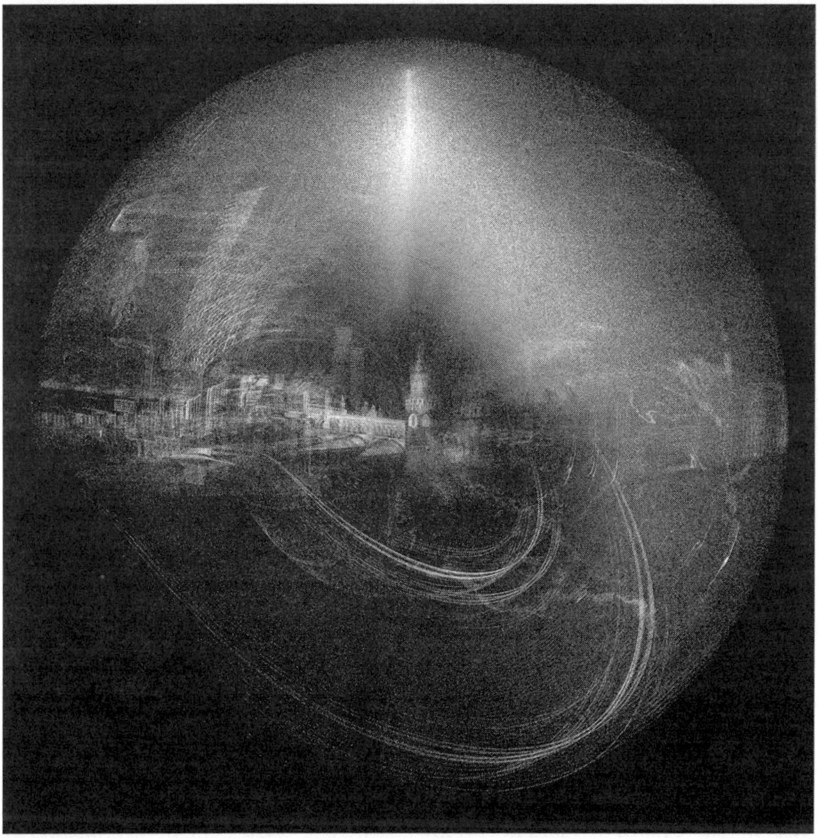

Figure 3.16
ScanLAB's *Noise: Error in the Void* (2013) series celebrates, rather than suppresses, the imperfections of long-range digital scans around Berlin. Image credit: *Noise: Berlin Oberbaum Bridge—The Spree*, by ScanLAB Projects.

ScanLAB often flouts the "millimeter accuracy" for which 3D scans are ordinarily deployed in favor of impressionistic interpretations of physical spaces. In their scans of Yosemite, for example, a single tree located just a few meters from the long-range scanner might cast a "data shadow" stretching for miles across the valley. The effect is to exaggerate the significance of an individual tree while obscuring vast contours of the landscape, but this strategy also preserves awareness of the location and the limitations of the scanning apparatus. Under "ideal" circumstances, point clouds do not reveal their point(s) of origin, constructing for viewers a deceptive sense of omniscience in relation to visible space. Among the other factors that are ordinarily suppressed in the interest of 3D modeling—but that ScanLAB embraces—are variables of time, movement, and atmospheric interference, all of which belie the capacity of static digital models to reflect lived realities.

Fascinatingly, ScanLAB conceived the Yosemite project in dialogue with past photographic projects by the likes of Eadweard Muybridge and Ansel Adams. They received permission to access areas of the park that are ordinarily off limits to visitors to create scans from the vantage points used for the original photographic documents. The project is thus a kind of variation on the practice of landscape rephotography. For this project, ScanLAB used a combination of long- and short-range laser scanners—one designed to capture data up to one thousand feet away, and another that captures features of the landscape up to seven miles away. While short-range scans may take as little as thirty minutes to complete, long-range scans may take several hours. In either case, the team has no way to preview the captured data until it is downloaded and processed into point clouds, marking yet another symmetry with the multistage process of nineteenth- (Muybridge) and twentieth- (Adams) century photochemical image making.

In contrast with the traditions of fine art photography—which reached its apotheosis in Adams's meticulous small-aperture large-format prints—ScanLAB refused to depict the wilderness as pristine and uninhabited. As any recent visitor to Yosemite can attest, the park's most popular viewpoints are overrun with tourists and other artifacts of human presence. Rather than suppress these intrusions on the natural world, ScanLAB included human bodies in the scans, resulting in blurry, noisy data that is nonetheless more representative of the park's lived environment. Similar challenges confronted the team when attempting to scan dynamic and amorphous elements such as streams, waterfalls, and fog banks. As with the tourists, ScanLAB deliberately captured a full range of these "unscannable" phenomena as part of their documentation, amplifying the indeterminacy that results when irresolute imagery mingles with noisy data. ScanLAB's deliberate misuse of expensive, highly specialized scanning technologies to create aesthetically stunning and enigmatic data-images marks an appropriate conclusion to this chapter's meditation on the perceptual transformations of space in the digital era. As ScanLAB's body of work continues to eloquently demonstrate, data need not continue to be posed as the solution to the unruliness of space; it is equally useful for highlighting problems we didn't even know we had.

Conclusion

Haunting the periphery of this chapter are twin specters of the media and technology industries. When we look to cinema for models to help understand virtual environments, we willingly inherit a logic predicated on the suppression of disruptions, gaps, and discontinuities. The spectacle of narrative cinema—which uses its own bag of technological and emotional tricks to generate feelings of immersion and empathy while concealing its apparatus—has always harbored totalitarian potentials. A different allure of totality may continue to lurk around every corner of the microprocessor, but it is rooted in an intellectual desire for encyclopedic knowledge and access, not the erasure of surfaces, edges, and materialities. For the persistent fetishization of immersion and visual plenitude, even within procedurally generated environments, we may blame cinema, not computers.

Edges have different meanings to artists than to corporations devoted to amassing and analyzing data. For Google, the limits of a data set exist only to be expanded. What matters is the comprehensiveness and accessibility of the data. From the outside, however, the edges and limits of information systems have a different valence and utility. Part of the lesson of this chapter is that those who are denied access to the interior functioning of an information system may still find ways to decode meanings latent in that system's omissions. Data that is deliberately excluded from—or otherwise indigestible by—an information system may still provide revealing glimpses of the processes and parameters by which that system functions.

As communications technologies have evolved, Americans have been acculturated to experience different kinds of relationships to the spaces we inhabit. For example, the differences between wired and wireless transmission of information contributes to an ongoing reconfiguration of the relationship between human bodies and physical environments. As we have seen, the evolution of these relationships does not follow a model of succession; but we may find eerie resonances in the repeated cycles of singular tracks and wires giving way to technologies predicated on the ubiquity of electromagnetic signals; these, in turn, revert to physical tracks and tethers to start the cycle anew. In such circuits, the obsolescence of each generation of hardware begins to seem not like an incidental artifact but the whole point. Another eerie parallel exists between the synthetic technologies used in the entertainment industries to create hybrid realities and the increasing instrumentation of urban environments. Where technologies such as motion capture and photogrammetry create the conditions of possibility for seamlessly blended realities in screen space, the ubiquity of electromagnetic signals in the lived environment (cell phone data, Wi-Fi, etc.) creates a kind of cloud chamber wherein both individual and collective data traces are clearly legible.

Somewhere along the line, the cyberpunk fantasy of dissolving one's body into the immaterial ethers of networked virtual reality seems to have lost its appeal. And that's not a bad thing. An earlier generation's fantasy of cyberspace as an egalitarian utopia is now a habitat for trolls and social misbehavior amplified by anonymity. In 2017, we may well feel desperate to escape from lived reality, but the current generation of "VR" offers little solace. Having a display apparatus mounted on our heads may bring temporary distraction, but we are more often in a world of isolation and stasis than remote presence or alternate identity. A different fantasy dominates algorithmic cartographies that aspire to synthesize a total record of image and data spaces, but the underlying message is the same. In data space, you may be able to run, but you definitely can't hide.

Conclusion

This book has been, in part, an exercise in speculative history. By "speculative history" I do not mean the kind of counterfactual historical fiction that asks what would have happened if the Nazis had won World War II.[1] Rather, I mean the sense suggested by Anthony Dunne and Fiona Raby, who, in their 2013 book *Speculative Everything*, argue that design should open the imagination, not constrain it; that being able to imagine—or even prototype—the future is crucial to thinking about the needs of the present. In proposing the metaphor of parallax as a means of investigating the historical evolution of data and images, I invite readers to speculate on the material consequences of a hypothetical framework that stretches from the early nineteenth century to the present. I do not suppose that applying any of my various "modes" of relating data to images consciously motivated the creator of any particular artwork or technology. But the process of taxonomizing these various strategies has helped pull several otherwise abstract tendencies, movements, and relationships into focus.

Moments of transition make for illuminating and contested histories. I hope it is no longer necessary to note that even the most rigorously researched accounts of the past are partial and idiosyncratic—and inevitably driven by the needs of their moment. Speculative history aspires not to comprehensive analysis, nor even narrative coherence, but to kernels of insight and unexpected connections that, at their best, extend beyond the immediate objects of study. The transition we are currently witnessing regarding data and images both draws attention to the forces of history and clouds our ability to perceive them. In particular, the cultural and industrial consensus around models of synthesis and convergence make it tempting to see this consensual vision as an inevitability. The parallax model was conceived specifically to complicate prevailing assumptions about technology and media. I hope that analyzing an eclectic range of examples—from the obscurity of experimental films and software art to the industrial strategies of media and technology giants—has demonstrated the value of looking closely at all of this.

Jonathan Crary once argued, "We will never really know what the stereoscope looked like to a 19th century viewer."[2] In part, this is because of the burden of historical certainty about "the way things turned out," but also because of the impossibility of fully reconstructing the subjectivity of nineteenth-century viewers. This book goes a step further to ask whether we really know what today's technologies of vision look like to viewers—us—in our own present. The strategy of defamiliarization, borrowed from Russian formalist literary theory, advocates viewing even the newest technology as if it were an artifact of the past, its users—us—as the product of our own material and social circumstances. This is easy if we imagine old technologies to be primitive and their users naïve, but this perspective is more difficult to sustain while being dazzled by our own innovations of the day.

In this book I deploy strategies of close reading and associative digression to analyze the shifting roles of digital media in articulations of space, visualization, and surveillance. I have also attempted to engage the tortured relationships between critical models devised to address visual, digital, and media cultures of the past quarter century. My goal has not been to reconcile these models—nor the generations of thinkers who deploy them—but to find points of intersection and resonance. I remain convinced that there is room for coexistence and benefit to be had from the cross-pollination of theories of pre- and postdigital visual culture.

The broader context for this investigation is about transience. The relation between data and images exists in a particularly rapid state of flux, but this is true for many domains. Transience offers an antidote to passive models of evolution and, worse, narratives of progress. I am also driven by other forms of transience, which in recent years have come to seem more urgent than ever. This includes the fragility and inequity of individual human lives as well as the fragility of our planet. In time, the Earth will be no more inherited by the wealthiest elites than by the meekest of the poor. The course we have charted during the last 150 years—roughly the same period of technological development this book is concerned with—shows few signs of reversing direction before we plunge headlong into a smorgasbord of dystopian science-fiction narratives in which our children will be cast, at best, as scrappy survivors.

That said, I have engaged only glancingly the environmental consequences wrought by the technology and entertainment industries responsible for most of my objects of study. In recent years, increasing attention has been paid to foregrounding the physical substrates and environmental consequences of being digital. The ideology of "virtuality," Jennifer Gabrys argues, "can even enable more extensive consumption and wasting." She sums up this contradiction: "When electronic devices shrink to the scale of paper-thin and handheld devices, they appear to be lightweight and free of material resources. But this sense of immateriality also enables the proliferation of waste, from the processes of manufacture to the development of disposable and transient devices in excess."[3] Gabrys cites Walter Benjamin's analysis of the "fossilized" nineteenth-century arcades as evidence of technocultural practices—a collection of obsolete, irrelevant, and ill-advised artifacts—that offer useful insights into times past and the mindsets of those immersed in their own era's frenzy of the technological.[4]

Jonathan Sterne has likewise put forward an unforgiving analysis of the material consequences of digital consumption. In an essay titled "Out with the Trash," Sterne writes, "Obsolescence is a nice word for disposability and waste."[5] For Sterne, the very definition of "new" media is predicated on the obsolescence—the literal burying—of the old. "The entire edifice of new communication technology is a giant trash heap waiting to happen, a monument to the hubris of computing and the peculiar shape of digital capitalism."[6] And in *The Stack*, Benjamin Bratton advocates attending to physical as well as virtual infrastructure when critiquing the digital. "Computation is not virtual; it is a deeply physical event, and The Stack has an enormous appetite for molecules of interest and distributing them into our pockets, our laps, and our landfills."[7] In this context, the concerns of this book related to the physicality of digital imaging and its reciprocal computationality of vision represent only a subgenre of these larger environmental issues.

Lastly, Sean Cubitt's *Finite Media* offers a sustained and erudite meditation on the imbrication of digital materialities and environmental consequences. The book is overtly dedicated to examining the "deep dependence of contemporary media on energy and materials." In our relentless development of technologies for communicating among ourselves, Cubitt argues, "we also inadvertently communicate our dismissive relation to the humans and natural environments who pay the terrible price for its efficiency, even for its poetry."[8] Cubitt further asserts that any hope of change lies in the social—not the technological—domain, noting that "it is essential to turn our gaze toward the polity—the assembly of human beings in action—as the site from which might arise any alternative. ... It is we ourselves who must become other in order to produce an other world."[9] The point to be taken from all this is the falseness of the once-prevalent material/immaterial binary. The digital has always been physical.

Recent years have brought an implicit reinscription of the physical/digital divide in the form of the "New Aesthetic." So-named by designer James Bridle, the New Aesthetic denotes a cluster of art practices that emerged in the 2010s seeking to manifest the unique attributes of digital imaging—especially pixelated 8-bit graphics—in the physical world. Describing this as a practice of "seeing like digital devices,"[10] Bridle valorized work by international artists, including Canadian novelist Douglas Coupland, whose life-sized *Pixellated Orca* (2009) sculpture is installed outside the Vancouver Convention Center; Dutch artist Helmut Smits, who dubbed a one-meter-square patch of dirt *Dead Pixel in Google Earth* (2008–2010); and Azerbaijani artist and rug maker Faig Ahmed, who creates traditionally woven carpets that evince distinctly digital distortion effects. These works are indeed seductive, and we may appreciate their perversity and idiosyncrasy as individual works, but as a movement, the New Aesthetic remains burdened by the combination of formalism and ahistoricism inherent in its name. Like firstness, few claims of newness are ever really justified.

To more productively theorize the impulse behind the New Aesthetic, several writers turned to the concept of "eversion."[11] Science-fiction author William Gibson coined the term in a *New York Times* op-ed piece in 2010 to signify the process by which cyberspace (another Gibson term) erupts from the virtual into the physical world. Gibson's op-ed came in response to the announcement that Google was moving from the ethers of the internet into brick-and-mortar corporate personhood. He wrote, "Now cyberspace has everted. Turned itself inside out. Colonized the physical.

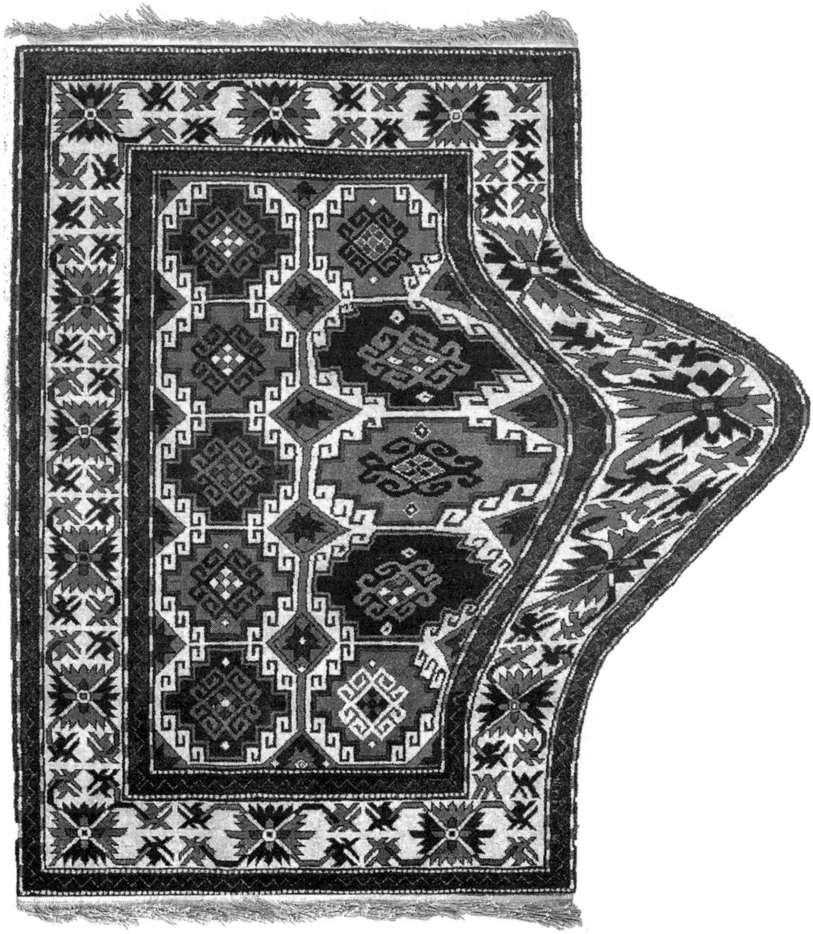

Figure 4.1

Azerbaijani artist Faig Ahmed creates traditionally woven carpets that resemble digital distortions. Faig Ahmed, *Expansion* (2011). Handmade woolen carpet, 100 × 150 cm. Image courtesy of Faig Ahmed Studio.

Making Google a central and evolving structural unit not only of the architecture of cyberspace, but of the world."[12] Echoing Gibson, Bruce Sterling dismissively noted that the New Aesthetic's eruption of the digital into the physical should have come as no surprise. "It's been going on for a generation. It should be much better acculturated than it is."[13] I do not always agree with Sterling's forays from the domain of science-fiction into cultural criticism, but despite his chastising tone, his point resonates with a core argument of this book. What is at stake in nearly all the media I have curated for this project is their integration in a long-term two-way process of acculturation. Whether media artifacts intend to do so or not, they teach us how to understand the technologies that make them possible.

In addition to the materiality of the digital, an underlying concern of this book has been the role of technology in producing neoliberal subjects ready to accept their role in the marketization of everyday life. A great many more factors are at play in this dynamic, of course, and I don't imagine that this book's warnings—however earnestly they might be issued—have much to offer in the absence of a related social movement. Given the imbrication of digital networks with the ideologies of neoliberalism, developing a sophisticated understanding of the functioning of digital systems may ultimately increase our agency in both domains. It is not only technologies whose secrets must be revealed, but the structure of the multiple social and political systems in which they are embedded. A thoroughly expanded view of the "war between data and images" would also take account of the many other wars, both literal and metaphorical, that we are now—or soon will be—engaged in.

What we choose to pay attention to when we create or study "digital culture" is an ethical matter, and the questions we don't ask are as important as the ones we do. So, why is it important to focus on data and images at this moment? Data can be used, as photographs once were, to awaken consciousness to systemic injustice and the need for social change. Where images are still frequently tied to the subjective position of an individual or the camera, understanding data necessitates thinking in terms of complex and interlocking systems. The message of this book is not meant to be pessimistic, even if my trust in the liberatory potentials of media and technology often wavers. I will say that the faith that even more technology can right the world's wrongs could only flourish in a cultural unconscious that has been too long soaking in the warm bath of Hollywood endings. Ultimately, my hope is that greater agency will follow from better understanding how our perceptions of the world are shaped by technologies of vision, specifically the entangled realms of computation and mimesis. As my repeated preference for the negotiated mode suggests, I do not view the function of data and images as an either/or proposition; by considering both at once and in relation to the other, we gain the greatest insight. If images allow us to see where we have been, and data reveals certain contours of the present, perhaps through juxtaposition of the two, we can identify the places that are worth struggling to go next.

Notes

Introduction

1. Susan Sontag, *On Photography* (New York: Farrar, Straus and Giroux, 1977), 2.

2. Ibid., 10.

3. Ibid., 11.

4. Although Negroponte's book was not published until January 1996, he articulated the transition from atoms to bits in a series of articles in *Wired* magazine beginning in January 1995. Nicholas Negroponte, *Being Digital* (New York: Vintage, 1996).

5. See Gitelman's introduction to her edited volume *"Raw Data" Is an Oxymoron* (Cambridge, MA: MIT Press, 2013), Kindle edition.

6. Geoffrey C. Bowker, "Data Flakes: An Afterword to *'Raw Data' Is an Oxymoron*," in *"Raw Data" Is an Oxymoron*, Kindle location 3892–3894.

7. Johanna Drucker, "Graphesis: Visual Knowledge Production and Representation," *Poetess Archive Journal* 2, no. 1 (December 2010): 1–50.

8. Chris Anderson, "The End of Theory: The Data Deluge Makes the Scientific Method Obsolete," *Wired*, June 23, 2008, https://www.wired.com/2008/06/pb-theory.

9. See, for example, danah boyd and Kate Crawford, "Critical Questions for Big Data," *Information, Communication & Society* 15, no. 5 (2012): 662–679, doi:10.1080/1369118X.2012.678878.

10. The full transcript of Cegłowski's "Haunted by Data" keynote address at the Strata + Hadoop World conference in New York City on October 1, 2015, in which he compares big data to radioactive waste, is available at: http://idlewords.com/talks/haunted_by_data.htm.

11. Theodor Adorno, *Minima Moralia: Reflections from Damaged Life*, trans. E. F. N. Jephcott (1951; reprint, London: Verso, 2006), 50.

12. See Janet Murray, *Inventing the Medium: Principles of Interaction Design as a Cultural Practice* (Cambridge, MA: MIT Press, 2011).

13. I have argued, regarding digital history, that computation is equally conducive to recombinant chaos as to totalizing order. See *Technologies of History* (Hanover, NH: Dartmouth College Press, 2011), chapter 5.

14. Gitelman, *Raw Data*, Kindle location 235–237.

15. Allan Sekula, "On the Invention of Photographic Meaning," in *Thinking Photography,* ed. Victor Burgin (London: Macmillan, 1982), 84–109. Originally published in *Artforum* 13, no. 5 (January 1975): 36–45.

16. Kate Crawford, "The Hidden Biases in Big Data," *Harvard Business Review,* April 1, 2013, http://hbr.org/2013/04/the-hidden-biases-in-big-data. Cited in Tom Boelstorff, "Making Big Data, in Theory," *First Monday* 18, no. 10 (2013), doi:10.5210/fm.v18i10.4869.

17. Crawford, "Hidden Biases."

18. This is the argument Tom Boelstorff makes in "Making Big Data." Lev Manovich's cultural analytics lab also aligns its methods with those of Geertz.

19. Michel Foucault, *The Archaeology of Knowledge: And the Discourse on Language* (New York: Vintage), 1982.

20. Facebook founder Mark Zuckerberg made this explicit in 2016 after receiving an award for entrepreneurial social responsibility. "What they're thinking about, what they're experiencing on a day-to-day basis, and the idea is that everyone has the power to share those things, then that makes the world more understanding, it helps people stay closer to the people who they love, all these good things that we value." Quoted in "Mark Zuckerberg Receives Axel Springer Award," *Axel Springer Award*, February 2016, http://axel-springer-award.com.

21. David Harvey, *A Brief History of Neoliberalism* (Oxford: Oxford University Press, 2005), 159.

22. Ibid., 3.

23. Timothy Shenk, "What Exactly Is Neoliberalism?" An interview with Wendy Brown in *Dissent*, April 2, 2015, https://www.dissentmagazine.org/blog/booked-3-what-exactly-is-neoliberalism-wendy-brown-undoing-the-demos.

24. Giorgio Agamben, *"What Is an Apparatus?" and Other Essays*, trans. D. Kishik and S. Pedatella (Palo Alto, CA: Stanford University Press, 2009), 22.

25. See Wendy Brown, *Undoing the Demos: Neoliberalism's Stealth Revolution* (New York: Zone Books, 2015).

26. Michel Foucault, "Omnes et Singulatim: Towards a Critique of Political Reason," in *Power: Essential Works of Michel Foucault, 1954–1984*, vol. 3 (New York: New Press, 2001).

27. Wendy Hui Kyong Chun, *Programmed Visions: Software and Memory* (Cambridge, MA: MIT Press, 2013), 15.

28. Sean Cubitt, *The Practice of Light: A Genealogy of Visual Technologies from Prints to Pixels* (Cambridge, MA: MIT Press, 2014), 6.

29. See Benjamin H. Bratton, *The Stack: On Software and Sovereignty* (Cambridge, MA: MIT Press, 2016).

30. In their introductory essay to the anthology *New Media, 1740–1915* (Cambridge, MA: MIT Press, 2004), Lisa Gitelman and Geoffrey Pingree ask bluntly "What's New About New Media?" Their conclusion, following the insights of Carolyn Marvin's *When Old Technologies Were New: Thinking About Electric Communication in the Late Nineteenth Century* (New York: Oxford University Press, 1990), was that we have much to learn about contemporary technology and culture by studying moments of emergence and disruption from the past.

31. In this book, I use "data" in the singular to maintain focus on its role as a technique or field of practice rather than a collection of individually meaningful datums.

32. See André Bazin, "The Ontology of the Photographic Image," trans. Hugh Gray, *Film Quarterly* 13, no. 4 (Summer 1960). 4–9.

33. Brian Winston, "A Mirror for Brunelleschi," *Daedalus: Journal of the American Academy of Arts and Sciences* 116, no. 3 (Summer 1987): 194.

34. I am indebted to Anne Friedberg for noting this concurrence in *The Virtual Window: From Alberti to Microsoft* (Cambridge, MA: MIT Press, 2009).

35. Christian Wurster, *Computers: An Illustrated History* (New York: Taschen, 2002), 12.

36. N. Katherine Hayles, *How We Think: Digital Media and Contemporary Technogenesis* (Chicago: University of Chicago Press, 2012).

37. The first instance of a criminal who had fled from one geographic region to another being identified by a telegraphically transmitted image took place in 1908.

38. For an extended study of Marey's focus on the trace as opposed to the image, see François Dagognet and Robert Galeta, *Etienne-Jules Marey: A Passion for the Trace* (New York: Zone Books, 1992).

39. Tom Boelstorff has eloquently argued that it is appropriate for writings on data to be dated, not only because the two share a root word, but also to mark the moment when particular applications of the notion of data seemed most relevant. See "Making Big Data."

40. Jonathan Crary, *Techniques of the Observer: On Vision and Modernity in the 19th Century* (Cambridge, MA: MIT Press, 1992), 110.

Chapter 1

1. Peter Meyer et al., "Painting by Numbers," *Nation*, March 14, 1994, 334–348.

2. JoAnn Wypijewski, ed., *Painting by Numbers: Komar and Melamid's Scientific Guide to Art* (Berkeley: University of California Press, 1998).

3. Sean Cubitt, "Cartographic Instruments, Narcissist Illusions, Regimes of Realism in CGI," *Millennium Film Journal* 34 (Fall 1999): 66.

4. Ibid., 68.

5. Andrew Ross, "Poll Stars," *Artforum* 33, no. 5 (January 1995): 72–77.

6. See the collection of essays published as *Thomas Kinkade: The Artist in the Mall*, ed. Alexis L. Boylan (Durham, NC: Duke University Press, 2011); and Wendy Katz and Thomas Kinkade, *Thomas Kinkade: Masterworks of Light* (Boston: Little, Brown, 2000).

7. "Description," *Terminal Time*, 1999, http://www.terminaltime.com.

8. See Anderson, *Technologies of History*.

9. Netflix promotional e-mail message received by the author, August 16, 2012.

10. Blake Hallinan and Ted Striphas, "Recommended for You: The Netflix Prize and the Production of Algorithmic Culture," *New Media and Society* 18, no. 1 (2014): 1–21.

11. Wendy Hui Kyong Chun, *Updating to Remain the Same: Habitual New Media* (Cambridge, MA: MIT Press, 2016).

12. For more on this, see Hallinan and Striphas, "Recommended for You."

13. Xavier Amatriain and Justin Basilico, "Netflix Recommendations: Beyond the 5 Stars (Part 1)," *Netflix Tech Blog*, April 6, 2012, http://techblog.netflix.com/2012/04/netflix-recommendations-beyond-5-stars.html.

14. Ben Fritz, "Cadre of Film Buffs Helps Netflix Viewers Sort through the Clutter," *Los Angeles Times*, September 3, 2012, http://articles.latimes.com/2012/sep/03/business/la-fi-0903-ct-netflix-taggers-20120903.

15. Ian Bogost, "The Cathedral of Computation," *Atlantic*, January 15, 2015, http://www.theatlantic.com/technology/archive/2015/01/the-cathedral-of-computation/384300.

16. Wendy Chun, in fact, argues in her article "Big Data as Drama" that user ratings were never an effective metric for the company, calling them "non-existent," even

before its interpretive emphasis shifted to real-time streaming analytics. "Big Data as Drama," *ELH* 83, no. 2 (Summer 2016): 363–382.

17. Todd Spangler, "Netflix Data Reveals Exactly When TV Shows Hook Viewers," *Variety*, September 23, 2015, http://variety.com/2015/digital/news/netflix-tv-show-data-viewer-episode-study-1201600746/.

18. Amatriain and Basilico, "Netflix Recommendations."

19. Jason Mittell, "Why Netflix Doesn't Release Its Ratings," *Atlantic*, February 23, 2016, https://www.theatlantic.com/entertainment/archive/2016/02/netflix-ratings/462447/.

20. Amatriain and Basilico, "Netflix Recommendations."

21. For a complete account of this project, see Alexis C. Madrigal, "How Netflix Reverse Engineered Hollywood," *Atlantic*, January 2, 2014, https://www.theatlantic.com/technology/archive/2014/01/how-netflix-reverse-engineered-hollywood/282679/.

22. Yves Raimond and Justin Basilico, "Recommending for the World," *Netflix Tech Blog*, February 17, 2016, http://techblog.netflix.com/2016/02/recommending-for-world.html.

23. See, for example, April Joyner, "Blackflix: How Netflix's Algorithm Exposes Technology's Racism," *Marie Claire*, February 29, 2016, http://www.marieclaire.com/culture/a18817/netflix-algorithms-black-movies.

24. Kevin Spacey, MacTaggart Lecture, transcript, Edinburgh International Television Festival 2013, *Guardian*, August 22, 2013, https://www.theguardian.com/media/interactive/2013/aug/22/kevin-spacey-mactaggart-lecture-full-text.

25. Although Komar and Melamid are, by every definition, professional artists, Tufte undoubtedly would have regarded their visual interpretations as "paintjunk," distracting from the visual economy of more directly presented, tabular survey data.

26. David Byrne, "Learning to Love PowerPoint," *Wired*, September 1, 2003, https://www.wired.com/2003/09/ppt1.

27. Byrne appears to be borrowing this text, reproduced verbatim but without attribution, from the Digital Physiognomy Software website by UNIPHIZ Lab Software (http://www.uniphiz.com/physiognomy.htm). Byrne's quotation is in the "Physiognomies" section, no page number, of his *Envisioning Emotional Epistemological Information* (Göttingen: Steidl, 2003).

28. Edward Tufte, "PowerPoint Is Evil," *Wired*, September 1, 2003, https://www.wired.com/2003/09/ppt2.

29. Ibid.

30. Daniel J. Boorstin, *The Image: A Guide to Pseudo-Events in America* (1962; repr., New York: Vintage Books 1992).

31. See, for example, Mitchell Stephens, *The Rise of the Image, The Fall of the Word* (Oxford: Oxford University Press, 1998).

32. See Franco Moretti and Alberto Piazza, *Graphs, Maps, Trees: Abstract Models for Literary History* (New York: Verso, 2007); and Franco Moretti, *Distant Reading* (New York: Verso, 2013).

33. See Matthew L. Jockers, *Macroanalysis: Digital Methods and Literary History* (Urbana: University of Illinois Press, 2013).

34. Gitelman, *Raw Data*, Kindle location 4.

35. Ibid., 121–122.

36. Ibid., 123–125.

37. Ibid.

38. See Erez Aiden and Jean-Baptiste Michel, *Uncharted: Big Data as a Lens on Human Culture* (New York: Riverhead Books, 2013), 31.

39. See, for example, Lior Shamir and Jane A. Tarakhovsky, "Computer Analysis of Art," *Journal on Computing and Cultural Heritage* 5, no. 2 (August 2012): 1–11.

40. See Tara McPherson, *Feminist in a Software Lab: Difference + Design* (Cambridge, MA: Harvard University Press, 2018).

41. See Steven E. Jones, *Roberto Busa, S. J., and the Emergence of Humanities Computing: The Priest and the Punched Cards* (New York: Routledge, 2016).

42. Holly Willis, "Writing Images and the Cinematic Humanities," *Visible Language* 49, no. 3 (December 2015): 74.

43. "Scientific Data Is Transformed into a Unique Visual Language for IBM's 'Smarter Planet' Campaign," *Motion Theory*, April 30, 2011, accessed October 9, 2015, http://www.motiontheory.com/content/437/ibm_data-films.

44. This is equally true of data sonification, but my concern for the moment is the visual.

45. Thomas H. Davenport and D. J. Patil, "Data Scientist: The Sexiest Job of the 21st Century," *Harvard Business Review,* October 2012, https://hbr.org/2012/10/data-scientist-the-sexiest-job-of-the-21st-century.

46. Koblin also distributes static images through Saatchi Art.

47. See Martin Wattenberg and VCL Team, "Many Eyes," *Fernanda B. Viégas*, accessed February 4, 2017, http://fernandaviegas.com/democratizing_viz.html.

48. Fernanda Viégas and Martin Wattenberg, abstract for "Shakespeare, God and Lonely Hearts: Transforming Data Access with Many Eyes," keynote talk for the Joint Conference on Digital Libraries, Pittsburgh, June 16–20, 2008.

49. Fernanda Viégas and Martin Wattenberg, "About," *Hint.FM*, accessed March 1, 2017, http://hint.fm/about/.

50. Fernanda Viégas and Martin Wattenberg, "About," *Fleshmap Touch*, accessed March 1, 2017, http://www.fleshmap.com/about.html.

51. 3D.SK is a widely used commercial repository of images and 3D models geared for artists and game developers.

52. Melissa Ragona, "Beauty and Danger: The Aestheticization of Information in Contemporary Art," in *Outrage: Art, Controversy, and Society*, ed. Richard Howells, Andreea Deciu Ritivoi, and Judith Schachter (New York: Palgrave Macmillan, 2012), 278–290.

53. In her attack on Wattenberg, who, for Ragona, "exemplifies the corporate-funded artist," Ragona strangely fails to acknowledge that the project was a collaboration and not Wattenberg's project alone.

54. Ragona, "Beauty and Danger," 287.

55. "Cultural Analytics," *Software Studies Initiative*, last updated December 2015, http://lab.softwarestudies.com/p/overview-slides-and-video-articles-why.html.

56. Lev Manovich, *Software Takes Command* (London: Bloomsbury Academic, 2013), 233.

57. Lev Manovich, "Visualizing Vertov," *Russian Journal of Communication* 5, no. 1 (2013): 44–55. Also available online: http://softwarestudies.com/cultural_analytics/Manovich.Visualizing_Vertov.2013.pdf.

58. For thorough documentation of the goals, challenges, and methods undertaken by cultural analytics, see Lev Manovich, "Media Visualization: Visual Techniques for Exploring Large Media Collections," in *Media Studies Futures*, ed. Kelly Gates (Malden, MA: Wiley-Blackwell, 2012).

59. Image Montage, available on the *ImageJ* website, last updated February 13, 2014, https://imagej.nih.gov/ij/plugins/image-montage/index.html.

60. These questions are all taken from the Selfiecity website, http://selfiecity.net.

61. Elizabeth Losh, "Feminism Reads Big Data: 'Social Physics,' Atomism, and Selfiecity," *International Journal of Communication* 9 (2015): 1647–1659.

62. These terms appear in the critical reflection published by Hochman and Manovich in *First Monday*. See Nadav Hochman and Lev Manovich, "Zooming into an

Instagram City: Reading the Local through Social Media," *First Monday* 18, no. 7 (2013), doi:10.5210/fm.v18i7.4711.

63. "About," *Phototrails*, 2013, http://phototrails.net/about.

64. Hochman and Manovich, "Zooming into an Instagram City."

65. Approximately 82 percent of the images uploaded to Instagram do not include geolocation data and are therefore automatically omitted from projects that are location-specific.

66. Lev Manovich, "Watching the World," *Aperture Magazine* 214 (Spring 2014), http://aperture.org/blog/watching-world.

67. These quotations are from a video interview by the Mark Moore Gallery with Jason Salavon in conjunction with his show *The Tragedy of the Commons* in April 2012, https://vimeo.com/40985624.

68. Nicholas Negroponte proposed a similar pairing of the fields of machine vision and computer graphics, but his interest was in missed opportunities among engineers working in isolation despite the proximity of their fields. See *Being Digital*, 59.

69. Jean-Louis Comolli, "Machines of the Visible," in *The Cinematic Apparatus*, ed. Teresa de Lauretis and Stephen Heath (London: Macmillan, 1980), 124.

70. Donna Haraway, "Situated Knowledges: The Science Question in Feminism and the Privilege of Partial Perspective," *Feminist Studies* 14, no. 3 (Autumn 1988), 581.

71. Donna Haraway, "Persistence of Vision," in *The Visual Culture Reader*, ed. Nicholas Mirzoeff (New York: Routledge, 2002), 679.

72. Haraway, "Situated Knowledges," 679.

73. Haraway, "Persistence of Vision," 585.

74. Benjamin Bratton, "Machine Vision: Benjamin Bratton in Conversation With Mike Pepi and Marvin Jordan," *DIS Magazine,* accessed March 2, 2017, http://dismagazine.com/discussion/73272/benjamin-bratton-machine-vision.

75. "How Google Uses Pattern Recognition," Google Privacy and Terms, accessed March 2, 2017, http://www.google.com/intl/en/policies/technologies/pattern-recognition.

76. This process was described with only minor variations by multiple participants in the Culture Analytics seminars held at UCLA's Institute for Pure and Applied Mathematics, March 7–June 10, 2016, https://www.ipam.ucla.edu/programs/long-programs/culture-analytics.

77. This sentence structure allows me to obliquely reference three texts that have been extremely influential for me: John Berger's *Ways of Seeing* (1972; repr., New York: Penguin, 2009); Marita Sturken and Lisa Cartwright's *Practices of Looking: An*

Introduction to Visual Culture (Oxford: Oxford University Press, 2001) and Crary's *Techniques of the Observer*.

78. Siegfried Kracauer, *The Mass Ornament: Weimar Essays*, trans. Thomas Y. Levin (Cambridge, MA: Harvard University Press, 2005), 75–76.

79. Ibid., 18.

80. Natalie Bookchin, *Databank of the Everyday*, 1996, http://bookchin.net/projects/databank-of-the-everyday.

81. Chun, *Updating to Remain the Same*, 173.

82. Ibid., 174.

83. For a rigorous reading of *The Clock* in terms of a different kind of dualism, related to its analog and digital resonances, see Homay King's "Christian Marclay's Two Clocks," in her book *Virtual Memory: Time-Based Art and the Dream of Digitality* (Durham, NC: Duke University Press, 2015).

84. David Golumbia, *The Cultural Logic of Computation* (Cambridge, MA: Harvard University Press, 2009), 221.

85. Grosser's interest in computer-made artwork dates to his *Interactive Robotic Painting Machine* (2011), in which a robotic arm holding a paint brush responds to sounds in the environment while applying paint to a canvas.

86. Grosser describes his process in an interview with Ben Valentine for *Hyperallergic*, "Computers Watching Movies," June 13, 2014, http://hyperallergic.com/131206/computers-watching-movies.

87. Benjamin Grosser, *Computers Watching Movies* (2013),*BenGrosser.com*, accessed March 2, 2017, https://bengrosser.com/projects/computers-watching-movies.

88. "Software for Digital Humanities," *Software Studies Initiative*, accessed March 2, 2017, http://lab.softwarestudies.com/p/software-for-digital-humanities.html.

89. Jeff Dean and Andrew Ng, "Using Large-Scale Brain Simulations for Machine Learning and A.I.," *Google Official Blog*, June 26, 2012, https://googleblog.blogspot.com/2012/06/using-large-scale-brain-simulations-for.html.

90. Ibid.

91. Ben Whitelaw, "Almost All YouTube Views Come from Just 30% of Films," *Telegraph*, April 20, 2011, http://www.telegraph.co.uk/technology/news/8464418/Almost-all-YouTube-views-come-from-just-30-of-films.html.

92. Rob Waugh, "Google Creates 'Computer Brain'—and It Immediately Starts Watching Cat Videos on YouTube," *Daily Mail Online*, June 26, 2012, http://www.dailymail.co.uk/sciencetech/article-2164832/Google-creates-artificial-brain--immediately-starts-watching-cat-videos.html.

93. Liat Clark, "Google's Artificial Brain Learns to Find Cat Videos," *Wired UK*, June 26, 2012, https://www.wired.com/2012/06/google-x-neural-network.

94. Dean and Ng, "Using Large-Scale Brain Simulations."

95. See Mercedes Bunz, "School Will Never End: On Infantilization in Digital Environments—Amplifying Empowerment or Propagating Stupidity?" in *Postdigital Aesthetics Art, Computation and Design*, ed. David M. Berry and Michael Dieter (New York: Palgrave Macmillan, 2015), 191–202.

96. Christian Szegedy et al., "Going Deeper with Convolutions," *Computing Research Repository* arXiv:1409.4842v1 (2014): 2, https://arxiv.org/abs/1409.4842.

97. Nor did I really expect it to; this was a thought experiment, not a real test of the Deep Dream system.

98. Valentino Braitenberg, *Vehicles: Experiments in Synthetic Psychology* (Cambridge, MA: A Bradford Book, 1986).

99. The latter interpretation is reinforced by the series title.

100. Reas follows the art world convention of numbered prints, a particularly necessary strategy given the acknowledged infinitude of "original" source images.

101. This term comes from Reas's historical overview of the project posted on his GitHub channel, "The History of the Process Works," June 15, 2016, https://github.com/REAS/studio/blob/master/ProcessHistory.md.

102. Generously documented and illustrated examples can be found in Reas's "Process Compendium," which describes the elements of which this series is composed and the instructions used to generate them. Casey Reas, "Process Compendium," last updated August 20, 2010, http://reas.com/compendium_text.

103. This is not to contradict Anna Lovatt's perceptive argument that LeWitt's work is, in fact, deeply entangled with human and architectural idiosyncrasies realized during the "transmission" from instruction to presentation. A similar variability occurs in Reas's work, as individual programmers may introduce a degree of improvisation when translating instructions into processing code. See Anna Lovatt, "Ideas in Transmission: LeWitt's Wall Drawings and the Question of Medium," *Tate Papers*, no. 14 (Autumn 2010), http://www.tate.org.uk/research/publications/tate-papers/14/ideas-in-transmission-lewitt-wall-drawings-and-the-question-of-medium.

104. The work is included on the DVD *Images 4 Music*, published in 2004.

105. The missing piece in this circuit is, of course, the executable Processing code by which Reas operationalizes the score. This code remains a kind of trade secret to be acknowledged but not shared.

106. This is also true of the *Linear Perspective* and *Today's Ideology* projects, in which editorial images from the *New York Times* are stretched and distorted in projected ribbons across gallery walls, unspooling at an excruciatingly slow pace.

107. A diptych format persists in some of Reas's work, including *Tox Screen* (2013) and *Ultraconcentrated* (2013), but the relationship between them is very different.

108. The first—and thus far only—undistorted photographic imagery in Reas's work appears in *Chronograph* (2011), a site-specific projection designed for the seven thousand-square-foot screen outside Miami's New World Symphony, created in collaboration with filmmaker Tal Rosner.

109. The concept of "algorithmic pleasure" is elaborated in my article "Aporias of the Digital Avant-Garde," *Digital Humanities Quarterly* 1, no. 2 (2007), http://www.digitalhumanities.org/dhq/vol/001/2/000011/000011.html.

110. *Century: Casey Reas* (Berlin: Deutsches Architekturmuseum, 2012), exhibition catalog, https://drive.google.com/file/d/0B9h469--G5OwYWt4XzF3OHNBd2M/view?usp=sharing.

111. These quotations appear in the Bitforms gallery description, "Casey Reas: Ultraconcentrated," accessed February 23, 2017, http://www.bitforms.com/reas-ultra/ultraconcentrated.

112. Another of Reas's works during this period was inspired by Claude Shannon's foundational text in information theory, "A Mathematical Theory of Communication," *Bell System Technical Journal* 27 (July 1948): 379–423; (October 1948): 623–656.

Chapter 2

1. In fact, the data encoded onto some punch cards afforded varying degrees of legibility to human readers, but the power of data stored in this way lay in its capacity for rapid processing and sorting by machines.

2. See Marshall McLuhan, *Understanding Media: The Extensions of Man* (New York: McGraw-Hill, 1964).

3. Lewis Mumford, *Technics and Civilization* (1934; repr., Chicago: University of Chicago Press, 2010), 321.

4. A partial exception may be found in the shift from magnetic disk drives to solid state memory, which traded decreased volume for faster, more stable data storage.

5. See Jeffrey Pomerantz, *Metadata* (Cambridge, MA: MIT Press, 2015).

6. See David Lyon, *Surveillance After Snowden* (Cambridge: Polity, 2015).

7. The complete text of Obama's speech on data collection reforms, "Remarks by the President on Review of Signals Intelligence," January 17, 2014, is available at the

Obama White House Archives, http://obamawhitehouse.archives.gov/the-press-office/2014/01/17/remarks-president-review-signals-intelligence.

8. This deflection did not go unnoticed in mainstream press. The *New Yorker,* for example, published Jane Mayer's article "What's the Matter with Metadata?" in which the author explains just how data-driven surveillance ignores capturing the content of phone calls in favor of tracking patterns. Jane Mayer, "What's the Matter with Metadata," *New Yorker,* June 6, 2013, http://www.newyorker.com/news/news-desk/whats-the-matter-with-metadata.

9. Lee Ferran, "Ex-NSA Chief: 'We Kill People Based on Metadata,'" *ABC News,* May 12, 2014, http://abcnews.go.com/blogs/headlines/2014/05/ex-nsa-chief-we-kill-people-based-on-metadata.

10. Hayden is quoted as saying, "In this debate, it's important to distinguish what might be done with what is being done." Ibid.

11. See Giorgio Agamben, *State of Exception,* trans. Kevin Attell (Chicago: University of Chicago Press, 2005).

12. Kelly Gates, *Our Biometric Future: Facial Recognition Technology and the Culture of Surveillance* (New York: New York University Press, 2011), Kindle location 2782–2784.

13. Giorgio Agamben, "No to Biopolitical Tattooing," trans. Stuart J. Murray, *Communication and Critical/Cultural Studies* 5, no. 2 (June 2008): 201–202.

14. "About DHS," U.S. Department of Homeland Security, last updated June 29, 2016, https://www.dhs.gov/about-dhs.

15. See Michel de Certeau, *The Practice of Everyday Life* (Berkeley: University of California Press, 1984).

16. "Threats & Protection: Homeland Security Advisory System," U.S. Department of Homeland Security archived page, April 2, 2003, https://web.archive.org/web/20030402130220/http://www.dhs.gov/dhspublic/display?theme=29.

17. In *Updating to Remain the Same,* Wendy Chun reflects on the online dynamic by which, "Whether or not YOU are aware of it, YOU are always following the mantra: If you see something, say something" (121). At the core of Chun's analysis, however, is not the overt admonition to public vigilance, but the internal structures of surveillance on social networks whereby the seemingly benign act of "friending" someone may result in "plac[ing] others at risk through the sometimes genuine care we show for them" (110).

18. Bush did not mention TIPS by name in the speech but concluded his segment on domestic security with the following: "As government works to better secure our homeland, America will continue to depend on the eyes and ears of alert citizens." George W. Bush, State of the Union Address, *George W. Bush White House* (archived),

January 29, 2002, https://georgewbush-whitehouse.archives.gov/news/releases/2002/01/20020129-11.html.

19. I do not mean to propose an equivalence between the Internet Archive's preservation of publicly available online information and the NSA's unwarranted harvesting of metadata traces describing private communications; it is the contrast between these two undertakings that is revealing.

20. See Arthur C. Danto, *Narration and Knowledge* (New York: Columbia University Press, 1985).

21. "First Wholly-Computerized Press Release Was Distributed Yesterday by Universal for Its 'Collosus' [*sic*] Feature, Science-Fiction Film," *Variety,* October 29, 1968.

22. This history is effectively synopsized, theorized, and exemplified in Allison de Fren's documentary *The Mechanical Bride* (2012).

23. Individual Privacy Protection Act of 1995, H. R. 184, 104th Cong., 1st sess. (January 4, 1995), file h184.ih, https://w2.eff.org/Legislation/Bills_by_number/hr184_95.bill.

24. Thomas Pynchon, *The Crying of Lot 49* (1966; repr., London: Picador, 1979), 125.

25. Ibid., 126.

26. Lynn Spigel, *Make Room for TV* (Chicago: University of Chicago Press, 1992), 118.

27. Katie Rogers, "Mark Zuckerberg Covers His Laptop Camera. You Should Consider It, Too," *New York Times,* June 22, 2016, https://www.nytimes.com/2016/06/23/technology/personaltech/mark-zuckerberg-covers-his-laptop-camera-you-should-consider-it-too.html.

28. Chris Matyszczyk, "Samsung Changes Smart TV Privacy Policy in Wake of Spying Fears," *CNET,* February 10, 2015, https://www.cnet.com/news/samsung-changes-smarttv-privacy-policy-in-wake-of-spying-fears. Samsung is not the only company to offer voice recognition systems. Similar concerns have been expressed about Amazon's Echo voice-activated computing system, Google's Home monitoring system, and voice controls in Microsoft's Xbox gaming console, to name just a few. Changes to Samsung's privacy policy were partially traceable thanks to the Internet Archive's Wayback Machine at http://archive.org/web.

29. Williams borrowed the term "frenzy of the visible" from Jean-Louis Comolli's 1980 essay "Machines of the Visible," in a passage that ends, "The whole world becomes visible at the same time that it becomes appropriatable" (122–123), cited in Linda Williams, *Hard Core: Power, Pleasure, and the "Frenzy of the Visible"* (Berkeley: University of California Press, 1999), 285.

30. Williams, *Hard Core,* 56–57.

31. Tung-Hui Hu, *A Prehistory of the Cloud* (Cambridge, MA: MIT Press, 2015), Kindle location 164.

32. Ibid., Kindle location 1590–1591.

33. I should clarify that I have adopted the industry vernacular of "mobile device" as an umbrella term for data-enabled "smart phones"; many of the generalizations made here do not apply to low-tech, outdated, or disposable cell phones that are not tied to data accounts or individual users.

34. A similar conceit underlies the development of a homicidal AI in Alex Garland's *Ex Machina* (2015). The creator of a Google-like search engine known as Blue Book reveals that his system was developed not for marketing purposes but to train a strong AI system to recognize and deploy nuanced human-style emotions, through mastery of language and facial expressions, by illegally capturing voice and visual data from every microphone and camera on every cell phone on the entire planet.

35. *The Dark Knight* preceded Google's announcement of its consumer-grade photogrammetry system *Project Tango* by nearly four years.

36. "How Google Uses Pattern Recognition."

37. Ibid.

38. Chun, *Updating to Remain the Same*, 94.

39. Sean Cubitt, Daniel Palmer, and Nathaniel Tkacz, eds., *Digital Light* (London: Open Humanities Press 2015), 216.

40. Matt Hicks, "Making Photo Tagging Easier," June 30, 2011, https://www.facebook.com/notes/facebook/making-photo-tagging-easier/467145887130/.

41. "Learn about Face Models," Google Photos Help, accessed March 2, 2017, https://support.google.com/photos/answer/6128838?hl=en&ref_topic=6128818.

42. Chun, "Big Data as Drama," 367.

43. Pasi Väliaho, *Biopolitical Screens: Image, Power, and the Neoliberal Brain* (Cambridge, MA: MIT Press, 2014), 25.

44. Ibid.

45. Michel Foucault, *Society Must Be Defended: Lectures at the Collège de France, 1975–1976* (New York: St. Martin's Press, 1997), 242.

46. Ibid., 246.

47. Agamben, *What Is an Apparatus?*, 14.

48. Adam Harvey, "Camouflage from Face Detection," *CV Dazzle*, last updated April 28, 2016, https://cvdazzle.com.

49. See Dick Hebdige, who writes in *Hiding in the Light: On Images and Things* (New York: Routledge, 1998) that to strike a pose is "to pose a threat" (18).

50. All quotations are from Sterling Crispin's project documentation at "*Data-Masks* (series)," accessed March 3, 2017, http://www.sterlingcrispin.com/data-masks.html.

51. All quotations in this paragraph are from the Leo Selvaggio's *URME Surveillance* website, accessed March 3, 2017, http://www.urmesurveillance.com.

52. See Simone Browne, *Dark Matters: On the Surveillance of Blackness* (Durham, NC: Duke University Press, 2015), Kindle edition.

53. Lisa Nakamura, *Digitizing Race: Visual Cultures of the Internet* (Minneapolis: University of Minnesota Press, 2008), 202, emphasis in original.

54. See Adam Rose, "Are Face-Detection Cameras Racist?" *Time*, January 22, 2010, http://content.time.com/time/business/article/0,8599,1954643,00.html.

55. Jocelyn "Joz" Wang, "Racist Camera! No, I Did Not Blink … I'm Just Asian!" *jozjozjoz* (blog), May 13, 2009, http://www.jozjozjoz.com/2009/05/13/racist-camera-no-i-did-not-blink-im-just-asian.

56. Browne, *Dark Matters*, Kindle location 162–163.

57. Tara McPherson, "Why Are the Digital Humanities So White? or Thinking the Histories of Race and Computation," in *Debates in the Digital Humanities*, ed. Matthew K. Gold (Minneapolis: University of Minnesota Press, 2012), http://dhdebates.gc.cuny.edu/debates/part/4.

58. This quotation comes from Simon Cole, *Suspect Identities: A History of Fingerprinting and Criminal Identifications* (Cambridge, MA: Harvard University Press, 2002), 64.

59. Joseph Pugliese, *Biometrics: Bodies, Technologies, Biopolitics* (New York: Routledge, 2012), 17.

60. "Home Soil," *Star Trek: The Next Generation*, season 1, episode 18 (1988).

61. See Paul Baker and Amanda Potts, "'Why Do White People Have Thin Lips?' Google and the Perpetuation of Stereotypes via Auto-complete Search Forms," *Critical Discourse Studies* 10, no. 2 (2013): 187–204, doi:10.1080/17405904.2012.744320.

62. See UN Women's report on the campaign by Memac Ogilvy & Mather Dubai, "UN Women Ad Series Reveals Widespread Sexism," *UN Women*, October 21, 2013, http://www.unwomen.org/en/news/stories/2013/10/women-should-ads.

63. Lorna Roth, "Looking at Shirley, the Ultimate Norm: Colour Balance, Image Technologies, and Cognitive Equity," *Canadian Journal of Communication* 34 (2009): 119.

64. Ibid., 120.

65. Rosalind Krauss, "Video: The Aesthetics of Narcissism," *October* 1 (Spring 1976): 52.

66. Ibid., 50.

67. Ibid., 52.

68. Artists who have explored this area through video include Vito Acconci, Bruce Nauman, Julia Scher, Harun Farocki, and Jordan Crandall.

69. At the time of Krauss's essay, of course, the visual vernacular of "surveillance video" had not yet been established. The images created by early consumer-grade video cameras *all* looked like low-res, low-contrast, black-and-white surveillance.

70. *Exposure* was first exhibited as part of a show titled *Blind Vision: Video and Limits of Perception*, at the San Jose Museum of Art, and was on display during the terrorist attacks of September 11, 2001.

71. "Seeing Surveillance: Kazys Varnelis and Trevor Paglen in Conversation with the *Straddler*," *Straddler*, Winter 2013, http://www.thestraddler.com/201412/piece2.php.

72. Bertolt Brecht, *Bertolt Brecht on Film and Radio*, ed. and trans. M. Silberman (London: Methuen, 2000), 164.

73. Brecht's focus on Krupp and AEG—Germany's largest arms manufacturer and electricity generator, respectively—is hardly accidental. The conjunction of heavy industry and electric power were defining of German industry in the years leading up to WWII. Further, the Weimar-era interrogation of its infrastructures was crucial to the Marxist critique of culture.

74. Hu, *A Prehistory of the Cloud*, Kindle location 1159–1160.

75. Ibid., Kindle location 1202.

76. Trevor Paglen, "New Photos of the NSA and Other Top Intelligence Agencies Revealed for First Time." *Intercept*, February 9, 2014, https://theintercept.com/2014/02/10/new-photos-of-nsa-and-others.

77. Trevor Paglen, *Blank Spots on the Map* (New York: Dutton, 2009), 275.

78. Paglen created "Unmarked Planes and Hidden Geographies" in collaboration with designers Craig Dietrich and Raegan Kelly for *Vectors* 2, no. 2 (2007), http://vectors.usc.edu/projects/index.php?project=59.

79. Paglen is credited with additional cinematography on Poitras's Oscar-winning documentary.

80. Trevor Paglen, "Is Photography Over?" Is Photography Over? post 1, *Still Searching* (blog), Fotomuseum, March 3, 2014, https://www.fotomuseum.ch/en/explore/still-searching/articles/26977_is_photography_over.

81. Paglen, "Seeing Machines," Is Photography Over? post 2, *Still Searching* (blog), Fotomuseum, March 13, 2014, https://www.fotomuseum.ch/en/explore/still-searching/articles/26978_seeing_machines.

82. Paglen, "Geographies of Photography," Is Photography Over? post4, *Still Searching* (blog), Fotomuseum, April 11, 2014, https://www.fotomuseum.ch/en/explore/still-searching/articles/26980_geographies_of_photography.

83. "Artist Snaps Creepy New Photos of the NSA," *Time*, February 11, 2014, http://newsfeed.time.com/2014/02/11/artist-snaps-creepy-new-photos-of-the-nsa.

84. Trevor Paglen, "Overhead: New Photos of the NSA and Other Top Intelligence Agencies Revealed," *Creative Time Reports*, February 10, 2014, http://creativetimereports.org/2014/02/10/overhead-new-photos-of-the-nsa-and-other-top-intelligence-agencies-revealed-trevor-paglen.

85. I once checked into a roadside motel in midcoastal Maine and was pleasantly surprised to find a gilt-framed print of Paglen's NSA photo hanging on a wall near the ice machine. Such is the power of refusing to allow copyright to interfere with distribution.

86. Laura Marks, *Enfoldment and Infinity: An Islamic Genealogy of New Media Art* (Cambridge, MA: MIT Press, 2010), 4.

87. Google's development of technologies for "synthetic cartography" is discussed in some detail in chapter 3.

88. Quotations are from project documentation for *Grow Finish Unit (near Elkhart, Kansas) 2008*, on the artist's site, *JohnGerrard.net*, accessed March 1, 2017, http://www.johngerrard.net/grow-finish-unit-elkhart.html.

89. Kevin Holmes, "An Artist and a Helicopter Capture Google's Off-Limits Data Farm," *Creators*, February 13, 2015, https://creators.vice.com/en_us/article/artist-and-helicopter-capture-off-limits-data-farm.

90. Timo Arnall, *Internet Machine* project page, *Elastic Space*, May 13, 2014, http://www.elasticspace.com/2014/05/internet-machine.

91. See Simon Norfolk's self-titled website, http://www.simonnorfolk.com.

Chapter 3

1. See Wolfgang Schivelbusch, *The Railway Journey: The Industrialization of Time and Space in the Nineteenth Century* (Berkeley: University of California Press, 2014).

2. Tung-Hui Hu identifies a different metaphorical resonance in the use of former railroad tracks to lay fiber optic cables. See Hu, *A Prehistory of the Cloud*, Kindle location 302.

3. These issues are addressed in greater depth in terms of surveillance in chapter 2.

4. All quotations are from "The Making of Drone 100," YouTube video, produced by the Intel Corporation (2015), posted by Ars Electronica, January 11, 2016, https://youtu.be/nTwX1Z68qMY.

5. Video documentation is available at "Drone 100," *Ars Electronica*, January 12, 2016, http://www.aec.at/feature/en/drone100.

6. Quotations and process descriptions from Tim Nackashi, "The Making-of 'House of Cards' video," YouTube video (2008), posted by Radiohead, July 9, 2008, https://www.youtube.com/watch?v=cyQoTGdQywY.

7. A Google X lab project that was announced publicly in 2014, Project Tango is led by computer scientist and Kinect developer-turned-internet-cult-icon Johnny Chung Lee.

8. William Uricchio, "The Algorithmic Turn: Photosynth, Augmented Reality and the Changing Implications of the Image," *Visual Studies* 26, no. 1 (March 2011): 34.

9. Ibid., 31.

10. "2012 Model Your Own Town Competition," *SketchUp*, last update May 15, 2012, http://www.sketchup.com/intl/en/competitions/modelyourtown/index.html.

11. "Google Acquires Keyhole Corp.," *News from Google*, October 27, 2004, http://googlepress.blogspot.com/2004/10/google-acquires-keyhole-corp.html.

12. The multiperspectival photographic apparatus used for the bullet-time effect was not invented for *The Matrix,* having appeared previously in numerous music videos and media artworks; what was new was the level of public attention drawn to its apparatus of production.

13. Jeff Sconce's *Haunted Media: Electronic Presence from Telegraphy to Television* (Durham, NC: Duke University Press, 2000) catalogs the public discourse surrounding these technologies.

14. Newton Minow used the phrase "vast wasteland" in a speech titled "Television and the Public Interest" (National Association of Broadcasters, Washington, DC, May 9, 1961).

15. Negroponte, *Being Digital*, 19.

16. Although the future of AI is clearly relevant to the evolving relation of data and images, it lies well beyond the scope of this project.

17. Howard Rheingold, *Tools for Thought: The History and Future of Mind-Expanding Technology* (Cambridge, MA: MIT Press, 2000), 337.

18. Scott S. Fisher, "Virtual Environments, Personal Simulation, and Telepresence," in *Virtual Reality: Theory, Practice and Promise*, ed. Sandra K. Helsel and Judith Roth (Darien, CT: Meckler Publishing, 1991), 101–110.

19. See Fred Turner, *From Counterculture to Cyberculture: Stewart Brand, the Whole Earth Network, and the Rise of Digital Utopianism* (Chicago: University of Chicago Press, 2008).

20. Scott S. Fisher, "Virtual Interface Environment" (paper presented at the Space Station Human Factors Research Review, NASA Ames Research Center, December 3–6, 1985).

21. Scott S. Fisher, "Virtual Environments, Personal Simulation, and Telepresence," in *Virtual Reality: Theory, Practice and Promise*, ed. Sandra K. Helsel and Judith Roth (Darien, CT: Meckler Publishing, 1991), 109.

22. Ibid., 266.

23. Ellen Strain, "Virtual VR," *Convergence* 5, no. 2 (June 1999): 10–15.

24. "Nintendo Introduces Video Game Players to Three-Dimensional Worlds with New Virtual Reality," *Tokyo Business Wire*, November 14, 1994, available on *Planet Virtual Boy*, http://www.planetvb.com/modules/advertising/?r17.

25. At this point in the discussion, attentive readers might well expect some mention of the technologies for augmented reality (AR) and mixed reality (MR). While I agree that such innovations have much to contribute to evolving perceptions of data/space, they do not as clearly manifest the perceptual tension between data and images underlying this book. The dynamic placement of images within an AR or MR user's field of view implies the existence of spatial coordinates by which images may appear while preserving—in contrast to VR—visual or tactile access to the physical environment. This creates a certain tension between perceptions of physical space and images that are not conventionally rasterized for display on a screen or projection surface. A similar visual dynamic occurs with technologies such as holography, light field capture and display, and projection mapping, all of which suggest compelling future objects of parallax analysis.

26. As such, I will limit my use of the term VR without quotation marks to those situations where I am referring to the cultural and marketing discourses surrounding the technology.

27. Milk is quoted by Josh Constine in "Virtual Reality, The Empathy Machine," *TechCrunch*, February 1, 2015, https://techcrunch.com/2015/02/01/what-it-feels-like.

28. For a useful reading of Davies's work, see Mark B. N. Hansen, *Bodies in Code: Interfaces with Digital Media* (New York: Routledge, 2006).

29. See Hal Foster, *The Return of the Real* (Cambridge, MA: MIT Press, 1997).

30. Ibid., 166.

31. Ibid.

32. Nonny de la Peña, "Project Syria: An Immersive Journalism Experience" project documentation, YouTube video, posted by Nonny de la Peña, January 28, 2014, https://youtu.be/jN_nbHnHDi4.

33. For a well-researched and inclusive oral history of first-generation VR, see "Voices from a Virtual Past: An Oral History of a Technology Whose Time Has Come Again," compiled by Adi Robertson and Michael Zelenko for the *Verge* (undated 2014), accessed February 19, 2017, http://www.theverge.com/a/virtual-reality/oral_history.

34. Sam Gregory, "Co-Presence: A New Way to Bring People Together for Human Rights Activism," *Witness* (blog), September 2013, http://blog.witness.org/2013/09/co-presence-for-human-rights.

35. Ibid.

36. Erkki Huhtamo, "Time Traveling in the Gallery," in *Immersed in Technology: Art and Virtual Environments*, ed. Mary Anne Moser and Douglas MacLeod (Cambridge, MA: MIT Press 1996), 244.

37. In 2009, ZKM rephotographed the entire system, creating the possibility of historical comparison across two decades.

38. Erkki Huhtamo, "Seeking Deeper Contact: Interactive Art as Metacommentary," in *European Media Art Festival Osnabruck 1993*, ed. Eckhard Diesing and Ralf Sausmikat (Osnabruck: EMAF 1993), 255–272, exhibition catalog. Also available on Ken Feingold's website: http://www.kenfeingold.com/seekingdeeper.html.

39. Michael Naimark, "Place Runs Deep: Virtuality, Place and Indigenousness" (paper presented at Virtual Museums Symposium, ARCH Foundation, Salzburg, Austria, 1998), http://www.naimark.net/writing/salzberg.html.

40. See chapter 6, "Digital Histories," in my *Technologies of History*, also published as "Past Indiscretions: Digital Archives and Recombinant History," in *Transmedia Frictions: The Digital, the Arts, and the Humanities,* ed. Marsha Kinder and Tara McPherson (Berkeley: University of California Press, 2014), 100–114.

41. Fred Turner, *The Democratic Surround: Multimedia and American Liberalism from World War II to the Psychedelic Sixties* (Chicago: University of Chicago Press, 2013), 16.

42. Ibid., 11.

43. For an insightful, historical overview of screen multiplicity, see chapter 5, "The Multiple," in Friedberg, *Virtual Window*, 191–239.

44. Turner, *Democratic Surround*, 237.

45. This term is borrowed from Sarah Pink, "Sensory Digital Photography: Re-Thinking 'Moving' and the Image," *Visual Studies* 26, no. 1 (2011): 4–13.

46. Kristin Roberts and Eric Auchard, "Google Pulls Some Map Images at Pentagon's Request," *Reuters,* March 6, 2008, http://www.reuters.com/article/us-usa-military-google-idUSN0625659220080306.

47. I am grateful to Michael Naimark for drawing my attention to this event and its aftermath.

48. Kei Kawai, "Never Ass-ume," *Google Maps Blog*, January 6, 2013, https://google-latlong.blogspot.com/2013/01/never-ass-ume.html. The post read: "Over the last 24-hours concerned members of the public and the media have been speculating on the fate of a donkey pictured in Street View in the Kweneng region of Botswana. Because of the way our 360-degree imagery is put together, it looked to some that our car had been involved in an unseemly hit and run, leaving the humble beast stranded in the road. As our imagery below shows, the donkey was lying in the path—perhaps enjoying a dust bath—before moving safely aside as our car drove past. I'm pleased to confirm the donkey is alive and well."

49. Although previous tools such as the "Spot-healing brush," which was designed for automated retouching of small areas of an image, had been available since 2005, "Content-aware fill" was not included in Adobe's Creative Suite until 2010.

50. A similar process of interpellation occurs with digital film restoration systems that fill in gaps in images with approximations based on adjacent frames. These include the Diamant system, which provides an opening parable in Sean Cubitt's *Finite Media: Environmental Implications of Digital Technologies* (Durham, NC: Duke University Press, 2016), Kindle edition.

51. The donkey incident was not the first time Street View ran afoul of a culturally situated controversy. Shortly after launching Street View in Germany, Google was found to be gathering not only panoramic images and volumetric data, but also data from Wi-Fi networks in homes and businesses. Ostensibly, the goal of this data acquisition was to verify and refine GPS locational data, but for German policy makers, Google's ability to capture such data represented a transgression of a more intrusive order. Google was ultimately fined a symbolic 145,000 euros by the German government and ordered to stop collecting Wi-Fi data. Google was also compelled to blur out images of more than two hundred thousand private residences whose owners opted out of the system, and in 2011, the company ceased its efforts to continue Street View documentation in Germany altogether. This is only one instance among many in which image-data and data-data are perceived differently, especially in public spaces.

52. Clement Valla, *Postcards from Google Earth* (2013), accessed March 4, 2017, http://www.postcards-from-google-earth.com.

53. I am grateful to Valla for noting the use of this term in a Google patent for texture mapping technology. See Clement Valla, "The Universal Texture," *Rhizome* (blog), July 31, 2012, http://rhizome.org/editorial/2012/jul/31/universal-texture.

54. Ibid.

55. Though most of Valla's images are distributed online or converted to large-scale inkjet prints for gallery display, he has also created a project that more directly attempts to illustrate the process by which these images are created. Titled *The Universal Texture Recreated (46°42′3.50″N, 120°26′28.59″W)* (2014), the project mimics the process of generating a digital landscape model using physical objects—specifically a wooden table with a gap in the middle representing a ravine. He printed the image texture onto a large piece of canvas and draped it over the table, allowing the canvas to hang down in the center. As a final touch to augment the gallery installation, Valla directed a live web cam at the installation, in effect returning the model to its native online habitat.

56. Masaki Fujihata, "Beyond Pages: Artist's Statement," *International Academy of Media Arts and Sciences*, accessed March 4, 2017, http://www.iamas.ac.jp/interaction/i97/artist_Fujihata.html.

57. "Noise: Error in the Void," ScanLAB Projects project documentation, accessed April 27, 2017, http://scanlabprojects.co.uk/projects/noise.

58. Manaugh also suggests that we can learn from "the delusions and hallucinations of sensing machines." Geoff Manaugh, "The Dream Life of Driverless Cars," *New York Times,* November 11, 2015, https://www.nytimes.com/2015/11/15/magazine/the-dream-life-of-driverless-cars.html.

59. Amy McCabe Heibel, "Following in the Footsteps of Innovators: Terrestrial Laser Scans of Yosemite," *Unframed,* LACMA, June 9, 2016, https://unframed.lacma.org/2016/06/09/following-footsteps-innovators-terrestrial-laser-scans-yosemite.

Conclusion

1. Much of my previous book *Technologies of History* was devoted to serious consideration of various strategies of eccentric historiography, including counterfactuals, but the playfulness that I once sought to redeem as part of the historiographical imagination has lately begun to seem less fun.

2. Crary, *Techniques of the Observer*, 124.

3. Jennifer Gabrys, *Digital Rubbish: A Natural History of Electronics* (Ann Arbor: University of Michigan Press, 2013), 5.

4. Scholars such as Lisa Parks and Nicole Starosielski likewise remind us of the physical infrastructures underlying data storage and transmission, including cell phone trees and transoceanic internet cables, as well as the environmental costs of power consumption. See their edited volume *Signal Traffic: Critical Studies of Media Infrastructures* (Champaign: University of Illinois Press, 2015).

5. Jonathan Sterne, "Out with the Trash," in *Residual Media*, ed. Charles R. Acland (Minneapolis: University of Minnesota Press, 2007), 17.

6. Ibid.

7. Bratton, *The Stack*, Kindle location 524–525.

8. Cubitt, *Finite Media*, Kindle location 165–167.

9. Ibid., 169–175.

10. See James Bridle, "The New Aesthetic: Seeing Like Digital Devices," *booktwo.org* (blog), March 15, 2012, http://booktwo.org/notebook/sxaesthetic.

11. See Steven E. Jones, *The Emergence of the Digital Humanities* (New York: Routledge, 2013).

12. William Gibson, "Google's Earth," *New York Times*, August 31, 2010, http://www.nytimes.com/2010/09/01/opinion/01gibson.html.

13. Bruce Sterling, "An Essay on the New Aesthetic," *Wired*, April 2, 2012, https://www.wired.com/2012/04/an-essay-on-the-new-aesthetic.

Bibliography

Adorno, Theodor. *Minima Moralia: Reflections from Damaged Life*. Translated by E. F. N. Jephcott. 1951. Reprint, London: Verso, 2006.

Agamben, Georgio. "No to Biopolitical Tattooing." Translated by Stuart J. Murray. *Communication and Critical/Cultural Studies* 5, no. 2 (June 2008): 201–202.

Agamben, Georgio. *State of Exception*. Translated by Kevin Attell. Chicago: University of Chicago Press, 2005.

Agamben, Georgio. *"What Is an Apparatus?" and Other Essays*. Translated by D. Kishik and S. Pedatella. Palo Alto, CA: Stanford University Press, 2009.

Aiden, Erez, and Jean-Baptiste Michel. "Netflix Recommendations: Beyond the 5 Stars (Part 2)." *Netflix Tech Blog*, June 20, 2012. http://techblog.netflix.com/2012/06/netflix-recommendations-beyond-5-stars.html.

Aiden, Erez, and Jean-Baptiste Michel. *Uncharted: Big Data as a Lens on Human Culture* . New York: Riverhead Books, 2013.

Amatriain, Xavier, and Justin Basilico. "Netflix Recommendations: Beyond the 5 Stars (Part 1)." *Netflix Tech Blog*, April 6, 2012. http://techblog.netflix.com/2012/04/netflix-recommendations-beyond-5-stars.html.

Anderson, Chris. "The End of Theory: The Data Deluge Makes the Scientific Method Obsolete." *Wired*, June 23, 2008. https://www.wired.com/2008/06/pb-theory.

Anderson, Steve. "Aporias of the Digital Avant-Garde." *Digital Humanities Quarterly* 1, no. 2 (2007). http://www.digitalhumanities.org/dhq/vol/001/2/000011.html.

Anderson, Steve. "Past Indiscretions: Digital Archives and Recombinant History." In *Transmedia Frictions: The Digital, the Arts, and the Humanities*, edited by Marsha Kinder and Tara McPherson, 100–114. Berkeley: University of California Press, 2014.

Anderson, Steve. *Technologies of History*. Hanover, NH: Dartmouth College Press, 2011.

"Artist Snaps Creepy New Photos of the NSA." *Time*, February 11, 2014. http://newsfeed.time.com/2014/02/11/artist-snaps-creepy-new-photos-of-the-nsa.

Baker, Paul, and Amanda Potts. "'Why Do White People Have Thin Lips?' Google and the Perpetuation of Stereotypes via Auto-complete Search Forms." *Critical Discourse Studies* 10, no. 2 (2013): 187–204. doi:10.1080/17405904.2012.744320.

Barthes, Roland. *Mythologies*. Translated by A. Lavers. New York: Farrar, Straus and Giroux, 1972.

Bazin, André. "The Ontology of the Photographic Image." Translated by Hugh Gray. *Film Quarterly* 13, no. 4 (Summer 1960): 4–9.

Berger, John. *Ways of Seeing*. 1972. Reprint, New York: Penguin, 1990.

Boelstorff, Tom. "Making Big Data, in Theory." *First Monday* 18, no. 10 (2013). doi:10.5210/fm.v18i10.4869.

Bogost, Ian. "The Cathedral of Computation." *Atlantic*, January 15, 2015. http://www.theatlantic.com/technology/archive/2015/01/the-cathedral-of-computation/384300.

Boorstin, Daniel J. *The Image: A Guide to Pseudo-Events in America*. 1962. Reprint, New York: Vintage Books, 1992.

Borenstein, Greg. "Ghosts and Underwear." *Holo*, no. 1 (2013): 104–109.

Bowker, Geoffrey C. "Data Flakes: An Afterword to *'Raw Data' Is an Oxymoron*." In *"Raw Data" Is an Oxymoron*, edited by Lisa Gitelman, Kindle edition location 3892–3990. Cambridge, MA: MIT Press, 2013.

boyd, danah, and Kate Crawford. "Critical Questions for Big Data." *Information, Communication & Society* 15, no. 5 (2012): 662–679. doi:10.1080/1369118X.2012.678878.

Boylan, A., ed. *Thomas Kinkade: The Artist in the Mall*. Durham, NC: Duke University Press, 2011.

Braitenberg, Valentino. *Vehicles: Experiments in Synthetic Psychology*. Reprint, Cambridge, MA: MIT Press, 1986.

Bratton, Benjamin. "Machine Vision: Benjamin Bratton in Conversation with Mike Pepi and Marvin Jordan." *DIS Magazine*. Accessed March 2, 2017. http://dismagazine.com/discussion/73272/benjamin-bratton-machine-vision.

Bratton, Benjamin H. *The Stack: On Software and Sovereignty*. Cambridge, MA: MIT Press, 2016.

Brecht, Bertolt. *Bertolt Brecht on Film and Radio*. Edited and translated by M. Silberman. London: Methuen, 2000.

Bridle, James. "The New Aesthetic: Seeing Like Digital Devices." *Booktwo.org* (blog), March 15, 2012. http://booktwo.org/notebook/sxaesthetic.

Brown, Wendy. *Undoing the Demos: Neoliberalism's Stealth Revolution.* New York: Zone Books, 2015.

Browne, Simone. *Dark Matters: On the Surveillance of Blackness.* Durham, NC: Duke University Press, 2015. Kindle edition.

Bunz, Mercedes. "School Will Never End: On Infantilization in Digital Environments—Amplifying Empowerment or Propagating Stupidity?" In *Postdigital Aesthetics Art, Computation and Design*, edited by David M. Berry and Michael Dieter, 191–202. New York: Palgrave Macmillan, 2015.

Bush, George W. State of the Union Address. *George W. Bush White House* (archived), January 29, 2002. https://georgewbush-whitehouse.archives.gov/news/releases/2002/01/20020129-11.html.

Byrne, David. *Envisioning Emotional Epistemological Information.* Göttingen: Steidl, 2003.

Byrne, David. "Learning to Love PowerPoint." *Wired*, September 1, 2003. https://www.wired.com/2003/09/ppt1.

Cegłowski, Maciej. "Haunted by Data" keynote address at Strata + Hadoop World conference, New York City October 1, 2015. http://idlewords.com/talks/haunted_by_data.htm.

Century: Casey Reas. Berlin: Deutsches Architekturmuseum, 2012. Exhibition catalog. PDF. https://drive.google.com/file/d/0B9h469--G5OwYWt4XzF3OHNBd2M/view?usp=sharing.

Chun, Wendy Hui Kyong. "Big Data as Drama." *ELH* 83, no. 2 (Summer 2016): 363–382.

Chun, Wendy Hui Kyong. *Programmed Visions: Software and Memory.* Cambridge, MA: MIT Press, 2013.

Chun, Wendy Hui Kyong. *Updating to Remain the Same: Habitual New Media.* Cambridge, MA: MIT Press, 2016.

Clark, Liat. "Google's Artificial Brain Learns to Find Cat Videos." *Wired UK*, June 26, 2012. https://www.wired.com/2012/06/google-x-neural-network.

Cole, Simon. *Suspect Identities: A History of Fingerprinting and Criminal Identifications.* Cambridge, MA: Harvard University Press, 2002.

Comolli, Jean-Louis. "Machines of the Visible." In *The Cinematic Apparatus*, edited by Teresa de Lauretis and Stephen Heath, 121–142. London: Macmillan, 1980.

Constine, Josh. "Virtual Reality, The Empathy Machine." *TechCrunch,* February 1, 2015. https://techcrunch.com/2015/02/01/what-it-feels-like.

Crary, Jonathan. *Techniques of the Observer: On Vision and Modernity in the 19th Century*. Cambridge, MA: MIT Press, 1992.

Crawford, Kate. "The Hidden Biases in Big Data." *Harvard Business Review,* April 1, 2013. http://hbr.org/2013/04/the-hidden-biases-in-big-data.

Cubitt, Sean. "Cartographic Instruments, Narcissist Illusions, Regimes of Realism in CGI." *Millennium Film Journal* 34 (Fall 1999): 66–81.

Cubitt, Sean, Daniel Palmer, and Nathaniel Tkacz, eds. *Digital Light.* London: Open Humanities Press, 2015.

Cubitt, Sean. *Finite Media: Environmental Implications of Digital Technologies* . Durham, NC: Duke University Press, 2016. Kindle edition.

Cubitt, Sean. *The Practice of Light: A Genealogy of Visual Technologies from Prints to Pixels*. Cambridge, MA: MIT Press, 2014.

Dagognet, François, and Robert Galeta. *Etienne-Jules Marey: A Passion for the Trace.* New York: Zone Books, 1992.

Danto, Arthur C. *Narration and Knowledge.* New York: Columbia University Press, 1985.

Davenport, Thomas H., and D. J. Patil. "Data Scientist: The Sexiest Job of the 21st Century." *Harvard Business Review,* October 2012. https://hbr.org/2012/10/data-scientist-the-sexiest-job-of-the-21st-century.

Dean, Jeff, and Andrew Ng. "Using Large-Scale Brain Simulations for Machine Learning and A.I." *Google Official Blog,* June 26, 2012. https://googleblog.blogspot.com/2012/06/using-large-scale-brain-simulations-for.html.

de Certeau, Michel. *The Practice of Everyday Life*. Berkeley: University of California Press, 1984.

Drucker, Johanna. "Graphesis: Visual Knowledge Production and Representation." *Poetess Archive Journal* 2, no. 1 (December 2010): 1–50.

Ferran, Lee. "Ex-NSA Chief: 'We Kill People Based on Metadata.'" *ABC News,* May 12, 2014. http://abcnews.go.com/blogs/headlines/2014/05/ex-nsa-chief-we-kill-people-based-on-metadata.

"First Wholly-Computerized Press Release Was Distributed Yesterday by Universal for Its 'Collosus' [*sic*] Feature, Science-Fiction Film." *Variety,* October 29, 1968.

Fisher, Scott S. "Virtual Environments, Personal Simulation, and Telepresence." In *Virtual Reality: Theory, Practice and Promise,* edited by Sandra K. Helsel and Judith Roth, 101–110. Darien, CT: Meckler Publishing, 1991.

Fisher, Scott S. "Virtual Interface Environment." Paper presented at the Space Station Human Factors Research Review, NASA Ames Research Center, December 3–December 6, 1985.

Foster, Hal. *The Return of the Real*. Cambridge, MA: MIT Press, 1997.

Foucault, Michel. *The Archaeology of Knowledge: And the Discourse on Language*. New York: Vintage, 1982.

Foucault, Michel. "Omnes et Singulatim: Towards a Criticism of Political Reason." In *Power: Essential Works of Michel Foucault, 1954–1984*, vol. 3. New York: New Press, 2001.

Foucault, Michel. *Society Must Be Defended: Lectures at the Collège de France, 1975–1976*. New York: St. Martin's Press, 1997.

Friedberg, Anne. *The Virtual Window: From Alberti to Microsoft*. Cambridge, MA: MIT Press, 2009.

Fritz, Ben. "Cadre of Film Buffs Helps Netflix Viewers Sort through the Clutter." *Los Angeles Times*, September 3, 2012. http://articles.latimes.com/2012/sep/03/business/la-fi-0903-ct-netflix-taggers-20120903.

Gabrys, Jennifer. *Digital Rubbish: A Natural History of Electronics*. Ann Arbor: University of Michigan Press, 2013.

Gates, Kelly. *Our Biometric Future: Facial Recognition Technology and the Culture of Surveillance*. New York: New York University Press, 2011. Kindle edition.

Gibson, William. "Google's Earth." *New York Times*, August 31, 2010. http://www.nytimes.com/2010/09/01/opinion/01gibson.html.

Gitelman, L., ed. *"Raw Data" Is an Oxymoron*. Cambridge, MA: MIT Press, 2013. Kindle edition.

Gitelman, L., and G. Pingree, eds. *New Media, 1740–1915*. Cambridge, MA: MIT Press, 2004.

Golumbia, David. *The Cultural Logic of Computation*. Cambridge, MA: Harvard University Press, 2009.

"Google Acquires Keyhole Corp." *News from Google*, October 27, 2004. http://googlepress.blogspot.com/2004/10/google-acquires-keyhole-corp.html.

Gregory, Sam. "Co-Presence: A New Way to Bring People Together for Human Rights Activism." *Witness* (blog), September 2013. http://blog.witness.org/2013/09/co-presence-for-human-rights.

Hallinan, Blake, and Ted Striphas. "Recommended for You: The Netflix Prize and the Production of Algorithmic Culture." *New Media and Society* 18, no. 1 (2014): 1–21.

Hansen, Mark B. N. *Bodies in Code: Interfaces with Digital Media*. New York: Routledge, 2006.

Haraway, Donna. "The Persistence of Vision." In *The Visual Culture Reader*, edited by Nicholas Mirzoeff, 191–198. New York: Routledge, 2002.

Haraway, Donna. "Situated Knowledges: The Science Question in Feminism and the Privilege of Partial Perspective." *Feminist Studies* 14, no. 3 (Autumn 1988): 575–599.

Harvey, Adam. "Camouflage from Face Detection." CV Dazzle. Last updated April 28, 2016. https://cvdazzle.com.

Harvey, David. *A Brief History of Neoliberalism*. Oxford: Oxford University Press, 2005.

Hayles, N. Katherine. *How We Think: Digital Media and Contemporary Technogenesis*. Chicago: University of Chicago Press, 2012.

Hebdige, Dick. *Hiding in the Light: On Images and Things*. New York: Routledge, 1998.

Heibel, Amy McCabe. "Following in the Footsteps of Innovators: Terrestrial Laser Scans of Yosemite." *Unframed*, LACMA, June 9, 2016. https://unframed.lacma.org/2016/06/09/following-footsteps-innovators-terrestrial-laser-scans-yosemite.

Heidegger, Martin. *The Question Concerning Technology and Other Essays*. Translated by W. Lovitt. New York: Garland, 1977.

Hicks, Matt. "Making Photo Tagging Easier," June 30, 2011. https://www.facebook.com/notes/facebook/making-photo-tagging-easier/467145887130/.

Hochman, Nadav, and Lev Manovich. "Zooming into an Instagram City: Reading the Local through Social Media." *First Monday* 18, no. 7 (2013). doi:10.5210/fm.v18i7.4711.

Holmes, Kevin. "An Artist and a Helicopter Capture Google's Off-Limits Data Farm." *Creators*, February 13, 2015. https://creators.vice.com/en_us/article/artist-and-helicopter-capture-off-limits-data-farm.

Hu, Tung-Hui. *A Prehistory of the Cloud*. Cambridge, MA: MIT Press, 2015.

Huhtamo, Erkki. "Seeking Deeper Contact: Interactive Art as Metacommentary." In *European Media Art Festival Osnabruck 1993*, edited by Eckhard Diesing and Ralf Sausmikat, 255–272. Osnabruck: EMAF, 1993. Exhibition catalog.

Huhtamo, Erkki. "Time Traveling in the Gallery." In *Immersed in Technology: Art and Virtual Environments*, edited by Mary Anne Moser and Douglas MacLeod, 233–268. Cambridge, MA: MIT Press, 1996.

Jockers, Matthew L. *Macroanalysis: Digital Methods and Literary History*. Urbana: University of Illinois Press, 2013.

Jones, Steven E. *The Emergence of the Digital Humanities*. New York: Routledge, 2013.

Jones, Steven E. *Roberto Busa, S. J., and the Emergence of Humanities Computing: The Priest and the Punched Cards*. New York: Routledge, 2016.

Joyner, April. "Blackflix: How Netflix's Algorithm Exposes Technology's Racism." *Marie Claire*, February 29, 2016. http://www.marieclaire.com/culture/a18817/netflix-algorithms-black-movies.

Katz, Wendy, and Thomas Kinkade. *Thomas Kinkade: Masterworks of Light*. Boston: Little, Brown, 2000.

Kawai, Kei. "Never Ass-ume." *Google Maps Blog*, January 6, 2013. https://google-latlong.blogspot.com/2013/01/never-ass-ume.html.

King, Homay. *Virtual Memory: Time-Based Art and the Dream of Digitality*. Durham, NC: Duke University Press, 2015.

Kirby, Lynne. *Parallel Tracks: The Railroad and Silent Cinema*. Durham, NC: Duke University Press, 1997.

Kracauer, Siegfried. *The Mass Ornament: Weimar Essays*. Translated by Thomas Y. Levin. Cambridge, MA: Harvard University Press, 2005.

Krauss, Rosalind. "Video: The Aesthetics of Narcissism." *October* 1 (Spring 1976): 50–64.

Losh, Elizabeth. "Feminism Reads Big Data: 'Social Physics,' Atomism, and *Selfiecity*." *International Journal of Communication* 9 (2015): 1647–1659.

Lovatt, Anna. "Ideas in Transmission: LeWitt's Wall Drawings and the Question of Medium." *Tate Papers*, no. 14 (Autumn 2010). http://www.tate.org.uk/research/publications/tate-papers/14/ideas-in-transmission-lewitt-wall-drawings-and-the-question-of-medium.

Lyon, David. *Surveillance After Snowden*. Cambridge: Polity, 2015.

Manaugh, Geoff. "The Dream Life of Driverless Cars." *New York Times*, November 11, 2015. https://www.nytimes.com/2015/11/15/magazine/the-dream-life-of-driverless-cars.html.

Madrigal, Alexis C. "How Netflix Reverse Engineered Hollywood." *Atlantic*, January 2, 2014. https://www.theatlantic.com/technology/archive/2014/01/how-netflix-reverse-engineered-hollywood/282679/.

Manovich, Lev. "Cinema and Digital Media." In *Media Art Perspectives*, edited by Hans-Peter Schwarz and Jeffrey Shaw. Ostfildern, Germany: Cantz Verlag, 1996.

Manovich, Lev. "Media Visualization: Visual Techniques for Exploring Large Media Collections." In *Media Studies Futures*, edited by Kelly Gates. Malden, MA: Wiley-Blackwell, 2012.

Manovich, Lev. *Software Takes Command.* London: Bloomsbury Academic, 2013.

Manovich, Lev. "Visualizing Vertov." *Russian Journal of Communication* 5, no. 1 (2013): 44–55. http://softwarestudies.com/cultural_analytics/Manovich.Visualizing_Vertov.2013.pdf.

Manovich, Lev. "Watching the World." *Aperture Magazine* 214 (Spring 2014). http://aperture.org/blog/watching-world.

Marks, Laura. *Enfoldment and Infinity: An Islamic Genealogy of New Media Art.* Cambridge, MA: MIT Press, 2010.

Marvin, Carolyn. *When Old Technologies Were New: Thinking About Electric Communication in the Late Nineteenth Century.* New York: Oxford University Press, 1990.

Matyszczyk, Chris. "Samsung Changes Smart TV Privacy Policy in Wake of Spying Fears." *CNET,* February 10, 2015. https://www.cnet.com/news/samsung-changes-smarttv-privacy-policy-in-wake-of-spying-fears.

Mayer, Jane. "What's the Matter with Metadata?" *New Yorker,* June 6, 2013. http://www.newyorker.com/news/news-desk/whats-the-matter-with-metadata.

McLuhan, Marshall. *Understanding Media: The Extensions of Man.* New York: McGraw-Hill, 1964.

McPherson, Tara. *Feminist in a Software Lab: Difference + Design.* Cambridge, MA: Harvard University Press, 2018.

McPherson, Tara. "Why Are the Digital Humanities So White? or Thinking the Histories of Race and Computation." In *Debates in the Digital Humanities,* edited by Matthew K. Gold. Minneapolis: University of Minnesota Press, 2012. http://dhdebates.gc.cuny.edu/debates/part/4.

Meyer, Peter, Victor Navasky, Katrina vanden Heuvel, and JoAnn Wypijewski. "Painting by Numbers." *Nation,* March 14, 1994, 334–348.

Minow, Newton. "Television and the Public Interest." Speech delivered to the National Association of Broadcasters, Washington, DC, May 9, 1961.

Mittell, Jason. "Why Netflix Doesn't Release Its Ratings." *Atlantic,* February 23, 2016. https://www.theatlantic.com/entertainment/archive/2016/02/netflix-ratings/462447.

Moretti, Franco. *Distant Reading* . New York: Verso, 2013.

Moretti, Franco, and Alberto Piazza. *Graphs, Maps, Trees: Abstract Models for Literary History.* New York: Verso, 2007.

Mumford, Lewis. *Technics and Civilization.* 1934. Reprint, Chicago: University of Chicago Press, 2010.

Murray, Janet. *Inventing the Medium: Principles of Interaction Design as a Cultural Practice*. Cambridge, MA.: MIT Press, 2011.

Naimark, Michael. "Place Runs Deep: Virtuality, Place and Indigenousness." Paper presented at Virtual Museums Symposium, ARCH Foundation, Salzburg, Austria, 1998. http://www.naimark.net/writing/salzberg.html.

Nakamura, Lisa. *Digitizing Race: Visual Cultures of the Internet*. Minneapolis: University of Minnesota Press, 2008.

Negroponte, Nicholas. *Being Digital*. New York: Vintage, 1996.

"Nintendo Introduces Video Game Players to Three-Dimensional Worlds with New Virtual Reality." *Tokyo Business Wire*, November 14, 1994. Available on *Planet Virtual Boy*. http://www.planetvb.com/modules/advertising/?r17.

Obama, Barack. "Remarks by the President on Review of Signals Intelligence." *Barack Obama White House* (archived), January 17, 2014. http://obamawhitehouse.archives.gov/the-press-office/2014/01/17/remarks-president-review-signals-intelligence.

Ohmer, Susan. *George Gallup in Hollywood*. New York: Columbia University Press, 2006.

Paglen, Trevor. *Blank Spots on the Map*. New York: Dutton, 2009.

Paglen, Trevor. "Geographies of Photography." Is Photography Over? post 4. *Still Searching* (blog). Fotomuseum. April 11, 2014. https://www.fotomuseum.ch/en/explore/still-searching/articles/26980_geographies_of_photography.

Paglen, Trevor. *I Could Tell You But Then You Would Have to Be Destroyed by Me: Emblems from the Pentagon's Black World*. Brooklyn, NY: Melville, 2007.

Paglen, Trevor. "Is Photography Over?" Is Photography Over? post 1. *Still Searching* (blog). Fotomuseum. March 3, 2014. https://www.fotomuseum.ch/en/explore/still-searching/articles/26977_is_photography_over.

Paglen, Trevor. "New Photos of the NSA and Other Top Intelligence Agencies Revealed for First Time." *Intercept*, February 9, 2014. https://theintercept.com/2014/02/10/new-photos-of-nsa-and-others.

Paglen, Trevor. "Overhead: New Photos of the NSA and Other Top Intelligence Agencies Revealed." *Creative Time Reports*, February 10, 2014. http://creativetimereports.org/2014/02/10/overhead-new-photos-of-the-nsa-and-other-top-intelligence-agencies-revealed-trevor-paglen.

Paglen, Trevor. "Seeing Machines." Is Photography Over? post 2. *Still Searching* (blog). Fotomuseum. March 13, 2014. https://www.fotomuseum.ch/en/explore/still-searching/articles/26978_seeing_machines.

Paglen, Trevor. "Unmarked Planes and Hidden Geographies." *Vectors* 2, no. 2 (2007). http://vectors.usc.edu/projects/index.php?project=59.

Parks, Lisa, and Nicole Starosielski, eds. *Signal Traffic: Critical Studies of Media Infrastructures* . Champaign: University of Illinois Press, 2015.

Pink, Sarah. "Sensory Digital Photography: Re-Thinking 'Moving' and the Image." *Visual Studies* 26, no. 1 (2011): 4–13.

Pomerantz, Jeffrey. *Metadata*. Cambridge, MA: MIT Press, 2015.

Pugliese, Joseph. *Biometrics: Bodies, Technologies, Biopolitics*. New York: Routledge, 2012.

Pynchon, Thomas. *The Crying of Lot 49*. 1966. Reprint, London: Picador, 1979.

Ragona, Melissa. "Beauty and Danger: The Aestheticization of Information in Contemporary Art." In *Outrage: Art, Controversy, and Society*, edited by Richard Howells, Andreea Deciu Ritivoi, and Judith Schachter, 278–290. New York: Palgrave Macmillan, 2012.

Raimond, Yves, and Justin Basilico. "Recommending for the World." *Netflix Tech Blog,* February 17, 2016. http://techblog.netflix.com/2016/02/recommending-for-world.html.

Reas, Casey. "The History of the Process Works." *GitHub*, June 15, 2016. https://github.com/REAS/studio/blob/master/ProcessHistory.md.

Reas, Casey. "Process Compendium." *Reas.com.* Last updated August 20, 2010. http://reas.com/compendium_text/.

Rheingold, Howard. *Tools for Thought: The History and Future of Mind-Expanding Technology*. Cambridge, MA: MIT Press, 2000.

Roberts, Kristin, and Eric Auchard. "Google Pulls Some Map Images at Pentagon's Request." *Reuters,* March 6, 2008. http://www.reuters.com/article/us-usa-military-google-idUSN0625659220080306.

Robertson, Adi, and Michael Zelenko. "Voices from a Virtual Past: An Oral History of a Technology Whose Time Has Come Again." *Verge* (undated 2014). Accessed February 19, 2017. http://www.theverge.com/a/virtual-reality/oral_history.

Rogers, Katie. "Mark Zuckerberg Covers His Laptop Camera. You Should Consider It, Too." *New York Times*, June 22, 2016. https://www.nytimes.com/2016/06/23/technology/personaltech/mark-zuckerberg-covers-his-laptop-camera-you-should-consider-it-too.html.

Rose, Adam. "Are Face-Detection Cameras Racist?" *Time*, January 22, 2010. http://content.time.com/time/business/article/0,8599,1954643,00.html.

Ross, Andrew. "Poll Stars." *Artforum* 33, no. 5 (January 1995), 72–77.

Roth, Lorna. "Looking at Shirley, the Ultimate Norm: Colour Balance, Image Technologies, and Cognitive Equity." *Canadian Journal of Communication* 34 (2009): 111–136.

Schivelbusch, Wolfgang. *The Railway Journey: The Industrialization of Time and Space in the Nineteenth Century*. Berkeley: University of California, 2014.

"Scientific Data Is Transformed into a Unique Visual Language for IBM's 'Smarter Planet' campaign." *Motion Theory*, April 30, 2011. http://www.motiontheory.com/content/437/ibm_data-films.

Sconce, Jeff. *Haunted Media: Electronic Presence from Telegraphy to Television*. Durham, NC: Duke University Press, 2000.

"Seeing Surveillance: Kazys Varnelis and Trevor Paglen in Conversation with the *Straddler*." *Straddler*, Winter 2013. http://www.thestraddler.com/201412/piece2.php.

Sekula, Allan. "On the Invention of Photographic Meaning." In *Thinking Photography* , edited by Victor Burgin, 84–109. London: Macmillan, 1982. Originally published in *Artforum* 13, no. 5 (January 1975): 36–45.

Shamir, Lior, and Jane A. Tarakhovsky. "Computer Analysis of Art." *Journal on Computing and Cultural Heritage* 5, no. 2 (August 2012): 1–11.

Shannon, Claude. "A Mathematical Theory of Communication." *Bell System Technical Journal* 27 (July 1948): 379–423; (October 1948): 623–656.

Shenk, Timothy. "What Exactly Is Neoliberalism?" *Dissent*, April 2, 2015. https://www.dissentmagazine.org/blog/booked-3-what-exactly-is-neoliberalism-wendy-brown-undoing-the-demos.

Sontag, Susan. *On Photography*. New York: Farrar, Straus and Giroux, 1977.

Spacey, Kevin. MacTaggart Lecture. Transcript. Edinburgh International Television Festival. *Guardian*, August 22, 2013. https://www.theguardian.com/media/interactive/2013/aug/22/kevin-spacey-mactaggart-lecture-full-text.

Spangler, Todd. "Netflix Data Reveals Exactly When TV Shows Hook Viewers." *Variety*, September 23, 2015. http://variety.com/2015/digital/news/netflix-tv-show-data-viewer-episode-study-1201600746/.

Spigel, Lynn. *Make Room for TV*. Chicago: University of Chicago Press, 1992.

Stephens, Mitchell. *The Rise of the Image, The Fall of the Word*. Oxford: Oxford University Press, 1998.

Sterling, Bruce. "An Essay on the New Aesthetic." *Wired*, April 2, 2012. https://www.wired.com/2012/04/an-essay-on-the-new-aesthetic.

Sterne, Jonathan. "Out with the Trash." In *Residual Media*, edited by Charles R. Acland, 16–31. Minneapolis: University of Minnesota Press, 2007.

Strain, Ellen. "Virtual VR." *Convergence* 5, no. 2 (June 1999): 10–15.

Sturken, Marita, and Lisa Cartwright. *Practices of Looking: An Introduction to Visual Culture*. Oxford: Oxford University Press, 2001.

Szegedy, Christian, Wei Liu, Yangqing Jia, Pierre Sermanet, Scott Reed, Dragomir Anguelov, Dumitru Erhan, Vincent Vanhoucke, and Andrew Rabinovich. "Going Deeper with Convolutions." *Computing Research Repository* arXiv:1409.4842v1 (2014). https://arxiv.org/abs/1409.4842.

Tufte, Edward. *Envisioning Information*. Cheshire, CT: Graphics Press, 1990.

Tufte, Edward. "PowerPoint Is Evil." *Wired*, September 1, 2003. https://www.wired.com/2003/09/ppt2.

Turner, Fred. *The Democratic Surround: Multimedia and American Liberalism From World War II to the Psychedelic Sixties*. Chicago: University of Chicago Press, 2013.

Turner, Fred. *From Counterculture to Cyberculture: Stewart Brand, the Whole Earth Network, and the Rise of Digital Utopianism*. Chicago: University of Chicago Press, 2008.

"UN Women Ad Series Reveals Widespread Sexism." *UN Women*, October 21, 2013. http://www.unwomen.org/en/news/stories/2013/10/women-should-ads.

Uricchio, William. "The Algorithmic Turn: Photosynth, Augmented Reality and the Changing Implications of the Image." *Visual Studies* 26, no. 1 (March 2011): 25–35.

Valla, Clement. "The Universal Texture." *Rhizome* (blog), July 31, 2012. http://rhizome.org/editorial/2012/jul/31/universal-texture.

Valentine, Ben. "Computers Watching Movies." *Hyperallergic*, June 13, 2014. http://hyperallergic.com/131206/computers-watching-movies.

Väliaho, Pasi. *Biopolitical Screens: Image, Power, and the Neoliberal Brain*. Cambridge, MA: MIT Press, 2014.

Viégas, Fernanda, and Martin Wattenberg. Abstract for "Shakespeare, God and Lonely Hearts: Transforming Data Access with Many Eyes." Keynote talk for the Joint Conference on Digital Libraries, Pittsburgh, Pennsylvania, June 16–20, 2008.

Wang, Jocelyn. "Racist Camera! No, I Did Not Blink … I'm Just Asian!" *jozjozjoz* (blog), May 13, 2009. http://www.jozjozjoz.com/2009/05/13/racist-camera-no-i-did-not-blink-im-just-asian.

Waugh, Rob. "Google Creates 'Computer Brain'—and It Immediately Starts Watching Cat Videos on YouTube." *Daily Mail Online*, June 26, 2012. http://www.dailymail.co.uk/sciencetech/article-2164832/Google-creates-artificial-brain--immediately-starts-watching-cat-videos.html.

Whitelaw, Ben. "Almost All YouTube Views Come from Just 30% of Films." *Telegraph,* April 20, 2011. http://www.telegraph.co.uk/technology/news/8464418/Almost-all-YouTube-views-come-from-just-30-of-films.html.

Williams, Linda. *Hard Core: Power, Pleasure, and the "Frenzy of the Visible."* Berkeley: University of California Press, 1999.

Willis, Holly. "Writing Images and the Cinematic Humanities." *Visible Language* 49, no. 3 (December 2015): 63–77.

Winston, Brian. "A Mirror for Brunelleschi." *Daedalus: Journal of the American Academy of Arts and Sciences* 116, no. 3 (Summer 1987): 187–201.

Winston, Brian. *Technologies of Seeing: Photography, Cinematography and Television.* London: British Film Institute, 1997.

Wurster, Christian. *Computers: An Illustrated History*. New York: Taschen, 2002.

Wypijewski, JoAnn, ed. *Painting by Numbers: Komar and Melamid's Scientific Guide to Art* . Berkeley: University of California Press, 1998.

Index